SPEECHES AND LETTERS OF ABRAHAM LINCOLN 1832-1865
BY
Abraham Lincoln

SPEECHES AND LETTERS OF ABRAHAM LINCOLN 1832-1865

Published by Firework Press

New York City, NY

First published 1865

Copyright © Firework Press, 2015

All rights reserved

Except in the United States of America, this book is sold subject to the condition that it shall not, by way of trade or otherwise, be lent, re-sold, hired out, or otherwise circulated without the publisher's prior consent in any form of binding or cover other than that in which it is published and without a similar condition including this condition being imposed on the subsequent purchaser.

ABOUT FIREWORK PRESS

Firework Press prints and publishes the greatest books about American history ever written, including seminal works written by our nation's most influential figures.

Introduction

*Includes all of Lincoln's classic speeches and letters, including the House Divided Speech, the Lincoln-Douglas Debates, the Inaugural Addresses, the Emancipation Proclamation, the Gettysburg Address, and dozens of other speeches and letters
*Includes an appendix of several anecdotes about Lincoln written by those who knew him.
*Includes a Table of Contents.
*Includes over 30 pictures of Lincoln, his life, and work, including pictures of Lincoln at Gettysburg and a copy of the Gettysburg Address. Also includes pictures of other famous leaders and generals of the Civil War.

Abraham Lincoln (1809–1865) is one of the most famous Americans in history and one of the country's most revered presidents. Schoolchildren can recite the life story of Lincoln, the "Westerner" who educated himself and became a self made man, rising from lawyer to leader of the new Republican Party before becoming the 16th President of the United States. Lincoln successfully navigated the Union through the Civil War but didn't live to witness his own accomplishment, becoming the first president assassinated when he was killed at Ford's Theater by John Wilkes Booth.

As impressive as his presidency was, one of his most lasting legacies was his writing. In addition to masterful writing for everything from orders to his generals and condolences to the aggrieved Mrs. Bixby, his Second Inaugural Address and Gettysburg Address are considered masterpieces that rate among the greatest writings in American history. Perhaps Lincoln's most impressive feat is that he was able to convey so much with so few words; after famous orator Edward Everett spoke for hours at Gettysburg, Lincoln's Gettysburg Address only took a few minutes.

In the generation after the Civil War, Lincoln became an American deity and one of the most written about men in history. Understandably, all of his speeches and writings were scoured and preserved. This collection includes all of Lincoln's classics, including the "House Divided" Speech, the Lincoln-Douglas Debates, his iconic Inaugural Addresses, the Emancipation Proclamation, and the Gettysburg Address. It is specially formatted with a Table of Contents and pictures of Lincoln and his life, along with other famous leaders and generals of the Civil War.

Pictures

Lincoln at Gettysburg before giving the Gettysburg Address

Lincoln with his son Tad

Lincoln in his 30s

Lincoln in 1860

Original handwritten copy of the Gettysburg Address

Presidents Abraham Lincoln and Jefferson Davis

Robert E. Lee during the war

John Bell Hood

James Longstreet

A.P. Hill

Stonewall Jackson

JEB Stuart

George Pickett

Albert Sydney Johnston
P.G.T. Beauregard
Braxton Bragg
Patrick Cleburne
Ulysses S. Grant
William Tecumseh Sherman
Don Carlos Buell

Lew Wallace
Joe Hooker

Oliver Howard

Winfield Scott Hancock

John Sedgwick

Speeches & Letters of Abraham Lincoln 1832-1865

INTRODUCTION

No man since Washington has become to Americans so familiar or so beloved a figure as Abraham Lincoln. He is to them the representative and typical American, the man who best embodies the political ideals of the nation. He is typical in the fact that he sprang from the masses of the people, that he remained through his whole career a man of the people, that his chief desire was to be in accord with the beliefs and wishes of the people, that he never failed to trust in the people and to rely on their support. Every native American knows his life and his speeches. His anecdotes and witticisms have passed into the thought and the conversation of the whole nation as those of no other statesman have done.

He belongs, however, not only to the United States, but to the whole of civilized mankind. It is no exaggeration to say that he has, within the last thirty years, grown to be a conspicuous figure in the history of the modern world. Without him, the course of events not only in the Western hemisphere but in Europe also would have been different, for he was called to guide at the greatest crisis of its fate a State already mighty, and now far more mighty than in his days, and the guidance he gave has affected the march of events ever since. A life and a character such as his ought to be known to and comprehended by Europeans as well as by Americans. Among Europeans, it is especially Englishmen who ought to appreciate him and understand the significance of his life, for he came of an English stock, he spoke the English tongue, his action told upon the progress of events and the shaping of opinion in all British communities everywhere more than it has done upon any other nation outside America itself.

This collection of Lincoln's speeches seeks to make him known by his words as readers of history know him by his deeds. In popularly-governed countries the great statesman is almost of necessity an orator, though his eminence as a speaker may be no true measure either of his momentary power or of his permanent fame, for wisdom, courage and tact bear little direct relation to the gift for speech. But whether that gift be present in greater or in lesser degree, the character and ideas of a statesman are best studied through his own words. This is particularly true of Lincoln, because he was not what may be called a professional orator. There have been famous orators whose speeches we may read for the beauty of their language or for the wealth of ideas they contain, with comparatively little regard to the circumstances of time and place that led to their being delivered. Lincoln is not one of these. His speeches need to be studied in close relation to the occasions which called them forth. They are not philosophical lucubrations or brilliant displays of rhetoric. They are a part of his life. They are the expression of his convictions, and derive no small part of their weight and dignity from the fact that they deal with grave and urgent questions, and express the spirit in which he approached those questions. Few great characters stand out so clearly revealed by their words, whether spoken or written, as he does.

Accordingly Lincoln's discourses are not like those of nearly all the men whose eloquence has won them fame. When we think of such men as Pericles, Demosthenes, Æschines, Cicero, Hortensius, Burke, Sheridan, Erskine, Canning, Webster, Gladstone, Bright, Massillon, Vergniaud, Castelar, we think of exuberance of ideas or of phrases, of a command of appropriate similes or metaphors, of the gifts of invention and of exposition, of imaginative flights, or outbursts of passion fit to stir and rouse an audience to like passion. We think of the orator as gifted with a powerful or finely-modulated voice, an imposing presence, a graceful delivery. Or if—remembering that Lincoln was by profession a lawyer and practised until he became President of the United States—we think of the special gifts which mark the forensic orator, we should expect to find a man full of ingenuity and subtlety, one dexterous in handling his case in such wise as to please and capture the judge or the jury whom he addresses, one skilled in those rhetorical devices and strokes of art which can be used, when need be, to engage the listener's feelings and distract his mind from the real merits of the issue.

Of all this kind of talent there was in Lincoln but little. He was not an artful pleader; indeed, it was said of him that he could argue well only those cases in the justice of which he personally believed, and was unable to make the worse appear the better reason. For most of the qualities which the world admires in Cicero or in Burke we should look in vain in Lincoln's speeches. They are not fine pieces of exquisite diction, fit to be declaimed as school exercises or set before students as models of composition.

What, then, are their merits? and why do they deserve to be valued and remembered? How comes it that a man of first-rate powers was deficient in qualities appertaining to his own profession which men less remarkable have possessed?

To answer this question, let us first ask what were the preparation and training Abraham Lincoln had for oratory, whether political or forensic.

Born in rude and abject poverty, he had never any education, except what he gave himself, till he was approaching manhood. Not even books wherewith to inform and train his mind were within his reach. No school, no university, no legal faculty had any part in training his powers. When he became a lawyer and a politician, the years most favourable to continuous study had already passed, and the opportunities he found for reading were very scanty. He knew but few authors in general literature, though he knew those few thoroughly. He taught himself a little mathematics, but he could read no language save his own, and can have had only the faintest acquaintance with European history or with any branch of philosophy.

The want of regular education was not made up for by the persons among whom his lot was cast. Till he was a grown man, he never moved in any society from which he could learn those things with which the mind of an orator or a statesman ought to be stored. Even after he had gained some legal practice, there was for many years no one for him to mix with except the petty practitioners of a petty town, men nearly all of whom knew little more than he did himself.

Schools gave him nothing, and society gave him nothing. But he had a powerful intellect and a resolute will. Isolation fostered not only self-reliance but the habit of reflection, and, indeed, of prolonged and intense reflection. He made all that he knew a part of himself. He thought everything out for himself. His convictions were his own—clear and coherent. He was not positive or opinionated, and he did not deny that at certain moments he pondered and hesitated long before he decided on his course. But though he could keep a policy in suspense, waiting for events to guide him, he did not waver. He paused and reconsidered, but it was never his way either to go back upon a decision once made, or to waste time in vain regrets that all he expected had not been attained. He took advice readily, and left many things to his ministers; but he did not lean upon his advisers. Without vanity or ostentation, he was always independent, self-contained, prepared to take full responsibility for his acts.

That he was keenly observant of all that passed under his eyes, that his mind played freely round everything it touched, we know from the accounts of his talk, which first made him famous in the town and neighbourhood where he lived. His humour, and his memory for anecdotes which he could bring out to good purpose, at the right moment, are qualities which Europe deems distinctively American, but no great man of action in the nineteenth century, even in America, possessed them in the same measure. Seldom has so acute a power of observation been found united to so abundant a power of sympathy.

These remarks may seem to belong to a study of his character rather than of his speeches, yet they are not irrelevant, because the interest of his speeches lies in their revelation of his character. Let us, however, return to the speeches and to the letters, some of which, given in this volume, are scarcely less noteworthy than are the speeches.

What are the distinctive merits of these speeches and letters? There is less humour in them than his reputation as a humorist would have led us to expect. They are serious, grave, practical. We feel that the man does not care to play over the surface of the subject, or to use it as a way of displaying his cleverness. He is trying to get right down to the very foundation of the matter and tell us what his real thoughts about it are. In this respect he sometimes reminds us of Bismarck's speeches, which, in their rude, broken, forth-darting way, always go straight to their destined aim; always hit the nail on the head. So too, in their effort to grapple with fundamental facts, Lincoln's bear a sort of likeness to Cromwell's speeches, though Cromwell has far less power of utterance, and always seems to be wrestling with the difficulty of finding language to convey to others what is plain, true and weighty to himself. This difficulty makes the great Protector, though we can usually see what he is driving at, frequently confused and obscure. Lincoln, however, is always clear. Simplicity, directness and breadth are the notes of his thought. Aptness, clearness, and again, simplicity, are the notes of his diction. The American speakers of his generation, like most of those of the preceding generation, but unlike those of that earlier generation to which Alexander Hamilton, John Adams, Marshall and Madison belonged, were generally infected by a floridity which made them a by-word in Europe. Even men of brilliant talent, such as Edward Everett, were by no means free from this straining after effect by highly-coloured phrases and theatrical effects. Such faults have to-day virtually vanished from the United States, largely from a change in public taste, to which perhaps the example set by Lincoln himself may have contributed. In the forties and fifties florid rhetoric was rampant, especially in the West and South, where taste was less polished than in the older States. That Lincoln escaped it is a striking mark of his independence as well as of his greatness. There is no superfluous ornament in his orations, nothing tawdry, nothing otiose. For the most part, he addresses the reason of his hearers, and credits them with desiring to have none but solid arguments laid before them. When he does appeal to emotion, he does it quietly, perhaps even solemnly. The note struck is always a high note. The impressiveness of the appeal comes not from fervid vehemence of language, but from the sincerity of his own convictions. Sometimes one can see that through its whole course the argument is suffused by the speaker's feeling, and when the time comes for the feeling to be directly expressed, it glows not with fitful flashes, but with the steady heat of an intense and strenuous soul.

The impression which most of the speeches leave on the reader is that their matter has been carefully thought over even when the words have not been learnt by heart. But there is an anecdote that on one occasion, early in his career, Lincoln went to a public meeting not in the least intending to speak, but presently being called for by the audience, rose in obedience to the call, and delivered a long address so ardent and thrilling that the reporters dropped their pencils and, absorbed in watching him, forgot to take down what he said. It has also been stated, on good authority, that on his way in the railroad cars, to the dedication of the monument on the field of Gettysburg, he turned to a Pennsylvanian gentleman who was sitting beside him and remarked, "I suppose I shall be expected to say something this afternoon; lend me a pencil and a bit of paper," and that he thereupon jotted down the notes of a speech which has become the best known and best remembered of all his utterances, so that some of its words and sentences have passed into the minds of all educated men everywhere.

That famous Gettysburg speech is the best example one could desire of the characteristic quality of Lincoln's eloquence. It is a short speech. It is wonderfully terse in expression. It is quiet, so quiet that at the moment it did not make upon the audience, an audience wrought up by a long and highly-decorated harangue from one of the prominent orators of the day, an impression at all commensurate to that which it began to make as soon as it was read over America and Europe. There is in it not a touch of what we call rhetoric, or of any striving after effect. Alike in thought and in language it is simple, plain, direct. But it states certain truths and principles in phrases so aptly chosen and so forcible, that one feels as if those truths could have been conveyed in no other words, and as if this deliverance of them were made for all time. Words so simple and so strong could have come only from one who had meditated so long upon the primal facts of American history and popular government that the truths those facts taught him had become like the truths of mathematics in their clearness, their breadth, and their precision.

The speeches on Slavery read strange to us now, when slavery as a living system has been dead for forty years, dead and buried hell deep under the detestation of mankind. It is hard for those whose memory does not go back to 1865 to realize that down till then it was not only a terrible fact, but was defended—defended by many otherwise good men, defended not only by pseudo-scientific anthropologists as being in the order of nature, but by ministers of the Gospel, out of the sacred Scriptures, as part of the ordinances of God. Lincoln's position, the position of one who had to induce slave-owning fellow-citizens to listen to him and admit persuasion into their heated and prejudiced minds, did not allow him to denounce it with horror, as we can all so easily do to-day. But though his language is calm and restrained, he never condescends to palter with slavery. He shows its innate evils and dangers with unanswerable force. The speech on the Dred Scott decision is a lucid, close and cogent piece of reasoning which, in its wide view of Constitutional issues, sometimes reminds one of Webster, sometimes even of Burke, though it does not equal the former in weight nor the latter in splendour of diction.

Among the letters, perhaps the most impressive is that written to Mrs. Bixley, the mother of five sons who had died fighting for the Union in the armies of the North. It is short, and it deals with a theme on which hundreds of letters are written daily. But I do not know where the nobility of self-sacrifice for a great cause, and of the consolation which the thought of a sacrifice so made should bring, is set forth with such simple and pathetic beauty. Deep must be the fountains from which there issues so pure a stream.

The career of Lincoln is often held up to ambitious young Americans as an example to show what a man may achieve by his native strength, with no advantages of birth or environment or education. In this there is nothing improper, nothing fanciful. The moral is one which may well be drawn, and in which those on whose early life Fortune has not smiled may find encouragement. But the example is, after all, no great encouragement to ordinary men, for Lincoln was an extraordinary man.

He triumphed over the adverse conditions of his early years because Nature had bestowed on him high and rare powers. Superficial observers who saw his homely aspect and plain manners, and noted that his fellow-townsmen, when asked why they so trusted him, answered that it was for his common-sense, failed to see that his common-sense was a part of his genius. What is common-sense but the power of seeing the fundamentals of any practical question, and of disengaging them from the accidental and transient features that may overlie these fundamentals—the power, to use a familiar expression, of getting down to bed rock? One part of this power is the faculty for perceiving what the average man will think and can be induced to do. This is what keeps the superior mind in touch with the ordinary mind, and this is perhaps why the name of "common-sense" is used, because the superior mind seems in its power of comprehending others to be itself a part of the general sense of the community. All men of high practical capacity have this power. It is the first condition of success. But in men who have received a philosophical or literary education there is a tendency to embellish, for purposes of persuasion, or perhaps for their own gratification, the language in which they recommend their conclusions, or to state those conclusions in the light of large general principles, a tendency which may, unless carefully watched, carry them too high above the heads of the crowd. Lincoln, never having had such an education, spoke to the people as one of themselves. He seemed to be saying not only what each felt, but expressing the feeling just as each would have expressed it. In reality, he was quite as much above his neighbours in insight as was the polished orator or writer, but the plain directness of his language seemed to keep him on their level. His strength lay less in the form and vesture of the thought than in the thought itself, in the large, simple, practical view which he took of the position. And thus, to repeat what has been said already, the sterling merit of these speeches of his, that which made them effective when they were delivered and makes them worth reading to-day, is to be found in the justness of his conclusions and their fitness to the circumstances of the time. When he rose into higher air, when his words were clothed with stateliness and solemnity, it was the force of his conviction and the emotion that thrilled through his utterance, that printed the words deep upon the minds and drove them home to the hearts of the people.

What is a great man? Common speech, which after all must be our guide to the sense of the terms which the world uses, gives this name to many sorts of men. How far greatness lies in the power and range of the intellect, how far in the strength of the will, how far in elevation of view and aim and purpose,—this is a question too large to be debated here. But of Abraham Lincoln it may be truly said that in his greatness all three elements were present. He had not the brilliance, either in thought or word or act, that dazzles, nor the restless activity that occasionally pushes to the front even persons with gifts not of the first order. He was a patient, thoughtful, melancholy man, whose intelligence, working sometimes slowly but always steadily and surely, was capacious enough to embrace and vigorous enough to master the incomparably difficult facts and problems he was called to deal with. His executive talent showed itself not in sudden and startling strokes, but in the calm serenity with which he formed his judgments and laid his plans, in the undismayed firmness with which he adhered to them in the face of popular clamour, of conflicting counsels from his advisers, sometimes, even, of what others deemed all but hopeless failure. These were the qualities needed in one who had to pilot the Republic through the heaviest storm that had ever broken upon it. But the mainspring of his power, and the truest evidence of his greatness, lay in the nobility of his aims, in the fervour of his conviction, in the stainless rectitude which guided his action and won for him the confidence of the people. Without these things neither the vigour of his intellect nor the firmness of his will would have availed.

There is a vulgar saying that all great men are unscrupulous. Of him it may rather be said that the note of greatness we feel in his thinking and his speech and his conduct had its source in the loftiness and purity of his character. Lincoln's is one of the careers that refute this imputation on human nature.

JAMES BRYCE

The following is a list of Lincoln's published works:

SELECTIONS.—Letters on Questions of National Policy, etc., 1863; Dedicatory Speech of President Lincoln, etc., at the Consecration of Gettysburg Cemetery, Nov. 19th, 1863, 1864; The Last Address of President Lincoln to the American People, 1865; The Martyr's Monument, 1865; In Memoriam, 1865; Gems from A. Lincoln, 1865; The President's Words, 1866; Emancipation Proclamation—Second Inaugural Address—Gettysburg Speech, 1878; Two Inaugural Addresses and Gettysburg Speech, 1889; The Gettysburg Speech and other Papers, with an essay on Lincoln by J.R. Lowell (Riverside Literature Series, 32), 1888; The Table Talk of Abraham Lincoln, ed. W.O. Stoddard, 1894; Political Debates between Abraham Lincoln and Stephen A. Douglas in the celebrated campaign of 1858 in Illinois, etc. Also the two great speeches of Abraham Lincoln at Ohio in 1859, 1894; Political Speeches and Debates of Abraham Lincoln and S.A. Douglas, 1854-1861, edited by A.T. Jones, 1895; Lincoln, Passages from his Speeches and Letters, with Introduction by R.W. Gilder, 1901.

COMPLETE EDITIONS OF WORKS, LETTERS, AND SPEECHES.—H.J. Raymond, History of the Administration of Abraham Lincoln (Speeches, Letters, etc.), 1864; Abraham Lincoln, Pen and Voice, being a Complete Compilation of his Letters, Public Addresses, Messages to Congress, ed. G.M. Van Buren, etc., 1890; Complete Works, ed. J.G. Nicolay and J. Hay, 2 vols., 1894; enlarged edition, with Introduction by R.W. Gilder, etc., 1905, etc.; A. Lincoln's Speeches, compiled by L.E. Chittenden, 1895; The Writings of A. Lincoln, ed. A.B. Lapsley, with an Introduction by Theodore Roosevelt, and a life by Noah Brooks, etc. (Federal Edition), 1905; etc.

LIFE.—H.J. Raymond; The Life and Public Services of A.L., etc., with Anecdotes and Personal Reminiscences, by F.B. Carpenter, 1865; J.H. Barrett, 1865; J.G. Holland, 1866; W.H. Lamon, 1872; W.O. Stoddard, 1884; I.N. Arnold, 1885; J.G. Nicolay and J. Hay, 1890; Condensed Edition, 1902; Recollections of President Lincoln and his Administration, 1891; C.C. Coffin, 1893; J.T. Morse, 1893; J. Hay (The Presidents of the United States), 1894; C.A. Dana, Lincoln and his Cabinet, etc., 1896; J.H. Choate, 1900; Address delivered before the Edinburgh Philosophical Institution, Nov. 13, 1900; I.M. Tarbell, 1900; W.E. Curtis, The True Abraham Lincoln, 1903; J.H. Barrett, A. Lincoln and his Presidency, 1904; J. Baldwin, 1904. A. Rothschild, Lincoln, Master of Men, 1906; F.T. Hill, Lincoln the Lawyer, 1906.

Among those who have written short lives are: Mrs. H. Beecher Stowe, D.W. Bartlett, C.G. Leland, J.C. Power, etc.

PUBLISHERS' NOTE

For permission to use extracts from "The Complete Works of Abraham Lincoln," edited by John G. Nicolay and John Hay, the Publishers wish to thank The Century Company.

They also wish to thank Mr. William H. Lambert, the owner of the copyright, and Mrs. Sarah A. Whitney for their courtesy in allowing them to publish "Lincoln's Lost Speech."

Lincoln's First Public Speech. From an Address to the People of Sangamon County. March 9, 1832

Upon the subject of education, not presuming to dictate any plan or system respecting it, I can only say that I view it as the most important subject which we, as a people, can be engaged in. That every man may receive at least a moderate education, and thereby be enabled to read the histories of his own and other countries, by which he may duly appreciate the value of our free institutions, appears to be an object of vital importance, even on this account alone, to say nothing of the advantages and satisfaction to be derived from all being able to read the Scriptures and other works, both of a religious and moral nature, for themselves.

For my part, I desire to see the time when education—and by its means morality, sobriety, enterprise, and industry—shall become much more general than at present; and should be gratified to have it in my power to contribute something to the advancement of any measure which might have a tendency to accelerate that happy period.

With regard to existing laws, some alterations are thought to be necessary. Many respectable men have suggested that our estray laws—the law respecting the issuing of executions, the road law, and some others—are deficient in their present form, and require alterations. But considering the great probability that the framers of those laws were wiser than myself, I should prefer not meddling with them, unless they were first attacked by others, in which case I should feel it both a privilege and a duty to take that stand which, in my view, might tend to the advancement of justice.

But, fellow-citizens, I shall conclude. Considering the great degree of modesty which should always attend youth, it is probable I have already been more presuming than becomes me. However, upon the subjects of which I have treated, I have spoken as I have thought. I may be wrong in regard to any or all of them; but, holding it a sound maxim that it is better only to be sometimes right than at all times wrong, so soon as I discover my opinions to be erroneous I shall be ready to renounce them.

Every man is said to have his peculiar ambition. Whether it be true or not, I can say, for one, that I have no other so great as that of being truly esteemed of my fellow-men by rendering myself worthy of their esteem. How far I shall succeed in gratifying this ambition is yet to be developed. I am young and unknown to many of you; I was born and have ever remained in the most humble walks of life. I have no wealthy or popular relations or friends to recommend me. My case is thrown exclusively upon the independent voters of the county, and if elected, they will have conferred a favour upon me for which I shall be unremitting in my labours to compensate. But if the good people in their wisdom shall see fit to keep me in the background, I have been too familiar with disappointments to be very much chagrined.

Your friend and fellow-citizen,
A. LINCOLN.

Letter to Colonel Robert Allen. June 21, 1836

Dear Colonel, I am told that during my absence last week you passed through this place, and stated publicly that you were in possession of a fact or facts which, if known to the public, would entirely destroy the prospects of N.W. Edwards and myself at the ensuing election; but that, through favour to us, you should forbear to divulge them. No one has needed favours more than I, and, generally, few have been less unwilling to accept them; but in this case favour to me would be injustice to the public, and therefore I must beg your pardon for declining it. That I once had the confidence of the people of Sangamon, is sufficiently evident; and if I have since done anything, either by design or misadventure, which if known would subject me to a forfeiture of that confidence, he that knows of that thing, and conceals it, is a traitor to his country's interest.

I find myself wholly unable to form any conjecture of what fact or facts, real or supposed, you spoke; but my opinion of your veracity will not permit me for a moment to doubt that you at least believed what you said. I am flattered with the personal regard you manifested for me; but I do hope that, on more mature reflection, you will view the public interest as a paramount consideration, and therefore determine to let the worst come. I here assure you that the candid statement of facts on your part, however low it may sink me, shall never break the tie of personal friendship between us. I wish an answer to this, and you are at liberty to publish both, if you choose.

Lincoln's Opinion on Universal Suffrage. From a Letter published in the Sangamon "Journal." June 13, 1836

I go for all sharing the privileges of the government who assist in bearing its burdens: consequently I go for admitting all whites to the right of suffrage who pay taxes or bear arms [by no means excluding females].

From an Address before the Young Men's Lyceum of Springfield, Illinois. January 27, 1837

As a subject for the remarks of the evening "The perpetuation of our political institutions" is selected. In the great journal of things happening under the sun, we, the American people, find our account running under the date of the nineteenth century of the Christian era. We find ourselves in the peaceful possession of the fairest portion of the earth, as regards extent of territory, fertility of soil, and salubrity of climate. We find ourselves under the government of a system of political institutions conducing more essentially to the ends of civil and religious liberty, than any of which the history of former times tells us. We, when remounting the stage of existence, found ourselves the legal inheritors of these fundamental blessings. We toiled not in the acquirement or the establishment of them; they are a legacy bequeathed to us by a once hardy, brave, and patriotic, but now lamented and departed race of ancestors.

Theirs was the task (and nobly they performed it) to possess themselves, and through themselves us, of this goodly land, and to rear upon its hills and valleys a political edifice of liberty and equal rights; 'tis ours only to transmit these,—the former unprofaned by the foot of the invader; the latter undecayed by lapse of time. This, our duty to ourselves and to our posterity, and love for our species in general, imperatively require us to perform.

How, then, shall we perform it? At what point shall we expect the approach of danger? By what means shall we fortify against it? Shall we expect some transatlantic military giant to step across the ocean and crush us at a blow? Never. All the armies of Europe, Asia and Africa combined, with all the treasure of the earth (our own excepted) in their military chest, with a Bonaparte for a commander, could not, by force, take a drink from the Ohio, or make a track on the Blue Ridge, in a trial of a thousand years.

At what point, then, is the approach of danger to be expected? I answer, if it ever reaches us, it must spring up among us. It cannot come from abroad. If destruction be our lot, we must ourselves be its author and finisher. As a nation of freemen, we must live through all time, or die by suicide.

There is even now something of ill omen among us. I mean the increasing disregard for law which pervades the country; the growing disposition to substitute wild and furious passions in lieu of the sober judgment of courts; and the worse than savage mobs for the executive ministers of justice. This disposition is awfully fearful in any community; and that it now exists in ours, though grating to our feelings to admit, it would be a violation of truth and an insult to our intelligence to deny.

I know the American people are *much* attached to their government. I know they would suffer *much* for its sake. I know they would endure evils long and patiently before they would ever think of exchanging it for another. Yet, notwithstanding all this, if the laws be continually despised and disregarded, if their rights to be secure in their persons and property are held by no better tenure than the caprice of a mob, the alienation of their affection for the government is the natural consequence, and to that sooner or later it must come.

Here, then, is one point at which danger may be expected. The question recurs, how shall we fortify against it? The answer is simple. Let every American, every lover of liberty, every well-wisher to his posterity, swear by the blood of the Revolution never to violate in the least particular the laws of the country, and never to tolerate their violation by others. As the patriots of seventy-six did to the support of the Declaration of Independence, so to the support of the Constitution and the Laws let every American pledge his life, his property, and his sacred honour; let every man remember that to violate the law is to trample on the blood of his father, and to tear the charter of his own and his children's liberty. Let reverence for the laws be breathed by every American mother to the lisping babe that prattles on her lap. Let it be taught in schools, in seminaries, and in colleges. Let it be written in primers, spelling-books, and in almanacs. Let it be preached from the pulpit, proclaimed in legislative halls, and enforced in courts of justice. And, in short, let it become the political religion of the nation.

When I so pressingly urge a strict observance of all the laws, let me not be understood as saying that there are no bad laws, or that grievances may not arise for the redress of which no legal provisions have been made. I mean to say no such thing. But I do mean to say that although bad laws, if they exist, should be repealed as soon as possible, still, while they continue in force, for the sake of example they should be religiously observed. So also in unprovided cases. If such arise, let proper legal provisions be made for them with the least possible delay, but till then let them, if not too intolerable, be borne with.

There is no grievance that is a fit object of redress by mob law. In any case that may arise, as, for instance, the promulgation of abolitionism, one of two positions is necessarily true—that is, the thing is right within itself, and therefore deserves the protection of all law and all good citizens, or it is wrong, and therefore proper to be prohibited by legal enactments; and in neither case is the interposition of mob law either necessary, justifiable, or excusable....

They (histories of the Revolution) were pillars of the temple of liberty; and now that they have crumbled away, that temple must fall unless we, their descendants, supply their places with other pillars, hewn from the solid quarry of sober reason. Passion has helped us, but can do so no more. It will in future be our enemy. Reason—cold, calculating, unimpassioned reason—must furnish all the materials for our future support and defence. Let those materials be moulded into general intelligence, sound morality, and, in particular, a reverence for the Constitution and laws; and that we improved to the last, that we remained free to the last, that we revered his name to the last, that during his long sleep we permitted no hostile foot to pass over or desecrate his resting-place, shall be that which to learn the last trump shall awaken our Washington.

Upon these let the proud fabric of freedom rest, as the rock of its basis; and as truly as has been said of the only greater institution, "the gates of hell shall not prevail against it."

Many great and good men, sufficiently qualified for any task they should undertake, may ever be found, whose ambition would aspire to nothing beyond a seat in Congress, a gubernatorial or a presidential chair. But such belong not to the family of the lion or the brood of the eagle. What? Think you these places would satisfy an Alexander, a Cæsar, or a Napoleon? Never! Towering genius disdains a beaten path. It seeks regions hitherto unexplored. It sees no distinction in adding story to story upon the monuments of fame erected to the memory of others. It denies that it is glory enough to serve under any chief. It scorns to tread in the footsteps of any predecessor, however illustrious. It thirsts and burns for distinction; and, if possible, it will have it, whether at the expense of emancipating slaves, or enslaving free men. Is it unreasonable, then, to expect that some men, possessed of the loftiest genius, coupled with ambition sufficient to push it to its utmost stretch, will at some time spring up among us? And when such a one does, it will require the people to be united with each other, attached to the government and laws, and generally intelligent, to successfully frustrate his design.

Distinction will be his paramount object, and although he would as willingly, perhaps more so, acquire it by doing good as harm, yet that opportunity being passed, and nothing left to be done in the way of building up, he would sit down boldly to the task of pulling down. Here, then, is a probable case, highly dangerous, and such a one as could not well have existed heretofore.

All honour to our Revolutionary ancestors, to whom we are indebted for these institutions. They will not be forgotten. In history we hope they will be read of, and recounted, so long as the Bible shall be read. But even granting that they will, their influence cannot be what it heretofore has been. Even then, they cannot be so universally known, nor so vividly felt, as they were by the generation just gone to rest. At the close of that struggle, nearly every adult male had been a participator in some of its scenes. The consequence was, that of those scenes, in the form of a husband, a father, a son, or a brother, a living history was to be found in every family,—a history bearing the indubitable testimonies to its own authenticity in the limbs mangled, in the scars of wounds received in the midst of the very scenes related; a history, too, that could be read and understood alike by all, the wise and the ignorant, the learned and the unlearned. But those histories are gone. They can be read no more for ever. They were a fortress of strength; but what the invading foemen could never do, the silent artillery of time has done,—the levelling of its walls. They are gone. They were a forest of giant oaks; but the resistless hurricane has swept over them, and left only here and there a lonely trunk, despoiled of its verdure, shorn of its foliage, unshading and unshaded, to murmur in a few more gentle breezes, and to combat with its mutilated limbs a few more ruder storms, and then to sink and be no more.

Humorous Account of His Experiences With a Lady He Was Requested to Marry

A Letter to Mrs. O.H. Browning. Springfield, Illinois. April 1, 1838

Dear Madam, Without apologising for being egotistical, I shall make the history of so much of my life as has elapsed since I saw you the subject of this letter. And, by the way, I now discover that in order to give a full and intelligible account of the things I have done and suffered since I saw you, I shall necessarily have to relate some that happened before.

It was, then, in the autumn of 1836 that a married lady of my acquaintance, and who was a great friend of mine, being about to pay a visit to her father and other relatives residing in Kentucky, proposed to me that on her return she would bring a sister of hers with her on condition that I would engage to become her brother-in-law with all convenient dispatch. I, of course, accepted the proposal, for you know I could not have done otherwise had I really been averse to it; but privately, between you and me, I was most confoundedly well pleased with the project. I had seen the said sister some three years before, thought her intelligent and agreeable, and saw no good objection to plodding life through hand-in-hand with her. Time passed on, the lady took her journey, and in due time returned, sister in company, sure enough. This astonished me a little, for it appeared to me that her coming so readily showed that she was a trifle too willing, but on reflection it occurred to me that she might have been prevailed on by her married sister to come, without anything concerning me having been mentioned to her, and so I concluded that if no other objection presented itself, I would consent to waive this. All this occurred to me on hearing of her arrival in the neighbourhood—for, be it remembered, I had not yet seen her, except about three years previous, as above mentioned. In a few days we had an interview, and, although I had seen her before, she did not look as my imagination had pictured her. I knew she was over-size, but she now appeared a fair match for Falstaff. I knew she was called an "old maid," and I felt no doubt of the truth of at least half of the appellation, but now, when I beheld her, I could not for my life avoid thinking of my mother; and this, not from withered features,—for her skin was too full of fat to permit of its contracting into wrinkles—but from her want of teeth, weather-beaten appearance in general, and from a kind of notion that ran in my head that nothing could have commenced at the size of infancy and reached her present bulk in less than thirty-five or forty years; and, in short, I was not at all pleased with her. But what could I do? I had told her sister that I would take her for better or for worse, and I made a point of honour and conscience in all things to stick to my word, especially if others had been induced to act on it, which in this case I had no doubt they had, for I was now fairly convinced that no other man on earth would have her, and hence the conclusion that they were bent on holding me to my bargain. "Well," thought I, "I have said it, and, be the consequences what they may, it shall not be my fault if I fail to do it." At once I determined to consider her my wife, and this done, all my powers of discovery were put to work in search of perfections in her which might be fairly set off against her defects. I tried to imagine her handsome, which, but for her unfortunate corpulency, was actually true. Exclusive of this, no woman that I have ever seen has a finer face. I also tried to convince myself that the mind was much more to be valued than the person, and in this she was not inferior, as I could discover, to any with whom I had been acquainted.

   Shortly after this, without attempting to come to any positive understanding with her, I set out for Vandalia, when and where you first saw me. During my stay there I had letters from her which did not change my opinion of either her intellect or intention, but, on the contrary, confirmed it in both.

   All this while, although I was fixed "firm as the surge-repelling rock" in my resolution, I found I was continually repenting the rashness which had led me to make it. Through life I have been in no bondage, either real or imaginary, from the thraldom of which I so much desired to be free. After my return home I saw nothing to change my opinion of her in any particular. She was the same, and so was I. I now spent my time in planning how I might get along in life after my contemplated change of circumstances should have taken place, and how I might procrastinate the evil day for a time, which I really dreaded as much, perhaps more, than an Irishman does the halter.

   After all my sufferings upon this deeply interesting subject, here I am, wholly, unexpectedly, completely out of the "scrape," and I now want to know if you can guess how I got out of it—out, clear, in every sense of the term—no violation of word, honour, or conscience. I don't believe you can guess, and so I might as well tell you at once. As the lawyer says, it was done in the manner following, to wit: After I had delayed the matter as long as I thought I could in honour do (which, by the way, had brought me round into the last fall), I concluded I might as well bring it to a consummation without further delay, and so I mustered my resolution and made the proposal to her direct; but, shocking to relate, she answered, No. At first I supposed she did it through an affectation of modesty, which I thought but ill became her under the peculiar circumstances of the case, but on my renewal of the charge I found she repelled it with greater firmness than before. I tried it again and again, but with the same success, or rather with the same want of success.

   I finally was forced to give it up, at which I very unexpectedly found myself mortified almost beyond endurance. I was mortified, it seemed to me, in a hundred different ways. My vanity was deeply wounded by the reflection that I had so long been too stupid to discover her intentions, and at the same time never doubting that I understood them perfectly; and also that she, whom I had taught myself to believe nobody else would have, had actually rejected me with all my fancied greatness. And, to cap the whole, I then for the first time began to suspect that I was really a little in love with her. But let it all go! I'll try and outlive it. Others have been made fools of by the girls, but this can never in truth be said of me. I most emphatically, in this instance, made a fool of myself. I have now come to the conclusion never again to think of marrying, and for this reason—I can never be satisfied with any one who would be blockhead enough to have me.

When you receive this, write me a long yarn about something to amuse me. Give my respects to Mr. Browning.

From a Debate between Lincoln, E.D. Baker, and others against Douglas, Lamborn, and others. Springfield. December 1839

... Mr. Lamborn insists that the difference between the Van Buren party and the Whigs is, that although the former sometimes err in practice, they are always correct in principle, whereas the latter are wrong in principle; and the better to impress this proposition, he uses a figurative expression in these words: "The Democrats are vulnerable in the heel, but they are sound in the heart and in the head." The first branch of the figure—that is, that the Democrats are vulnerable in the heel—I admit is not merely figuratively but literally true. Who that looks but for a moment at their Swartwouts, their Prices, their Harringtons, and their hundreds of others, scampering away with the public money to Texas, to Europe, and to every spot of the earth where a villain may hope to find refuge from justice, can at all doubt that they are most distressingly affected in their heels with a species of running fever? It seems that this malady of their heels operates on the sound-headed and honest-hearted creatures very much like the cork leg in the song did on its owner, which, when he had once got started on it, the more he tried to stop it, the more it would run away. At the hazard of wearing this point threadbare, I will relate an anecdote which seems to be too strikingly in point to be omitted. A witty Irish soldier who was always boasting of his bravery when no danger was near, but who invariably retreated without orders at the first charge of the engagement, being asked by his captain why he did so, replied, "Captain, I have as brave a heart as Julius Cæsar ever had; but somehow or other, whenever danger approaches, my cowardly legs will run away with it." So it is with Mr. Lamborn's party. They take the public money into their hands for the most laudable purpose that wise heads and honest hearts can dictate, but before they can possibly get it out again, their rascally vulnerable heels will run away with them....

Letter to W.G. Anderson. Lawrenceville, Illinois. October 31, 1840

Dear Sir, Your note of yesterday is received. In the difficulty between us of which you speak, you say you think I was the aggressor. I do not think I was. You say my "words imported insult." I meant them as a fair set-off to your own statements, and not otherwise; and in that light alone I now wish you to understand them. You ask for my present "feelings on the subject." I entertain no unkind feelings to you, and none of any sort upon the subject, except a sincere regret that I permitted myself to get into such an altercation.

Extract from a Letter to John T. Stuart. Springfield Illinois. January 23, 1841

For not giving you a general summary of news, you must pardon me; it is not in my power to do so. I am now the most miserable man living. If what I feel were equally distributed to the whole human family, there would not be one cheerful face on earth. Whether I shall ever be better, I cannot tell; I awfully forebode I shall not. To remain as I am is impossible; I must die or be better, it appears to me. The matter you speak of on my account you may attend to as you say, unless you shall hear of my condition forbidding it. I say this because I fear I shall be unable to attend to any business here, and a change of scene might help me. If I could be myself, I would rather remain at home with Judge Logan. I can write no more.

From an Address before the Washingtonian Temperance Society. Springfield, Illinois. February 22, 1842

Although the temperance cause has been in progress for nearly twenty years, it is apparent to all that it is just now being crowned with a degree of success hitherto unparalleled.

The list of its friends is daily swelled by the additions of fifties, of hundreds, and of thousands. The cause itself seems suddenly transformed from a cold abstract theory to a living, breathing, active and powerful chieftain, going forth conquering and to conquer. The citadels of his great adversary are daily being stormed and dismantled; his temples and his altars, where the rites of his idolatrous worship have long been performed, and where human sacrifices have long been wont to be made, are daily desecrated and deserted. The trump of the conqueror's fame is sounding from hill to hill, from sea to sea, and from land to land, and calling millions to his standard at a blast.

"But," say some, "we are no drunkards, and we shall not acknowledge ourselves such by joining a reform drunkard's society, whatever our influence might be." Surely no Christian will adhere to this objection.

If they believe, as they profess, that Omnipotence condescended to take on himself the form of sinful man, and, as such, to die an ignominious death for their sakes, surely they will not refuse submission to the infinitely lesser condescension for the temporal and perhaps eternal salvation of a large, erring, and unfortunate class of their fellow-creatures; nor is the condescension very great. In my judgment, such of us as have never fallen victims have been spared more from the absence of appetite, than from any mental or moral superiority over those who have. Indeed I believe, if we take habitual drunkards as a class, their heads and their hearts will bear an advantageous comparison with those of any other class. There seems ever to have been a proneness in the brilliant and warm-blooded to fall into this vice. The demon of intemperance ever seems to have delighted in sucking the blood of genius and generosity. What one of us but can call to mind some relative more promising in youth than all his fellows, who has fallen a sacrifice to his rapacity? He ever seems to have gone forth like the Egyptian angel of death, commissioned to slay, if not the first, the fairest born of every family. Shall he now be arrested in his desolating career? In that arrest all can give aid that will; and who shall be excused that can and will not? Far around as human breath has ever blown, he keeps our fathers, our brothers, our sons, and our friends prostrate in the chains of moral death....

When the conduct of men is designed to be influenced, persuasion, kind, unassuming persuasion, should ever be adopted. It is an old and a true maxim "that a drop of honey catches more flies than a gallon of gall." So with men. If you would win a man to your cause, first convince him that you are his sincere friend. Therein is a drop of honey that catches his heart, which, say what you will, is the great high-road to his reason, and which, when once gained, you will find but little trouble in convincing his judgment of the justice of your cause, if indeed that cause really be a just one. On the contrary, assume to dictate to his judgment, or to command his action, or to mark him as one to be shunned and despised, and he will retreat within himself, close all the avenues to his head and his heart; and though your cause be naked truth itself, transformed to the heaviest lance, harder than steel, and sharper than steel can be made, and though you throw it with more than herculean force and precision, you shall be no more able to pierce him than to penetrate the hard shell of a tortoise with a rye straw. Such is man, and so must he be understood by those who would lead him, even to his own best interests....

Another error, as it seems to me, into which the old reformers fell, was the position that all habitual drunkards were utterly incorrigible, and therefore must be turned adrift and damned without remedy in order that the grace of temperance might abound, to the temperate then, and to all mankind some hundreds of years thereafter. There is in this something so repugnant to humanity, so uncharitable, so cold-blooded and feelingless, that it never did, nor never can enlist the enthusiasm of a popular cause. We could not love the man who taught it—we could not hear him with patience. The heart could not throw open its portals to it, the generous man could not adopt it—it could not mix with his blood. It looked so fiendishly selfish, so like throwing fathers and brothers overboard to lighten the boat for our security, that the noble-minded shrank from the manifest meanness of the thing. And besides this, the benefits of a reformation to be effected by such a system were too remote in point of time to warmly engage many in its behalf. Few can be induced to labour exclusively for posterity; and none will do it enthusiastically. Posterity has done nothing for us; and theorize on it as we may, practically we shall do very little for it, unless we are made to think we are at the same time doing something for ourselves.

What an ignorance of human nature does it exhibit, to ask or expect a whole community to rise up and labour for the temporal happiness of others, after themselves shall be consigned to the dust, a majority of which community take no pains whatever to secure their own eternal welfare at no more distant day! Great distance in either time or space has wonderful power to lull and render quiescent the human mind. Pleasures to be enjoyed, or pains to be endured, after we shall be dead and gone, are but little regarded even in our own cases, and much less in the cases of others. Still, in addition to this there is something so ludicrous in promises of good or threats of evil a great way off as to render the whole subject with which they are connected easily turned into ridicule. "Better lay down that spade you are stealing, Paddy; if you don't you'll pay for it at the day of judgment." "Be the powers, if ye'll credit me so long I'll take another jist."

From the Circular of the Whig Committee. An Address to the People of Illinois. March 4, 1843

... The system of loans is but temporary in its nature, and must soon explode. It is a system not only ruinous while it lasts, but one that must soon fail and leave us destitute.

As an individual who undertakes to live by borrowing soon finds his original means devoured by interest, and next, no one left to borrow from, so must it be with a government.

We repeat, then, that a tariff sufficient for revenue, or a direct tax, must soon be resorted to; and, indeed, we believe this alternative is now denied by no one. But which system shall be adopted? Some of our opponents in theory admit the propriety of a tariff sufficient for revenue, but even they will not in practice vote for such a tariff; while others boldly advocate direct taxation. Inasmuch, therefore, as some of them boldly advocate direct taxation, and all the rest—or so nearly all as to make exceptions needless—refuse to adopt the tariff, we think it is doing them no injustice to class them all as advocates of direct taxation. Indeed, we believe they are only delaying an open avowal of the system till they can assure themselves that the people will tolerate it. Let us, then, briefly compare the two systems. The tariff is the cheaper system, because the duties, being collected in large parcels, at a few commercial points, will require comparatively few officers in their collection; while by the direct tax system the land must be literally covered with assessors and collectors, going forth like swarms of Egyptian locusts, devouring every blade of grass and other green thing. And, again, by the tariff system the whole revenue is paid by the consumers of foreign goods, and those chiefly the luxuries and not the necessaries of life. By this system, the man who contents himself to live upon the products of his own country pays nothing at all. And surely that country is extensive enough, and its products abundant and varied enough, to answer all the real wants of its people. In short, by this system the burden of revenue falls almost entirely on the wealthy and luxurious few, while the substantial and labouring many, who live at home and upon home products, go entirely free. By the direct tax system, none can escape. However strictly the citizen may exclude from his premises all foreign luxuries, fine cloths, fine silks, rich wines, golden chains, and diamond rings,—still, for the possession of his house, his barn, and his homespun he is to be perpetually haunted and harassed by the tax-gatherer. With these views, we leave it to be determined whether we or our opponents are more truly democratic on the subject.

From a Letter to Martin M. Morris. Springfield, Illinois. March 26, 1843

It is truly gratifying to me to learn that while the people of Sangamon have cast me off, my old friends of Menard, who have known me longest and best, stick to me. It would astonish, if not amuse, the older citizens to learn that I (a stranger, friendless, uneducated, penniless boy, working on a flatboat at ten dollars per month) have been put down here as the candidate of pride, wealth, and aristocratic family distinction. Yet so, chiefly, it was. There was, too, the strangest combination of church influence against me. Baker is a Campbellite; and therefore, as I suppose, with few exceptions, got all that church. My wife has some relations in the Presbyterian churches, and some with the Episcopal churches; and therefore, wherever it would tell, I was set down as either the one or the other, while it was everywhere contended that no Christian ought to go for me, because I belonged to no church, was suspected of being a deist, and had talked about fighting a duel. With all these things, Baker, of course, had nothing to do. Nor do I complain of them. As to his own church going for him, I think that was right enough, and as to the influences I have spoken of in the other, though they were very strong, it would be grossly untrue and unjust to charge that they acted upon them in a body, or were very near so. I only mean that those influences levied a tax of a considerable per cent. upon my strength throughout the religious controversy. But enough of this.

From a Letter to Joshua F. Speed. Springfield. October 22, 1846

We have another boy, born the 10th of March. He is very much such a child as Bob was at his age, rather of a longer order. Bob is "short and low," and I expect always will be. He talks very plainly—almost as plainly as anybody. He is quite smart enough. I sometimes fear that he is one of the little rare-ripe sort that are smarter at about five than ever after. He has a great deal of that sort of mischief that is the offspring of such animal spirits. Since I began this letter, a messenger came to tell me Bob was lost; but by the time I reached the house his mother had found him and had him whipped, and by now, very likely, he is run away again.

From a Letter to William H. Herndon. Washington. January 8, 1848

Dear William, Your letter of December 27th was received a day or two ago. I am much obliged to you for the trouble you have taken, and promise to take in my little business there. As to speech-making, by way of getting the hang of the House, I made a little speech two or three days ago on a post-office question of no general interest. I find speaking here and elsewhere about the same thing. I was about as badly scared, and no worse, as I am when I speak in court. I expect to make one within a week or two, in which I hope to succeed well enough to wish you to see it.

It is very pleasant to learn from you that there are some who desire that I should be re-elected. I most heartily thank them for their partiality; and I can say, as Mr. Clay said of the annexation of Texas, that "personally I would not object" to a re-election, although I thought at the time, and still think, it would be quite as well for me to return to the law at the end of a single term. I made the declaration that I would not be a candidate again, more from a wish to deal fairly with others, to keep peace among our friends, and to keep the district from going to the enemy, than for any cause personal to myself; so that, if it should so happen that nobody else wishes to be elected, I could refuse the people the right of sending me again. But to enter myself as a competitor of others, or to authorize any one so to enter me, is what my word and honour forbid.

From a Letter to William H. Herndon. Washington. June 22, 1848

As to the young men. You must not wait to be brought forward by the older men. For instance, do you suppose that I should ever have got into notice if I had waited to be hunted up and pushed forward by older men? You young men get together and form a "Rough and Ready Club," and have regular meetings and speeches. Take in everybody you can get. Harrison Grimsley, L.A. Enos, Lee Kimball and C.W. Matheny will do to begin the thing; but as you go along gather up all the shrewd, wild boys about town, whether just of age or a little under age—Chris. Logan, Reddick Ridgley, Lewis Zwizler, and hundreds such. Let every one play the part he can play best,—some speak, some sing, and all "holler." Your meetings will be of evenings; the older men, and the women, will go to hear you; so that it will not only contribute to the election of "Old Zach," but will be an interesting pastime, and improving to the intellectual faculties of all engaged. Don't fail to do this.

From a Letter to William H. Herndon. Washington, July 10, 1848

The way for a young man to rise is to improve himself every way he can, never suspecting that anybody wishes to hinder him. Allow me to assure you that suspicion and jealousy never did help any man in any situation. There may sometimes be ungenerous attempts to keep a young man down; and they will succeed, too, if he allows his mind to be diverted from its true channel to brood over the attempted injury. Cast about, and see if this feeling has not injured every person you have ever known to fall into it.

Letter to John D. Johnston. January 2, 1851

Dear Johnston, Your request for eighty dollars I do not think it best to comply with now. At the various times when I have helped you a little you have said to me, "We can get along very well now"; but in a very short time I find you in the same difficulty again. Now, this can only happen by some defect in your conduct. What that defect is, I think I know. You are not lazy, and still you are an idler. I doubt whether, since I saw you, you have done a good whole day's work in any one day. You do not very much dislike to work, and still you do not work much, merely because it does not seem to you that you could get much for it. This habit of uselessly wasting time is the whole difficulty; it is vastly important to you, and still more so to your children, that you should break the habit. It is more important to them, because they have longer to live, and can keep out of an idle habit before they are in it, easier than they can get out after they are in.

You are now in need of some money; and what I propose is, that you shall go to work, "tooth and nail," for somebody who will give you money for it. Let father and your boys take charge of your things at home, prepare for a crop, and make the crop, and you go to work for the best money wages, or in discharge of any debt you owe, that you can get; and, to secure you a fair reward for your labour, I now promise you, that for every dollar you will, between this and the first of May, get for your own labour, either in money or as your own indebtedness, I will then give you one other dollar. By this, if you hire yourself at ten dollars a month, from me you will get ten more, making twenty dollars a month for your work. In this I do not mean you shall go off to St. Louis, or the lead mines, or the gold mines in California, but I mean for you to go at it for the best wages you can get close to home in Coles County. Now, if you will do this, you will be soon out of debt, and, what is better, you will have a habit that will keep you from getting in debt again. But, if I should now clear you out of debt, next year you would be just as deep in as ever. You say you would almost give your place in heaven for seventy or eighty dollars. Then you value your place in heaven very cheap, for I am sure you can, with the offer I make, get the seventy or eighty dollars for four or five months' work. You say if I will furnish you the money you will deed me the land, and, if you don't pay the money back, you will deliver possession. Nonsense! If you can't now live with the land, how will you then live without it? You have always been kind to me, and I do not mean to be unkind to you. On the contrary, if you will but follow my advice, you will find it worth more than eighty times eighty dollars to you.

Letter to John D. Johnston. Shelbyville. November 4, 1851

Dear Brother, When I came into Charleston day before yesterday, I learned that you are anxious to sell the land where you live and move to Missouri. I have been thinking of this ever since, and cannot but think such a notion is utterly foolish. What can you do in Missouri better than here? Is the land any richer? Can you there, any more than here, raise corn and wheat and oats without work? Will anybody there, any more than here, do your work for you? If you intend to go to work, there is no better place than right where you are; if you do not intend to go to work, you cannot get along anywhere. Squirming and crawling about from place to place can do no good. You have raised no crop this year; and what you really want is to sell the land, get the money, and spend it. Part with the land you have, and, my life upon it, you will never after own a spot big enough to bury you in. Half you will get for the land you will spend in moving to Missouri, and the other half you will eat, drink, and wear out, and no foot of land will be bought. Now, I feel it my duty to have no hand in such a piece of foolery. I feel that it is so even on your own account, and particularly on mother's account. The eastern forty acres I intend to keep for mother while she lives; if you will not cultivate it, it will rent for enough to support her—at least, it will rent for something. Her dower in the other two forties she can let you have, and no thanks to me. Now, do not misunderstand this letter; I do not write it in any unkindness. I write it in order, if possible, to get you to face the truth, which truth is, you are destitute because you have idled away all your time. Your thousand pretences for not getting along better are all nonsense; they deceive nobody but yourself. Go to work is the only cure for your case.

A word to mother. Chapman tells me he wants you to go and live with him. If I were you I would try it awhile. If you get tired of it (as I think you will not), you can return to your own home. Chapman feels very kindly to you, and I have no doubt he will make your situation very pleasant.

Note for Law Lecture. Written about July 1, 1850

I am not an accomplished lawyer. I find quite as much material for a lecture in those points wherein I have failed, as in those wherein I have been moderately successful. The leading rule for a lawyer, as for the man of every other calling, is diligence. Leave nothing for to-morrow which can be done to-day. Never let your correspondence fall behind. Whatever piece of business you have in hand, before stopping, do all the labour pertaining to it which can then be done. When you bring a common law-suit, if you have the facts for doing so, write the declaration at once. If a law point be involved, examine the books, and note the authority you rely on upon the declaration itself, where you are sure to find it when wanted. The same of defences and pleas. In business not likely to be litigated,—ordinary collection cases, foreclosures, partitions, and the like,—make all examinations of titles, and note them and even draft orders and decrees in advance. The course has a triple advantage; it avoids omissions and neglect, saves your labour when once done, performs the labour out of court when you have leisure, rather than in court when you have not.

Extemporaneous speaking should be practised and cultivated. It is the lawyer's avenue to the public. However able and faithful he may be in other respects, people are slow to bring him business if he cannot make a speech. And yet there is not a more fatal error to young lawyers than relying too much on speech-making. If any one, upon his rare powers of speaking, shall claim an exemption from the drudgery of the law, his case is a failure in advance.

Discourage litigation. Persuade your neighbours to compromise whenever you can. Point out to them how the nominal winner is often a real loser—in fees, expenses, and waste of time. As a peace-maker the lawyer has a superior opportunity of being a good man. There will still be business enough.

Never stir up litigation. A worse man can scarcely be found than one who does this. Who can be more nearly a fiend than he who habitually overhauls the register of deeds in search of defects in titles, whereon to stir up strife, and put money in his pocket? A moral tone ought to be infused into the profession which should drive such men out of it.

The matter of fees is important, far beyond the mere question of bread and butter involved. Properly attended to, fuller justice is done to both lawyer and client. An exorbitant fee should never be claimed. As a general rule, never take your whole fee in advance, nor any more than a small retainer. When fully paid beforehand, you are more than a common mortal if you can feel the same interest in the case as if something was still in prospect for you, as well as for your client. And when you lack interest in the case the job will very likely lack skill and diligence in the performance. Settle the amount of fee and take a note in advance. Then you will feel that you are working for something, and you are sure to do your work faithfully and well. Never sell a fee-note—at least not before the consideration service is performed. It leads to negligence and dishonesty—negligence by losing interest in the case, and dishonesty in refusing to refund when you have allowed the consideration to fail.

There is a vague popular belief that lawyers are necessarily dishonest. I say vague, because when we consider to what extent confidence and honours are reposed in and conferred upon lawyers by the people, it appears improbable that their impression of dishonesty is very distinct and vivid. Yet the impression is common, almost universal. Let no young man choosing the law for a calling for a moment yield to the popular belief. Resolve to be honest at all events; and if in your own judgment you cannot be an honest lawyer, resolve to be honest without being a lawyer. Choose some other occupation, rather than one in the choosing of which you do, in advance, consent to be a knave.

A Fragment. Written about July 1, 1854

Equality in society alike beats inequality, whether the latter be of the British aristocratic sort or of the domestic slavery sort.

We know Southern men declare that their slaves are better off than hired labourers amongst us. How little they know whereof they speak! There is no permanent class of hired labourers amongst us. Twenty-five years ago I was a hired labourer. The hired labourer of yesterday labours on his own account to-day, and will hire others to labour for him to-morrow.

Advancement—improvement in condition—is the order of things in a society of equals. As labour is the common burden of our race, so the effort of some to shift their share of the burden on to the shoulders of others is the great durable curse of the race. Originally a curse for transgression upon the whole race, when, as by slavery, it is concentrated on a part only, it becomes the double-refined curse of God upon his creatures.

Free labour has the inspiration of hope; pure slavery has no hope. The power of hope upon human exertion and happiness is wonderful. The slave-master himself has a conception of it, and hence the system of tasks among slaves. The slave whom you cannot drive with the lash to break seventy-five pounds of hemp in a day, if you will task him to break a hundred, and promise him pay for all he does over, he will break you a hundred and fifty. You have substituted hope for the rod.

And yet perhaps it does not occur to you that, to the extent of your gain in the case, you have given up the slave system and adopted the free system of labour.

A Fragment on Slavery. July 1854

If A can prove, however conclusively, that he may of right enslave B, why may not B snatch the same argument and prove equally that he may enslave A? You say A is white and B is black. It is colour, then; the lighter having the right to enslave the darker? Take care. By this rule you are to be slave to the first man you meet with a fairer skin than your own.

You do not mean colour exactly? You mean the whites are intellectually the superiors of the blacks, and therefore have the right to enslave them? Take care again. By this rule you are to be slave to the first man you meet with an intellect superior to your own.

But, say you, it is a question of interest, and if you make it your interest you have the right to enslave another. Very well. And if he can make it his interest he has the right to enslave you.

Lincoln's Reply to Senator Douglas at Peoria, Illinois. The Origin of the Wilmot Proviso. October 16, 1854

... Our war with Mexico broke out in 1846. When Congress was about adjourning that session, President Polk asked them to place two millions of dollars under his control, to be used by him in the recess, if found practicable and expedient, in negotiating a treaty of peace with Mexico, and acquiring some part of her territory. A bill was duly gotten up for the purpose, and was progressing swimmingly in the House of Representatives, when a Democratic member from Pennsylvania by the name of David Wilmot moved as an amendment, "Provided, that in any territory thus acquired there shall never be slavery." *This is the origin of the far-famed Wilmot Proviso.* It created a great flutter; but it stuck like wax, was voted into the bill, and the bill passed with it through the House. The Senate, however, adjourned without final action on it, and so both the appropriation and the proviso were lost for the time.

... This declared indifference, but, as I must think, real, covert zeal, for the spread of slavery, I cannot but hate. I hate it because of the monstrous injustice of slavery itself. I hate it because it deprives our republican example of its just influence in the world, enables the enemies of free institutions with plausibility to taunt us as hypocrites, causes the real friends of freedom to doubt our sincerity, and especially because it forces so many good men amongst ourselves into an open war with the very fundamental principles of civil liberty, criticizing the Declaration of Independence, and insisting that there is no right principle of action but self-interest.

Before proceeding let me say that I think I have no prejudice against the Southern people. They are just what we would be in their situation. If slavery did not now exist among them, they would not introduce it. If it did now exist among us, we should not instantly give it up. This I believe of the masses North and South. Doubtless there are individuals on both sides who would not hold slaves under any circumstances, and others who would gladly introduce slavery anew if it were out of existence. We know that some Southern men do free their slaves, go North and become tip-top Abolitionists, while some Northern ones go South and become most cruel slave-masters.

When Southern people tell us they are no more responsible for the origin of slavery than we are, I acknowledge the fact. When it is said that the institution exists, and that it is very difficult to get rid of it in any satisfactory way, I can understand and appreciate the saying. I surely will not blame them for not doing what I should not know how to do myself. If all earthly power were given me, I should not know what to do as to the existing institution. My first impulse would be to free all the slaves, and send them to Liberia, to their own native land. But a moment's reflection would convince me that whatever of high hope (as I think there is) there may be in this in the long run, its sudden execution is impossible. If they were all landed there in a day, they would all perish in the next ten days; and there are not surplus shipping and surplus money enough to carry them there in many times ten days. What then? Free them all, and keep them among us as underlings? Is it quite certain that this betters their condition? I think I would not hold one in slavery at any rate, yet the point is not clear enough for me to denounce people upon. What next? Free them, and make them politically and socially our equals? My own feelings will not admit of this, and if mine would, we well know that those of the great mass of whites will not. Whether this feeling accords with justice and sound judgment is not the sole question, if indeed it is any part of it. A universal feeling, whether well or ill founded, cannot be safely disregarded. We cannot then make them equals. It does seem to me that systems of gradual emancipation might be adopted, but for their tardiness in this I will not undertake to judge our brethren of the South.

Equal justice to the South, it is said, requires us to consent to the extension of slavery to new countries. That is to say, that inasmuch as you do not object to my taking my hog to Nebraska, therefore I must not object to your taking your slave. Now, I admit that this is perfectly logical, if there is no difference between hogs and slaves. But while you thus require me to deny the humanity of the negro, I wish to ask whether you of the South, yourselves, have ever been willing to do as much? It is kindly provided that of all those who come into the world, only a small percentage are natural tyrants. That percentage is no larger in the slave States than in the free. The great majority, South as well as North, have human sympathies, of which they can no more divest themselves than they can of their sensibility to physical pain. These sympathies in the bosoms of the Southern people manifest in many ways their sense of the wrong of slavery, and their consciousness that, after all, there is humanity in the negro. If they deny this let me address them a few plain questions.

In 1820 you joined the North almost unanimously in declaring the African slave-trade piracy, and in annexing to it the punishment of death. Why did you do this? If you did not feel that it was wrong, why did you join in providing that men should be hung for it? The practice was no more than bringing wild negroes from Africa to such as would buy them. But you never thought of hanging men for catching and selling wild horses, wild buffaloes, or wild bears.

Again, you have among you a sneaking individual of the class of native tyrants known as the *slave-dealer*. He watches your necessities, and crawls up to buy your slave at a speculating price. If you cannot help it, you sell to him; but if you can help it, you drive him from your door. You despise him utterly; you do not recognize him as a friend, or even as an honest man. Your children must not play with his; they may rollick freely with the little negroes, but not with the slave-dealer's children. If you are obliged to deal with him, you try to get through the job without so much as touching him. It is common with you to join hands with the men you meet; but with the slave-dealer you avoid the ceremony,—instinctively shrinking from the snaky contact. If he grows rich and retires from business, you still remember him, and still keep up the ban of non-intercourse upon him and his family. Now, why is this? You do not so treat the man who deals in cotton, corn, or tobacco.

And yet again. There are in the United States and Territories, including the District of Columbia, over four hundred and thirty thousand free blacks. At five hundred dollars per head, they are worth over two hundred millions of dollars. How comes this vast amount of property to be running about without owners? We do not see free horses or free cattle running at large. How is this? All these free blacks are the descendants of slaves, or have been slaves themselves; and they would be slaves now but for something that has operated on their white owners, inducing them at vast pecuniary sacrifice to liberate them. What is that something? Is there any mistaking it? In all these cases it is your sense of justice and human sympathy continually telling you that the poor negro has some natural right to himself,—that those who deny it and make mere merchandise of him deserve kickings, contempt, and death.

And now why will you ask us to deny the humanity of the slave, and estimate him as only the equal of the hog? Why ask us to do what you will not do yourselves? Why ask us to do for nothing what two hundred millions of dollars could not induce you to do?

But one great argument in support of the repeal of the Missouri Compromise is still to come. That argument is "the sacred right of self-government." ... Some poet has said,—

"Fools rush in where angels fear to tread."

At the hazard of being thought one of the fools of this quotation, I meet that argument,—I rush in,—I take that bull by the horns.... My faith in the proposition that each man should do precisely as he pleases with all which is exclusively his own, lies at the foundation of the sense of justice there is in me. I extend the principle to communities of men as well as to individuals. I so extend it because it is politically wise as well as naturally just,—politically wise in saving us from broils about matters which do not concern us. Here, or at Washington, I would not trouble myself with the oyster laws of Virginia, or the cranberry laws of Indiana. The doctrine of self-government is right,—absolutely and internally right; but it has no just application as here attempted. Or perhaps I should rather say that whether it has any application here depends upon whether a negro is not or is a man. If he is not a man, in that case he who is a man may, as a matter of self-government, do just what he pleases with him. But if the negro is a man, is it not to that extent a total destruction of self-government to say that he, too, shall not govern himself? When the white man governs himself, that is self-government; but when he governs himself and also governs another man, that is more than self-government,—that is despotism. If the negro is a man, then my ancient faith teaches me that "all men are created equal," and that there can be no moral right in connection with one man's making a slave of another.

Judge Douglas frequently, with bitter irony and sarcasm, paraphrases our argument by saying: "The white people of Nebraska are good enough to govern themselves, but they are not good enough to govern a few miserable negroes!"

Well, I doubt not that the people of Nebraska are and will continue to be as good as the average of people elsewhere. I do not say the contrary. What I do say is that no man is good enough to govern another man without that other's consent. I say this is the leading principle,—the sheet-anchor of American republicanism.

Slavery is founded in the selfishness of man's nature,—opposition to it in his love of justice. These principles are in eternal antagonism, and when brought into collision so fiercely as slavery extension brings them, shocks and throes and convulsions must ceaselessly follow. Repeal the Missouri Compromise; repeal all compromises; repeal the Declaration of Independence; repeal all past history,—you still cannot repeal human nature. It still will be the abundance of man's heart that slavery extension is wrong, and out of the abundance of his heart his mouth will continue to speak....

The Missouri Compromise ought to be restored. Slavery may or may not be established in Nebraska. But whether it be or not, we shall have repudiated—discarded from the councils of the nation—the spirit of compromise; for who, after this, will ever trust in a national compromise? The spirit of mutual concession—that spirit which first gave us the Constitution, and has thrice saved the Union—we shall have strangled and cast from us for ever. And what shall we have in lieu of it? The South flushed with triumph and tempted to excess; the North betrayed, as they believed, brooding on wrong and burning for revenge. One side will provoke, the other resent. The one will taunt, the other defy; one aggresses, the other retaliates. Already a few in the North defy all constitutional restraints, resist the execution of the Fugitive Slave Law, and even menace the institution of slavery in the States where it exists. Already a few in the South claim the constitutional right to take and hold slaves in the free States, demand the revival of the slave-trade, and demand a treaty with Great Britain by which fugitive slaves may be reclaimed from Canada. As yet they are but few on either side. It is a grave question for lovers of the Union, whether the final destruction of the Missouri Compromise, and with it the spirit of all compromise, will or will not embolden and embitter each of these, and fatally increase the number of both.

... Some men, mostly Whigs, who condemn the repeal of the Missouri Compromise, nevertheless hesitate to go for its restoration, lest they be thrown in company with the Abolitionists. Will they allow me, as an old Whig, to tell them good-humouredly that I think this is very silly? Stand with anybody that stands right. Stand with him while he is right, and part with him when he goes wrong. Stand with the Abolitionist in restoring the Missouri Compromise, and stand against him when he attempts to repeal the Fugitive Slave Law. In the latter case you stand with the Southern disunionist. What of that? You are still right. In both cases you are right In both cases you expose the dangerous extremes. In both you stand on the middle ground and hold the ship level and steady. In both you are national, and nothing less than national. This is the good old Whig ground. To desert such ground because of any company is to be less than a Whig, less than a man, less than an American.

I particularly object to the new position which the avowed principle of this Nebraska law gives to slavery in the body politic. I object to it because it assumes that there can be moral right in the enslaving of one man by another. I object to it as a dangerous dalliance for free people—a sad evidence that, feeling over-prosperity, we forget right; that liberty as a principle we have ceased to revere. I object to it because the Fathers of the Republic eschewed and rejected it. The argument of "necessity" was the only argument they ever admitted in favour of slavery, and so far, and so far only as it carried them, did they ever go. They found the institution existing among us, which they could not help, and they cast the blame on the British king for having permitted its introduction. Thus we see the plain, unmistakable spirit of their age towards slavery was hostility to the principle, and toleration only by necessity.

But now it is to be transformed into a *sacred right*.... Henceforth it is to be the chief jewel of the nation,—the very figure-head of the ship of State. Little by little, but steadily as man's march to the grave, we have been giving up the old for the new faith. Near eighty years ago we began by declaring that all men are created equal; but now from that beginning we have run down to the other declaration, that for some men to enslave others is a sacred right of self-government. These principles cannot stand together. They are as opposite as God and Mammon; and whoever holds to the one must despise the other....

Our Republican robe is soiled and trailed in the dust. Let us purify it. Let us turn and wash it white in the spirit if not the blood of the Revolution. Let us turn slavery from its claims of moral right, back upon its existing legal rights and its arguments of necessity. Let us return it to the position our fathers gave it, and there let it rest in peace. Let us re-adopt the Declaration of Independence, and with it the practices and policy which harmonize with it. Let North and South, let all Americans, let all lovers of liberty everywhere, join in the great and good work. If we do this, we shall not only have saved the Union, but we shall have so saved it as to make and to keep it for ever worthy of the saving.

From Letter to the Hon. Geo. Robertson, Lexington, Kentucky. Springfield, Illinois. August 15, 1855

My dear Sir, ... You are not a friend of slavery in the abstract. In that speech you spoke of "the peaceful extinction of slavery" and used other expressions indicating your belief that the thing was, at some time, to have an end. Since then we have had thirty-six years of experience; and this experience has demonstrated, I think, that there is no peaceful extinction of slavery in prospect for us. The signal failure of Henry Clay and other good and great men, in 1849, to effect anything in favour of gradual emancipation in Kentucky, together with a thousand other signs, extinguishes that hope utterly. On the question of liberty, as a principle, we are not what we have been. When we were the political slaves of King George, and wanted to be free, we called the maxim that "all men are created equal" a self-evident truth; but now when we have grown fat, and have lost all dread of being slaves ourselves, we have become so greedy to be *masters* that we call the same maxim "a self-evident lie." The Fourth of July has not quite dwindled away; it is still a great day for burning fire-crackers!

That spirit which desired the peaceful extinction of slavery has itself become extinct with the *occasion* and the *men* of the Revolution. Under the impulse of that occasion, nearly half the States adopted systems of emancipation at once; and it is a significant fact that not a single State has done the like since. So far as peaceful, voluntary emancipation is concerned, the condition of the negro slave in America, scarcely less terrible to the contemplation of the free mind, is now as fixed and hopeless of change for the better as that of the lost souls of the finally impenitent. The Autocrat of all the Russias will resign his crown and proclaim his subjects free republicans, sooner than will our American masters voluntarily give up their slaves.

Our political problem now is, "Can we as a nation continue together *permanently—for ever—* half slave, and half free?" The problem is too mighty for me. May God in his mercy superintend the solution.

Your much obliged friend, and humble servant,
A. LINCOLN.

Extracts from Letter to Joshua F. Speed. August 24, 1855

You suggest that in political action now, you and I would differ. I suppose we would; not quite so much, however, as you may think. You know I dislike slavery, and you fully admit the abstract wrong of it. So far there is no cause of difference. But you say that sooner than yield your legal right to the slave, especially at the bidding of those who are not themselves interested, you would see the Union dissolved. I am not aware that any one is bidding you yield that right; very certainly I am not. I leave that matter entirely to yourself. I also acknowledge your rights and my obligations under the Constitution in regard to your slaves. I confess I hate to see the poor creatures hunted down and caught and carried back to their stripes and unrequited toil; but I bite my lips and keep quiet. In 1841, you and I had together a tedious low-water trip on a steamboat, from Louisville to St. Louis. You may remember, as I well do, that from Louisville to the mouth of the Ohio, there were on board ten or a dozen slaves shackled together with irons. That sight was a continued torment to me, and I see something like it every time I touch the Ohio or any other slave border. It is not fair for you to assume that I have no interest in a thing which has, and continually exercises, the power of making me miserable. You ought rather to appreciate how much the great body of the Northern people do crucify their feelings in order to maintain their loyalty to the Constitution and the Union. I do oppose the extension of slavery, because my judgment and feeling so prompt me, and I am under no obligations to the contrary. If for this you and I must differ, differ we must. You say if you were President, you would send an army and hang the leaders of the Missouri outrages upon the Kansas elections; still, if Kansas fairly votes herself a slave State she must be admitted, or the Union must be dissolved. But how if she votes herself a slave State unfairly; that is, by the very means for which you say you would hang men? Must she still be admitted, or the Union dissolved? That will be the phase of the question when it first becomes a practical one. In your assumption that there may be a fair decision of the slavery question in Kansas, I plainly see that you and I would differ about the Nebraska law. I look upon that enactment, not as a law, but as a violence from the beginning. It was conceived in violence, is maintained in violence, and is being executed in violence. I say it was conceived in violence, because the destruction of the Missouri Compromise, under the circumstances, was nothing less than violence. It was passed in violence, because it could not have passed at all but for the votes of many members in violence of the known will of their constituents. It is maintained in violence, because the elections since clearly demand its repeal, and the demand is openly disregarded.

You say men ought to be hung for the way they are executing the law; I say that the way it is being executed is quite as good as any of its antecedents. It is being executed in the precise way which was intended from the first, else why does no Nebraska man express astonishment or condemnation? Poor Reeder is the only public man who has been silly enough to believe that anything like fairness was ever intended, and he has been bravely undeceived.

That Kansas will form a slave constitution, and with it ask to be admitted into the Union, I take to be already a settled question, and so settled by the very means you so pointedly condemn. By every principle of law ever held by any court North or South, every negro taken to Kansas *is* free; yet in utter disregard of this—in the spirit of violence merely—that beautiful Legislature gravely passes a law to hang any man who shall venture to inform a negro of his legal rights. This is the subject and real object of the law. If, like Haman, they should hang upon the gallows of their own building, I shall not be among the mourners for their fate. In my humble sphere, I shall advocate the restoration of the Missouri Compromise so long as Kansas remains a Territory; and when, by all these foul means, it seeks to come into the Union as a slave State, I shall oppose it. I am very loath in any case to withhold my assent to the enjoyment of property acquired or located in good faith; but I do not admit that good faith in taking a negro to Kansas to be held in slavery is a probability with any man. Any man who has sense enough to be the controller of his own property has too much sense to misunderstand the outrageous character of the whole Nebraska business. But I digress. In my opposition to the admission of Kansas, I shall have some company, but we may be beaten. If we are, I shall not, on that account, attempt to dissolve the Union. I think it probable, however, we shall be beaten. Standing as a unit among yourselves, you can, directly and indirectly, bribe enough of our men to carry the day, as you could on the open proposition to establish a monarchy. Get hold of some man in the North whose position and ability are such that he can make the support of your measure, whatever it may be, a Democratic-party necessity, and the thing is done. Apropos of this, let me tell you an anecdote. Douglas introduced the Nebraska Bill in January. In February afterward, there was a called session of the Illinois Legislature. Of the one hundred members composing the two branches of that body, about seventy were Democrats. These latter held a caucus, in which the Nebraska Bill was talked of, if not formally discussed. It was thereby discovered that just three, and no more, were in favour of the measure. In a day or two Douglas's orders came on to have resolutions passed approving the bill; and they were passed by large majorities! The truth of this is vouched for by a bolting Democratic member. The masses too, Democratic as well as Whig, were even nearer unanimous against it; but as soon as the party necessity of supporting it became apparent, the way the Democrats began to see the wisdom and justice of it was perfectly astonishing.

You say that if Kansas fairly votes herself a free State, as a Christian you will rejoice at it. All decent slaveholders talk that way, and I do not doubt their candour; but they never vote that way. Although in a private letter or conversation you will express your preference that Kansas should be free, you would vote for no man for Congress who would say the same thing publicly. No such man could be elected from any district in a slave State. You think Stringfellow and company ought to be hung.... The slave-breeders and slave-traders are a small, odious, and detested class among you; and yet in politics they dictate the course of all of you, and are as completely your masters as you are the master of your own negroes. You inquire where I now stand. That is a disputed point. I think I am a Whig; but others say there are no Whigs, and that I am an Abolitionist. When I was at Washington, I voted for the Wilmot Proviso as good as forty times; and I never heard of any one attempting to unwhig me for that. I now do no more than oppose the extension of slavery. I am not a Know-nothing; that is certain. How could I be? How can any one who abhors the oppression of negroes be in favour of degrading classes of white people? Our progress in degeneracy appears to me to be pretty rapid. As a nation, we began by declaring that *all men are created equal*. We now practically read it, *all men are created equal except negroes*. When the Know-nothings get control, it will read, *all men are created equal except negroes* and foreigners and Catholics. When it comes to this, I shall prefer emigrating to some country where they make no pretence of loving liberty—to Russia, for instance, where despotism can be taken pure, and without the base alloy of hypocrisy.... My kindest regards to Mrs. Speed. On the leading subject of this letter I have more of her sympathy than I have of yours; and yet let me say I am your friend for ever.

A. LINCOLN.

Mr. Lincoln's Speech. May 19, 1856

Mr. Chairman and Gentlemen, I was over at [cries of "Platform!" "Take the platform!"]—I say, that while I was at Danville Court, some of our friends of anti-Nebraska got together in Springfield and elected me as one delegate to represent old Sangamon with them in this convention, and I am here certainly as a sympathizer in this movement and by virtue of that meeting and selection. But we can hardly be called delegates strictly, inasmuch as, properly speaking, we represent nobody but ourselves. I think it altogether fair to say that we have no anti-Nebraska party in Sangamon, although there is a good deal of anti-Nebraska feeling there; but I say for myself, and I think I may speak also for my colleagues, that we who are here fully approve of the platform and of all that has been done [A voice: "Yes!"]; and even if we are not regularly delegates, it will be right for me to answer your call to speak. I suppose we truly stand for the public sentiment of Sangamon on the great question of the repeal, although we do not yet represent many numbers who have taken a distinct position on the question.

We are in a trying time—it ranges above mere party—and this movement to call a halt and turn our steps backward needs all the help and good counsels it can get; for unless popular opinion makes itself very strongly felt, and a change is made in our present course, *blood will flow on account of Nebraska, and brother's hand will be raised against brother*! [The last sentence was uttered in such an earnest, impressive, if not, indeed, tragic, manner, as to make a cold chill creep over me. Others gave a similar experience.]

I have listened with great interest to the earnest appeal made to Illinois men by the gentleman from Lawrence [James S. Emery] who has just addressed us so eloquently and forcibly. I was deeply moved by his statement of the wrongs done to free-State men out there. I think it just to say that all true men North should sympathize with them, and ought to be willing to do any possible and needful thing to right their wrongs. But we must not promise what we ought not, lest we be called on to perform what we cannot; we must be calm and moderate, and consider the whole difficulty, and determine what is possible and just. We must not be led by excitement and passion to do that which our sober judgments would not approve in our cooler moments. We have higher aims; we will have more serious business than to dally with temporary measures.

We are here to stand firmly for a principle—to stand firmly for a right. We know that great political and moral wrongs are done, and outrages committed, and we denounce those wrongs and outrages, although we cannot, at present, do much more. But we desire to reach out beyond those personal outrages and establish a rule that will apply to all, and so prevent any future outrages.

We have seen to-day that every shade of popular opinion is represented here, with *Freedom* or rather *Free-Soil* as the basis. We have come together as in some sort representatives of popular opinion against the extension of slavery into territory now free in fact as well as by law, and the pledged word of the statesmen of the nation who are now no more. We come—we are here assembled together—to protest as well as we can against a great wrong, and to take measures, as well as we now can, to make that wrong right; to place the nation, as far as it may be possible now, as it was before the repeal of the Missouri Compromise; and the plain way to do this is to restore the Compromise, and to demand and determine that *Kansas shall be free!* [Immense applause.] While we affirm, and reaffirm, if necessary, our devotion to the principles of the Declaration of Independence, let our practical work here be limited to the above. We know that there is not a perfect agreement of sentiment here on the public questions which might be rightfully considered in this convention, and that the indignation which we all must feel cannot be helped; but all of us must give up something for the good of the cause. There is one desire which is uppermost in the mind, one wish common to us all—to which no dissent will be made; and I counsel you earnestly to bury all resentment, to sink all personal feeling, make all things work to a common purpose in which we are united and agreed about, and which all present will agree is absolutely necessary—which *must* be done by any rightful mode if there be such: *Slavery must be kept out of Kansas*! [Applause.] The test—the pinch—is right there. If we lose Kansas to freedom, an example will be set which will prove fatal to freedom in the end. We, therefore, in the language of the *Bible*, must "lay the axe to the root of the tree." Temporizing will not do longer; now is the time for decision—for firm, persistent, resolute action. [Applause.]

The Nebraska bill, or rather Nebraska law, is not one of wholesome legislation, but was and is an act of legislative usurpation, whose result, if not indeed intention, is to make slavery national; and unless headed off in some effective way, we are in a fair way to see this land of boasted freedom converted into a land of slavery in fact. [Sensation.] Just open your two eyes, and see if this be not so. I need do no more than state, to command universal approval, that almost the entire North, as well as a large following in the border States, is radically opposed to the planting of slavery in free territory. Probably in a popular vote throughout the nation nine-tenths of the voters in the free States, and at least one-half in the border States, if they could express their sentiments freely, would vote NO on such an issue; and it is safe to say that two-thirds of the votes of the entire nation would be opposed to it. And yet, in spite of this overbalancing of sentiment in this free country, we are in a fair way to see Kansas present itself for admission as a slave State. Indeed, it is a felony, by the local law of Kansas, to deny that slavery exists there even now. By every principle of law, a negro in Kansas is free; yet the *bogus* legislature makes it an infamous crime to tell him that he is free!

The party lash and the fear of ridicule will overawe justice and liberty; for it is a singular fact, but none the less a fact, and well known by the most common experience, that men will do things under the terror of the party lash that they would not on any account or for any consideration do otherwise; while men who will march up to the mouth of a loaded cannon without shrinking, will run from the terrible name of "Abolitionist," even when pronounced by a worthless creature whom they, with good reason, despise. For instance—to press this point a little—Judge Douglas introduced his anti-Nebraska bill in January; and we had an extra session of our legislature in the succeeding February, in which were seventy-five Democrats; and at a party caucus, fully attended, there were just three votes out of the whole seventy-five, for the measure. But in a few days orders came on from Washington, commanding them to approve the measure; the party lash was applied, and it was brought up again in caucus, and passed by a large majority. The masses were against it, but party necessity carried it; and it was passed through the lower house of Congress against the will of the people, for the same reason. Here is where the greatest danger lies—that, while we profess to be a government of law and reason, law will give way to violence on demand of this awful and crushing power. Like the great Juggernaut—I think that is the name—the great idol, it crushes everything that comes in its way, and makes a—or as I read once, in a black-letter law book, "a slave is a human being who is legally not a *person*, but a *thing*." And if the safeguards to liberty are broken down, as is now attempted, when they have made *things* of all the free negroes, how long, think you, before they will begin to make *things* of poor white men? [Applause.] Be not deceived. Revolutions do not go backward. The founder of the Democratic party declared that *all* men were created equal. His successor in the leadership has written the word "white" before men, making it read "all *white* men are created equal." Pray, will or may not the Know-nothings, if they should get in power, add the word "protestant," making it read "*all protestant white men*"?

Meanwhile the hapless negro is the fruitful subject of reprisals in other quarters. John Pettit, whom Tom Benton paid his respects to, you will recollect, calls the immortal Declaration "a self-evident lie;" while at the birth-place of freedom—in the shadow of Bunker Hill and of the "cradle of liberty," at the home of the Adamses and Warren and Otis—Choate, from our side of the house, dares to fritter away the birthday promise of liberty by proclaiming the Declaration to be "a string of glittering generalities;" and the Southern Whigs, working hand in hand with pro-slavery Democrats, are making Choate's theories practical. Thomas Jefferson, a slaveholder, mindful of the moral element in slavery, solemnly declared that he "trembled for his country when he remembered that God is just;" while Judge Douglas, with an insignificant wave of the hand, "don't care whether slavery is voted up or voted down." Now, if slavery is right, or even negative, he has a right to treat it in this trifling manner. But if it is a moral and political wrong, as all Christendom considers it to be, how can he answer to God for this attempt to spread and fortify it? [Applause.]

But no man, and Judge Douglas no more than any other, can maintain a negative, or merely neutral, position on this question; and, accordingly, he avows that the Union was made *by* white men and *for* white men and their descendants. As matter of fact, the first branch of the proposition is historically true; the government was made by white men, and they were and are the superior race. This I admit. But the corner-stone of the government, so to speak, was the declaration that "*all* men are created equal," and all entitled to "life, liberty, and the pursuit of happiness." [Applause.]

And not only so, but the framers of the Constitution were particular to keep out of that instrument the word "slave," the reason being that slavery would ultimately come to an end, and they did not wish to have any reminder that in this free country human beings were ever prostituted to slavery. [Applause.] Nor is it any argument that we are superior and the negro inferior—that he has but one talent while we have ten. Let the negro possess the little he has in independence; if he has but one talent, he should be permitted to keep the little he has. [Applause.] But slavery will endure no test of reason or logic; and yet its advocates, like Douglas, use a sort of bastard logic, or noisy assumption, it might better be termed, like the above, in order to prepare the mind for the gradual, but none the less certain, encroachments of the Moloch of slavery upon, the fair domain of freedom. But however much you may argue upon it, or smother it in soft phrases, slavery can only be maintained by force—by violence. The repeal of the Missouri Compromise was by violence. It was a violation of both law and the sacred obligations of honour, to overthrow and trample underfoot a solemn compromise, obtained by the fearful loss to freedom of one of the fairest of our Western domains. Congress violated the will and confidence of its constituents in voting for the bill; and while public sentiment, as shown by the elections of 1854, demanded the restoration of this compromise, Congress violated its trust by refusing, simply because it had the force of numbers to hold on to it. And murderous violence is being used now, in order to force slavery on to Kansas; for it cannot be done in any other way. [Sensation.]

The necessary result was to establish the rule of violence—force, instead of the rule of law and reason; to perpetuate and spread slavery, and, in time, to make it general. We see it at both ends of the line. In Washington, on the very spot where the outrage was started, the fearless Sumner is beaten to insensibility, and is now slowly dying; while senators who claim to be gentlemen and Christians stood by, countenancing the act, and even applauding it afterward in their places in the Senate. Even Douglas, our man, saw it all and was within helping distance, yet let the murderous blows fall unopposed. Then, at the other end of the line, at the very time Sumner was being murdered, Lawrence was being destroyed for the crime of Freedom. It was the most prominent stronghold of liberty in Kansas, and must give way to the all-dominating power of slavery. Only two days ago, Judge Trumbull found it necessary to propose a bill in the Senate to prevent a general civil war and to restore peace in Kansas.

We live in the midst of alarms; anxiety beclouds the future; we expect some new disaster with each newspaper we read. Are we in a healthful political state? Are not the tendencies plain? Do not the signs of the times point plainly the way in which we are going? [Sensation.]

In the early days of the Constitution slavery was recognized, by South and North alike, as an evil, and the division of sentiment about it was not controlled by geographical lines or considerations of climate, but by moral and philanthropic views. Petitions for the abolition of slavery were presented to the very first Congress by Virginia and Massachusetts alike. To show the harmony which prevailed, I will state that a fugitive slave law was passed in 1793, with no dissenting voice in the Senate, and but seven dissenting votes in the House. It was, however, a wise law, moderate, and, under the Constitution, a just one. Twenty-five years later, a more stringent law was proposed and defeated; and thirty-five years after that, the present law, drafted by Mason of Virginia, was passed by Northern votes. I am not, just now, complaining of this law, but I am trying to show how the current sets; for the proposed law of 1817 was far less offensive than the present one. In 1774 the Continental Congress pledged itself, without a dissenting vote, to wholly discontinue the slave trade, and to neither purchase nor import any slave: and less than three months before the passage of the Declaration of Independence, the same Congress which adopted that declaration unanimously resolved "that *no slave be imported into any of the thirteen United Colonies.*" [Great applause.]

On the second day of July, 1776, the draft of a Declaration of Independence was reported to Congress by the committee, and in it the slave trade was characterized as "an execrable commerce," as "a piratical warfare," as the "opprobrium of infidel powers," and as "a cruel war against human nature." [Applause.] All agreed on this except South Carolina and Georgia, and in order to preserve harmony, and from the necessity of the case, these expressions were omitted. Indeed, abolition societies existed as far south as Virginia; and it is a well-known fact that Washington, Jefferson, Madison, Lee, Henry, Mason, and Pendleton were qualified abolitionists, and much more radical on that subject than we of the Whig and Democratic parties claim to be to-day. On March 1, 1784, Virginia ceded to the confederation all its lands lying northwest of the Ohio River. Jefferson, Chase of Maryland, and Howell of Rhode Island, as a committee on that and territory thereafter *to be ceded*, reported that no slavery should exist after the year 1800. Had this report been adopted, not only the Northwest, but Kentucky, Tennessee, Alabama, and Mississippi also would have been free; but it required the assent of nine States to ratify it. North Carolina was divided, and thus its vote was lost; and Delaware, Georgia, and New Jersey refused to vote. In point of fact, as it was, it was assented to by six States. Three years later, on a square vote to exclude slavery from the Northwest, only one vote, and that from New York, was against it. And yet, thirty-seven years later, five thousand citizens of Illinois out of a voting mass of less than twelve thousand, deliberately, after a long and heated contest, voted to introduce slavery in Illinois; and, to-day, a large party in the free State of Illinois are willing to vote to fasten the shackles of slavery on the fair domain of Kansas, notwithstanding it received the dowry of freedom long before its birth as a political community. I repeat, therefore, the question, Is it not plain in what direction we are tending? [Sensation.] In the colonial time, Mason, Pendleton, and Jefferson were as hostile to slavery in Virginia as Otis, Ames, and the Adamses were in Massachusetts; and Virginia made as earnest an effort to get rid of it as old Massachusetts did. But circumstances were against them and they failed; but not that the good-will of its leading men was lacking. Yet within less than fifty years Virginia changed its tune, and made negro-breeding for the cotton and sugar States one of its leading industries. [Laughter and applause.]

In the Constitutional Convention, George Mason of Virginia made a more violent abolition speech than my friends Lovejoy or Codding would desire to make here to-day—a speech which could not be safely repeated anywhere on Southern soil in this enlightened year. But while there were some differences of opinion on this subject even then, discussion was allowed; but as you see by the Kansas slave code, which, as you know, is the Missouri slave code, merely ferried across the river, it is a felony to even express an opinion hostile to that foul blot in the land of Washington and the Declaration of Independence. [Sensation.]

In Kentucky—my State—in 1849, on a test vote, the mighty influence of Henry Clay and many other good men there could not get a symptom of expression in favour of gradual emancipation on a plain issue of marching toward the light of civilization with Ohio and Illinois; but the State of Boone and Hardin and Henry Clay, with a *nigger* under each arm, took the black trail toward the deadly swamps of barbarism. Is there—can there be—any doubt about this thing? And is there any doubt that we must all lay aside our prejudices and march, shoulder to shoulder, in the great army of Freedom? [Applause.]

Every Fourth of July our young orators all proclaim this to be "the land of the *free* and the home of the brave!" Well, now, when you orators get that off next year, and, may be, this very year, how would you like some old grizzled farmer to get up in the grove and deny it? [Laughter.] How would you like that? But suppose Kansas comes in as a slave State, and all the "border ruffians" have barbecues about it, and free-State men come trailing back to the dishonoured North, like whipped dogs with their tails between their legs, it is—ain't it?—evident that this is no more the "land of the free;" and if we let it go so, we won't dare to say "home of the brave" out loud. [Sensation and confusion.]

Can any man doubt that, even in spite of the people's will, slavery will triumph through violence, unless that will be made manifest and enforced? Even Governor Reeder claimed at the outset that the contest in Kansas was to be fair, but he got his eyes open at last; and I believe that, as a result of this moral and physical violence, Kansas will soon apply for admission as a slave State. And yet we can't mistake that the people don't want it so, and that it is a land which is free both by natural and political law. *No law is free law!* Such is the understanding of all Christendom. In the Somerset case, decided nearly a century ago, the great Lord Mansfield held that slavery was of such a nature that it must take its rise in *positive* (as distinguished from *natural*) law; and that in no country or age could it be traced back to any other source. Will some one please tell me where is the *positive* law that establishes slavery in Kansas? [A voice: "The *bogus* laws."] Aye, the *bogus* laws! And, on the same principle, a gang of Missouri horse-thieves could come into Illinois and declare horse-stealing to be legal [Laughter], and it would be just as legal as slavery is in Kansas. But by express statute, in the land of Washington and Jefferson, we may soon be brought face to face with the discreditable fact of showing to the world by our acts that we prefer slavery to freedom—darkness to light! [Sensation.]

It is, I believe, a principle in law that when one party to a contract violates it so grossly as to chiefly destroy the object for which it is made, the other party may rescind it. I will ask

Browning if that ain't good law. [Voices: "Yes!"] Well, now if that be right, I go for rescinding the whole, entire Missouri Compromise and thus turning Missouri into a free State; and I should like to know the difference—should like for any one to point out the difference—between *our* making a free State of Missouri and *their* making a slave State of Kansas. [Great applause.] There ain't one bit of difference, except that our way would be a great mercy to humanity. But I have never said—and the Whig party has never said—and those who oppose the Nebraska bill do not as a body say, that they have any intention of interfering with slavery in the slave States. Our platform says just the contrary. We allow slavery to exist in the slave States—not because slavery is right or good, but from the necessities of our Union. We grant a fugitive slave law because it is so "nominated in the bond;" because our fathers so stipulated—had to—and we are bound to carry out this agreement. But they did not agree to introduce slavery in regions where it did not previously exist. On the contrary, they said by their example and teachings that they did not deem it expedient—did not consider it right—to do so; and it is wise and right to do just as they did about it [Voices: "Good!"], and that is what we propose—not to interfere with slavery where it exists (we have never tried to do it), and to give them a reasonable and efficient fugitive slave law. [A voice: "No!"] I say YES! [Applause.] It was part of the bargain, and I'm for living up to it; but I go no further; I'm not bound to do more, and I won't agree any further. [Great applause.]

We, here in Illinois, should feel especially proud of the provision of the Missouri Compromise excluding slavery from what is now Kansas; for an Illinois man, Jesse B. Thomas, was its father. Henry Clay, who is credited with the authorship of the Compromise in general terms, did not even vote for that provision, but only advocated the ultimate admission by a second compromise; and, Thomas was, beyond all controversy, the real author of the "slavery restriction" branch of the Compromise. To show the generosity of the Northern members toward the Southern side; on a test vote to exclude slavery from Missouri, ninety voted not to exclude, and eighty-seven to exclude, every vote from the slave States being ranged with the former and fourteen votes from the free States, of whom seven were from New England alone; while on a vote to exclude slavery from what is now Kansas, the vote was one hundred and thirty-four *for* to forty-two *against*. The scheme, as a whole, was, of course, a Southern triumph. It is idle to contend otherwise, as is now being done by the Nebraskaites; it was so shown by the votes and quite as emphatically by the expressions of representative men. Mr. Lowndes of South Carolina was never known to commit a political mistake; his was the great judgment of that section; and he declared that this measure "would restore tranquillity to the country—a result demanded by every consideration of discretion, of moderation, of wisdom, and of virtue." When the measure came before President Monroe for his approval, he put to each member of his cabinet this question: "Has Congress the constitutional power to prohibit slavery in a territory?" And John C. Calhoun and William H. Crawford from the South, equally with John Quincy Adams, Benjamin Rush, and Smith Thompson from the North, alike answered, "*Yes!*" without qualification or equivocation; and this measure, of so great consequence to the South, was passed; and Missouri was, by means of it, finally enabled to knock at the door of the Republic for an open passage to its brood of slaves.

And, in spite of this, Freedom's share is about to be taken by violence—by the force of misrepresentative votes, not called for by the popular will. What name can I, in common decency, give to this wicked transaction? [Sensation.]

But even then the contest was not over; for when the Missouri constitution came before Congress for its approval, it forbade any free negro or mulatto from entering the State. In short, our Illinois "black laws" were hidden away in their constitution [Laughter], and the controversy was thus revived. Then it was that Mr. Clay's talents shone out conspicuously, and the controversy that shook the Union to its foundation was finally settled to the satisfaction of the conservative parties on both sides of the line, though not to the extremists on either, and Missouri was admitted by the small majority of six in the lower House. How great a majority, do you think, would have been given had Kansas also been secured for slavery? [A voice: "A majority the other way."] "A majority the other way," is answered. Do you think it would have been safe for a Northern man to have confronted his constituents after having voted to consign both Missouri and Kansas to hopeless slavery? And yet this man Douglas, who misrepresents his constituents, and who has exerted his highest talents in that direction, will be carried in triumph through the State, and hailed with honour while applauding that act. [Three groans for "*Dug*!"] And this shows whither we are tending. This thing of slavery is more powerful than its supporters—even than the high priests that minister at its altar. It debauches even our greatest men. It gathers strength, like a rolling snow-ball, by its own infamy. Monstrous crimes are committed in its name by persons collectively which they would not dare to commit as individuals. Its aggressions and encroachments almost surpass belief. In a despotism, one might not wonder to see slavery advance steadily and remorselessly into new dominions; but is it not wonderful, is it not even alarming, to see its steady advance in a land dedicated to the proposition that "all men are created equal"? [Sensation.]

It yields nothing itself; it keeps all it has, and gets all it can besides. It really came dangerously near securing Illinois in 1824; it did get Missouri in 1821. The first proposition was to admit what is now Arkansas *and* Missouri as one slave State. But the territory was divided, and Arkansas came in, without serious question, as a slave State; and afterward Missouri, not as a sort of equality, *free*, but also as a slave State. Then we had Florida and Texas; and now Kansas is about to be forced into the dismal procession. [Sensation.] And so it is wherever you look. We have not forgotten—it is but six years since—how dangerously near California came to being a slave State. Texas is a slave State, and four other slave States may be carved from its vast domain. And yet, in the year 1829, slavery was abolished throughout that vast region by a royal decree of the then sovereign of Mexico. Will you please tell me by what *right* slavery exists in Texas to-day? By the same right as, and no higher or greater than, slavery is seeking dominion in Kansas: by political force—peaceful, if that will suffice; by the torch (as in Kansas) and the bludgeon (as in the Senate chamber), if required. And so history repeats itself; and even as slavery has kept its course by craft, intimidation, and violence in the past, so it will persist, in my judgment, until met and dominated by the will of a people bent on its restriction.

We have, this very afternoon, heard bitter denunciations of Brooks in Washington, and Titus, Stringfellow, Atchison, Jones, and Shannon in Kansas—the battle-ground of slavery. I certainly am not going to advocate or shield them; but they and their acts are but the necessary outcome of the Nebraska law. We should reserve our highest censure for the authors of the mischief, and not for the catspaws which they use. I believe it was Shakespeare who said, "Where the offence lies, there let the axe fall;" and, in my opinion, this man Douglas and the Northern men in Congress who advocate "Nebraska" are more guilty than a thousand Joneses and Stringfellows, with all their murderous practices, can be. [Applause.]

We have made a good beginning here to-day. As our Methodist friends would say, "I feel it is good to be here." While extremists may find some fault with the moderation of our platform, they should recollect that "the battle is not always to the strong, nor the race to the swift." In grave emergencies, moderation is generally safer than radicalism: and as this struggle is likely to be long and earnest, we must not, by our action, repel any who are in sympathy with us in the main, but rather win all that we can to our standard. We must not belittle nor overlook the facts of our condition—that we are new and comparatively weak, while our enemies are entrenched and relatively strong. They have the administration and the political power; and, right or wrong, at present they have the numbers. Our friends who urge an appeal to arms with so much force and eloquence, should recollect that the government is arrayed against us, and that the numbers are now arrayed against us as well; or, to state it nearer to the truth, they are not yet expressly and affirmatively for us; and we should repel friends rather than gain them by anything savouring of revolutionary methods. As it now stands, we must appeal to the sober sense and patriotism of the people. We will make converts day by day; we will grow strong by calmness and moderation; we will grow strong by the violence and injustice of our adversaries. And, unless truth be a mockery and justice a hollow lie, we will be in the majority after a while, and then the revolution which we will accomplish will be none the less radical from being the result of pacific measures. The battle of freedom is to be fought out on principle. Slavery is a violation of the eternal right. We have temporized with it from the necessities of our condition; but *as sure as God reigns and school children read*, THAT BLACK FOUL LIE CAN NEVER BE CONSECRATED INTO GOD'S HALLOWED TRUTH! [Immense applause lasting some time.] One of our greatest difficulties is, that men who *know* that slavery is a detestable crime and ruinous to the nation, are compelled, by our peculiar condition and other circumstances, to advocate it concretely, though damning it in the raw. Henry Clay was a brilliant example of this tendency; others of our purest statesmen are compelled to do so; and thus slavery secures actual support from those who detest it at heart. Yet Henry Clay perfected and forced through the Compromise which secured to slavery a great State as well as a political advantage. Not that he hated slavery less, but that he loved the whole Union more. As long as slavery profited by his great Compromise, the hosts of pro-slavery could not sufficiently cover him with praise; but now that this Compromise stands in their way—

"...they never mention him,

His name is never heard:
Their lips are now forbid to speak
That once familiar word."

They have slaughtered one of his most cherished measures, and his ghost would arise to rebuke them. [Great applause.]

Now, let us harmonize, my friends, and appeal to the moderation and patriotism of the people: to the sober second thought; to the awakened public conscience. The repeal of the sacred Missouri Compromise has installed the weapons of violence: the bludgeon, the incendiary torch, the death-dealing rifle, the bristling cannon—the weapons of kingcraft, of the inquisition, of ignorance, of barbarism, of oppression. We see its fruits in the dying bed of the heroic Sumner; in the ruins of the "Free State" hotel; in the smoking embers of the *Herald of Freedom*; in the free-State Governor of Kansas chained to a stake on freedom's soil like a horse-thief, for the crime of freedom. [Applause.] We see it in Christian statesmen, and Christian newspapers, and Christian pulpits, applauding *the cowardly act of a low bully*, WHO CRAWLED UPON HIS VICTIM BEHIND HIS BACK AND DEALT THE DEADLY BLOW. [Sensation and applause.] We note our political demoralization in the catch-words that are coming into such common use; on the one hand, "freedom-shriekers," and sometimes "freedom-screechers" [Laughter]; and, on the other hand, "border ruffians," and that fully deserved. And the significance of catch-words cannot pass unheeded, for they constitute a sign of the times. Everything in this world "jibes" in with everything else, and all the fruits of this Nebraska bill are like the poisoned source from which they come. I will not say that we may not sooner or later be compelled to meet force by force; but the time has not yet come, and if we are true to ourselves, may never come. Do not mistake that the ballot is stronger than the bullet. Therefore let the legions of slavery use bullets; but let us wait patiently till November, and fire ballots at them in return; and by that peaceful policy, I believe we shall ultimately win. [Applause.]

It was by that policy that here in Illinois the early fathers fought the good fight and gained the victory. In 1824 the free men of our State, led by Governor Coles (who was a native of Maryland and President Madison's private secretary), determined that those beautiful groves should never re-echo the dirge of one who has no title to himself. By their resolute determination, the winds that sweep across our broad prairies shall never cool the parched brow, nor shall the unfettered streams that bring joy and gladness to our free soil water the tired feet, of a *slave*; but so long as those heavenly breezes and sparkling streams bless the land, or the groves and their fragrance or their memory remain, the humanity to which they minister SHALL BE FOR EVER FREE! [Great applause.] Palmer, Yates, Williams, Browning, and some more in this convention came from Kentucky to Illinois (instead of going to Missouri), not only to better their conditions, but also to get away from slavery. They have said so to me, and it is understood among us Kentuckians that we don't like it one bit. Now, can we, mindful of the blessings of liberty which the early men of Illinois left to us, refuse a like privilege to the free men who seek to plant

Freedom's banner on our Western outposts? ["No! No!"] Should we not stand by our neighbours who seek to better their conditions in Kansas and Nebraska? ["Yes! Yes!"] Can we as Christian men, and strong and free ourselves, wield the sledge or hold the iron which is to manacle anew an already oppressed race? ["No! No!"] "Woe unto them," it is written, "that decree unrighteous decrees and that write grievousness which they have prescribed." Can we afford to sin any more deeply against human liberty? ["No! No!"]

One great trouble in the matter is, that slavery is an insidious and crafty power, and gains equally by open violence of the brutal as well as by sly management of the peaceful. Even after the ordinance of 1787, the settlers in Indiana and Illinois (it was all one government then) tried to get Congress to allow slavery temporarily, and petitions to that end were sent from Kaskaskia, and General Harrison, the Governor, urged it from Vincennes the capital. If that had succeeded, good-bye to liberty here. But John Randolph of Virginia made a vigorous report against it; and although they persevered so well as to get three favourable reports for it, yet the United States Senate, with the aid of some slave States, finally *squelched* it for good. [Applause.] And that is why this hall is to-day a temple for free men instead of a negro livery stable. [Great applause and laughter.] Once let slavery get planted in a locality, by ever so weak or doubtful a title, and in ever so small numbers, and it is like the Canada thistle or Bermuda grass—you can't root it out. You yourself may detest slavery; but your neighbour has five or six slaves, and he is an excellent neighbour, or your son has married his daughter, and they beg you to help save their property, and you vote against your interest and principles to accommodate a neighbour, hoping that your vote will be on the losing side. And others do the same; and in those ways slavery gets a sure foothold. And when that is done the whole mighty Union—the force of the nation—is committed to its support. And that very process is working in Kansas to-day. And you must recollect that the slave property is worth a billion of dollars ($1,000,000,000); while free-State men must work for sentiment alone. Then there are "blue lodges"—as they call them—everywhere doing their secret and deadly work.

It is a very strange thing, and not solvable by any moral law that I know of, that if a man loses his horse, the whole country will turn out to help hang the thief; but if a man but a shade or two darker than I am is himself stolen, the same crowd will hang one who aids in restoring him to liberty. Such are the inconsistencies of slavery, where a horse is more sacred than a man; and the essence of *squatter* or popular sovereignty—I don't care how you call it—is that if one man chooses to make a slave of another, no third man shall be allowed to object. And if you can do this in free Kansas, and it is allowed to stand, the next thing you will see is ship-loads of negroes from Africa at the wharf at Charleston; for one thing is as truly lawful as the other; and these are the bastard notions we have got to stamp out, else they will stamp us out. [Sensation and applause.]

Two years ago, at Springfield, Judge Douglas avowed that Illinois came into the Union as a slave State, and that slavery was weeded out by the operation of his great, patent, everlasting principle of "popular sovereignty." [Laughter.] Well, now, that argument must be answered, for it has a little grain of truth at the bottom. I do not mean that it is true in essence, as he would have us believe. It could not be essentially true if the ordinance of '87 was valid. But, in point of fact, there were some degraded beings called slaves in Kaskaskia and the other French settlements when our first State constitution was adopted; that is a fact, and I don't deny it. Slaves were brought here as early as 1720, and were kept here in spite of the ordinance of 1787 against it. But slavery did not thrive here. On the contrary, under the influence of the ordinance, the number *decreased* fifty-one from 1810 to 1820; while under the influence of *squatter* sovereignty, right across the river in Missouri, they *increased* seven thousand two hundred and eleven in the same time; and slavery finally faded out in Illinois, under the influence of the law of freedom, while it grew stronger and stronger in Missouri, under the law or practice of "popular sovereignty." In point of fact there were but one hundred and seventeen slaves in Illinois one year after its admission, or one to every four hundred and seventy of its population; or, to state it in another way, if Illinois was a slave State in 1820, so were New York and New Jersey much greater slave States from having had greater numbers, slavery having been established there in very early times. But there is this vital difference between all these States and the judge's Kansas experiment: that they sought to disestablish slavery which had been already established, while the judge seeks, so far as he can, to disestablish freedom, which had been established there by the Missouri Compromise. [Voices: "Good!"]

The Union is undergoing a fearful strain; but it is a stout old ship, and has weathered many a hard blow, and "the stars in their courses," aye, an invisible power, greater than the puny efforts of men, will fight for us. But we ourselves must not decline the burden of responsibility, nor take counsel of unworthy passions. Whatever duty urges us to do or to omit, must be done or omitted; and the recklessness with which our adversaries break the laws, or counsel their violation, should afford no example for us. Therefore, let us revere the Declaration of Independence; let us continue to obey the Constitution and the laws; let us keep step to the music of the Union. Let us draw a cordon, so to speak, around the slave States, and the hateful institution, like a reptile poisoning itself, will perish by its own infamy. [Applause.]

But we cannot be free men if this is, by our national choice, to be a land of slavery. Those who deny freedom to others, deserve it not for themselves; and, under the rule of a just God, cannot long retain it. [Loud applause.]

Did you ever, my friends, seriously reflect upon the speed with which we are tending downward? Within the memory of men now present the leading statesmen of Virginia could make genuine, red-hot abolitionist speeches in old Virginia; and, as I have said, now even in "free Kansas" it is a crime to declare that it is "free Kansas." The very sentiments that I and others have just uttered would entitle us, and each of us, to the ignominy and seclusion of a dungeon; and yet I suppose that, like Paul, we were "free born." But if this thing is allowed to continue, it will be but one step further to impress the same rule in Illinois. [Sensation.]

The conclusion of all is, that we must restore the Missouri Compromise. We must highly resolve that *Kansas must be free*! [Great applause.] We must reinstate the birthday promise of the Republic; we must reaffirm the Declaration of Independence; we must make good in essence as well as in form Madison's vowal that "the word *slave* ought not to appear in the Constitution;" and we must even go further, and decree that only local law, and not that time-honoured instrument, shall shelter a slave-holder. We must make this a land of liberty in fact, as it is in name. But in seeking to attain these results—so indispensable if the liberty which is our pride and boast shall endure—we will be loyal to the Constitution and to the "flag of our Union," and no matter what our grievance—even though Kansas shall come in as a slave State; and no matter what theirs—even if we shall restore the Compromise—WE WILL SAY TO THE SOUTHERN DISUNIONISTS, WE WON'T GO OUT OF THE UNION, AND YOU SHAN'T!!! [This was the climax; the audience rose to its feet *en masse*, applauded, stamped, waved handkerchiefs, threw hats in the air, and ran riot for several minutes. The arch-enchanter who wrought this transformation looked, meanwhile, like the personification of political justice.]

But let us, meanwhile, appeal to the sense and patriotism of the people, and not to their prejudices; let us spread the floods of enthusiasm here aroused all over these vast prairies, so suggestive of freedom. Let us commence by electing the gallant soldier Governor (Colonel) Bissell who stood for the honour of our State alike on the plains and amidst the chaparral of Mexico and on the floor of Congress, while he defied the Southern Hotspur; and that will have a greater moral effect than all the border ruffians can accomplish in all their raids on Kansas. There is both a power and a magic in popular opinion. To that let us now appeal; and while, in all probability, no resort to force will be needed, our moderation and forbearance will stand us in good stead when, if ever, WE MUST MAKE AN APPEAL TO BATTLE AND TO THE GOD OF HOSTS!! [Immense applause and a rush for the orator.]

This speech has been called Lincoln's "Lost Speech," because all the reporters present were so carried away by his eloquence that they one and all forgot to take any notes. If it had not been for a young lawyer, a Mr. H.C. Whitney, who kept his head sufficiently to take notes, we would have no record of it. Mr. Whitney wrote out the speech for McClure's Magazine in 1896. It was submitted to several people who were present at the Bloomington Convention, and they said it was remarkably accurate considering that it was not taken down stenographically.

From his Speech on the Dred Scott Decision. Springfield, Illinois. June 26, 1857

... And now as to the Dred Scott decision. That decision declares two propositions,—first, that a negro cannot sue in the United States courts; and secondly, that Congress cannot prohibit slavery in the Territories. It was made by a divided court,—dividing differently on the different points. Judge Douglas does not discuss the merits of the decision, and in that respect I shall follow his example, believing I could no more improve on McLean and Curtis than he could on Taney.

He denounces all who question the correctness of that decision, as offering violent resistance to it. But who resists it? Who has, in spite of the decision, declared Dred Scott free, and resisted the authority of his master over him?

Judicial decisions have two uses: first, to absolutely determine the case decided; and secondly, to indicate to the public how other similar cases will be decided when they arise. For the latter use, they are called "precedents" and "authorities."

We believe as much as Judge Douglas (perhaps more) in obedience to and respect for the judicial department of government. We think its decisions on constitutional questions, when fully settled, should control not only the particular cases decided, but the general policy of the country, subject to be disturbed only by amendments of the Constitution, as provided in that instrument itself. More than this would be revolution. But we think the Dred Scott decision is erroneous. We know the court that made it has often overruled its own decisions, and we shall do what we can to have it overrule this. We offer no resistance to it.

Judicial decisions are of greater or less authority as precedents according to circumstances. That this should be so, accords both with common-sense and the customary understanding of the legal profession.

If this important decision had been made by the unanimous concurrence of the judges, and without any apparent partisan bias, and in accordance with legal public expectation, and with the steady practice of the departments throughout our history, and had been in no part based on assumed historical facts, which are not really true; or if wanting in some of these, it had been before the court more than once, and had there been affirmed and reaffirmed through a course of years,—it then might be, perhaps would be factious, nay, even revolutionary, not to acquiesce in it as a precedent.

But when, as is true, we find it wanting in all these claims to the public confidence, it is not resistance, it is not factious, it is not even disrespectful to treat it as not having yet quite established a settled doctrine for the country.

I have said in substance, that the Dred Scott decision was in part based on assumed historical facts which were not really true, and I ought not to leave the subject without giving some reasons for saying this, I therefore give an instance or two, which I think fully sustain me. Chief Justice Taney, in delivering the opinion of the majority of the court, insists at great length that negroes were no part of the people who made, or for whom was made, the Declaration of Independence, or the Constitution of the United States.

On the contrary, Judge Curtis, in his dissenting opinion, shows that in five of the then thirteen States—to wit, New Hampshire, Massachusetts, New York, New Jersey, and North Carolina—free negroes were voters, and in proportion to their numbers had the same part in making the Constitution that the white people had. He shows this with so much particularity as to leave no doubt of its truth; and as a sort of conclusion on that point, holds the following language:

"The Constitution was ordained and established by the people of the United States, through the action, in each State, of those persons who were qualified by its laws to act thereon in behalf of themselves and all other citizens of the State. In some of the States, as we have seen, coloured persons were among those qualified by law to act on the subject. These coloured persons were not only included in the body of 'the people of the United States' by whom the Constitution was ordained and established; but in at least five of the States they had the power to act, and doubtless did act, by their suffrages, upon the question of its adoption."

Again, Chief Justice Taney says:

"It is difficult at this day to realize the state of public opinion, in relation to that unfortunate race, which prevailed in the civilized and enlightened portions of the world at the time of the Declaration of Independence, and when the Constitution of the United States was framed and adopted."

And again, after quoting from the Declaration, he says:

"The general words above quoted would seem to include the whole human family, and if they were used in a similar instrument at this day, would be so understood."

In these the Chief Justice does not directly assert, but plainly assumes as a fact, that the public estimate of the black man is more favourable now than it was in the days of the Revolution. This assumption is a mistake. In some trifling particulars the condition of that race has been ameliorated; but as a whole, in this country, the change between then and now is decidedly the other way; and their ultimate destiny has never appeared so hopeless as in the last three or four years. In two of the five States—New Jersey and North Carolina—that then gave the free negro the right of voting, the right has since been taken away; and in a third—New York—it has been greatly abridged; while it has not been extended, so far as I know, to a single additional State, though the number of the States has more than doubled. In those days, as I understand, masters could, at their own pleasure, emancipate their slaves; but since then such legal restraints have been made upon emancipation as to amount almost to prohibition. In those days legislatures held the unquestioned power to abolish slavery in their respective States; but now it is becoming quite fashionable for State constitutions to withhold that power from the legislatures. In those days, by common consent, the spread of the black man's bondage to the new countries was prohibited; but now Congress decides that it will not continue the prohibition, and the Supreme Court decides that it could not if it would. In those days our Declaration of Independence was held sacred by all, and thought to include all; but now, to aid in making the bondage of the negro universal and eternal, it is assailed and sneered at, and construed, and hawked at, and torn, till, if its framers could rise from their graves, they could not at all recognize it. All the powers of earth seem rapidly combining against him. Mammon is after him; ambition follows, philosophy follows, and the theology of the day is fast joining in the cry. They have him in his prison-house; they have searched his person, and left no prying instrument with him. One after another they have closed the heavy iron doors upon him; and now they have him, as it were, bolted in with a lock of a hundred keys, which can never be unlocked without the concurrence of every key; the keys in the hands of a hundred different men, and they scattered to a hundred different and distant places; and they stand musing as to what invention, in all the dominions of mind and matter, can be produced to make the impossibility of escape more complete than it is. It is grossly incorrect to say or assume that the public estimate of the negro is more favourable now than it was at the origin of the government.

... There is a natural disgust in the minds of nearly all white people at the idea of an indiscriminate amalgamation of the white and black races; and Judge Douglas evidently is basing his chief hope upon the chances of his being able to appropriate the benefit of this disgust to himself. If he can, by much drumming and repeating, fasten the odium of that idea upon his adversaries, he thinks he can struggle through the storm. He therefore clings to this hope as a drowning man to the last plank. He makes an occasion for lugging it in from the opposition to the Dred Scott decision. He finds the Republicans insisting that the Declaration of Independence includes *all* men, black as well as white; and forthwith he boldly denies that it includes negroes at all, and proceeds to argue gravely that all who contend it does, do so only because they want to vote, and eat, and sleep, and marry with negroes! He will have it that they cannot be consistent else. Now I protest against the counterfeit logic which concludes that because I do not want a black woman for a slave, I must necessarily want her for a wife. I need not have her for either. I can just leave her alone. In some respects she certainly is not my equal; but in her natural right to eat the bread she earns with her own hands without asking leave of any one else, she is my equal, and the equal of all others.

Chief Justice Taney, in his opinion in the Dred Scott case, admits that the language of the Declaration is broad enough to include the whole human family; but he and Judge Douglas argue that the authors of that instrument did not intend to include negroes, by the fact that they did not at once actually place them on an equality with the whites. Now this grave argument comes to just nothing at all, by the other fact that they did not at once, nor ever afterward, actually place all white people on an equality with one another. And this is the staple argument of both the Chief Justice and the senator, for doing this obvious violence to the plain, unmistakable language of the Declaration.

I think the authors of that notable instrument intended to include *all* men, but they did not intend to declare all men equal *in all respects*. They did not mean to say that all were equal in colour, size, intellect, moral developments, or social capacity. They defined with tolerable distinctness in what respects they did consider all men created equal,—equal with "certain inalienable rights, among which are life, liberty, and the pursuit of happiness." This they said, and this they meant. They did not mean to assert the obvious untruth that all were then actually enjoying that equality, nor yet that they were about to confer it immediately upon them. In fact, they had no power to confer such a boon. They meant simply to declare the right, so that the enforcement of it might follow as fast as circumstances should permit.

They meant to set up a standard maxim for free society, which should be familiar to all and revered by all,—constantly looked to, constantly laboured for, and, even though never perfectly attained, constantly approximated, and thereby constantly spreading and deepening its influence, and augmenting the happiness and value of life to all people of all colours everywhere. The assertion that "all men are created equal," was of no practical use in effecting our separation from Great Britain; and it was placed in the Declaration, not for that, but for future use. Its authors meant it to be as, thank God, it is now proving itself, a stumbling-block to all those who in after times might seek to turn a free people back into the hateful paths of despotism. They knew the proneness of prosperity to breed tyrants, and they meant, when such should reappear in this fair land and commence their vocation, that they should find left for them at least one hard nut to crack.

I have now briefly expressed my view of the meaning and object of that part of the Declaration of Independence which declares that all men are created equal. Now let us hear Judge Douglas's view of the same subject, as I find it in the printed report of his late speech. Here it is:

"No man can vindicate the character, motives and conduct of the signers of the Declaration of Independence except upon the hypothesis that they referred to the white race alone, and not to the African, when they declared all men to have been created equal; that they were speaking of British subjects on this continent being equal to British subjects born and residing in Great Britain; that they were entitled to the same inalienable rights, and among them were enumerated life, liberty, and the pursuit of happiness. The Declaration was adopted for the purpose of justifying the colonists in the eyes of the civilized world in withdrawing their allegiance from the British crown, and dissolving their connection with the mother-country."

My good friends, read that carefully over some leisure hour, and ponder well upon it; see what a mere wreck and mangled ruin Judge Douglas makes of our once glorious Declaration. He says "they were speaking of British subjects on this continent being equal to British subjects born and residing in Great Britain!" Why, according to this, not only negroes but white people outside of Great Britain and America were not spoken of in that instrument. The English, Irish, and Scotch, along with white Americans, were included, to be sure; but the French, Germans, and other white people of the world are all gone to pot along with the Judge's inferior races!

I had thought that the Declaration promised something better than the condition of British subjects; but no, it only meant that we should be equal to them in their own oppressed and unequal condition. According to that, it gave no promise that, having kicked off the king and lords of Great Britain, we should not at once be saddled with a king and lords of our own.

I had thought the Declaration contemplated the progressive improvement in the condition of all men, everywhere; but no, it merely "was adopted for the purpose of justifying the colonists in the eyes of the civilized world in withdrawing their allegiance from the British crown, and dissolving their connection with the mother-country." Why, that object having been effected some eighty years ago, the Declaration is of no practical use now—mere rubbish—old wadding, left to rot on the battle-field after the victory is won.

I understand you are preparing to celebrate the "Fourth," to-morrow week. What for? The doings of that day had no reference to the present; and quite half of you are not even descendants of those who were referred to at that day. But I suppose you will celebrate, and will even go so far as to read the Declaration. Suppose, after you read it once in the old-fashioned way, you read it once more with Judge Douglas's version. It will then run thus: "We told these truths to be self-evident, that all British subjects who were on this continent eighty-one years ago, were created equal to all British subjects born and then residing in Great Britain!"

... The very Dred Scott case affords a strong test as to which party most favours amalgamation, the Republicans or the dear Union-saving Democracy. Dred Scott, his wife and two daughters, were all involved in the suit. We desired the court to have held that they were citizens, so far at least as to entitle them to a hearing as to whether they were free or not; and then also, that they were in fact and in law really free. Could we have had our way, the chances of these black girls ever mixing their blood with that of white people would have been diminished at least to the extent that it could not have been without their consent. But Judge Douglas is delighted to have them decided to be slaves, and not human enough to have a hearing, even if they were free, and thus left subject to the forced concubinage of their masters, and liable to become the mothers of mulattoes in spite of themselves,—the very state of the case that produces nine-tenths of all the mulattoes, all the mixing of the blood of the nation.

"A house divided against itself cannot stand." On Lincoln's Nomination to the United States Senate. Springfield, Illinois. June 17, 1858

If we could first know where we are, and whither we are tending, we could better judge what to do, and how to do it. We are now far into the fifth year since a policy was initiated with the avowed object and confident promise of putting an end to slavery agitation. Under the operation of that policy, that agitation has not only not ceased, but has constantly augmented. In my opinion it will not cease until a crisis shall have been reached and passed. "A house divided against itself cannot stand." I believe this government cannot endure permanently, half slave and half free. I do not expect the Union to be dissolved,—I do not expect the house to fall; but I do expect it will cease to be divided. It will become all one thing, or all the other. Either the opponents of slavery will arrest the further spread of it, and place it where the public mind shall rest in the belief that it is in the course of ultimate extinction; or its advocates will push it forward till it shall become alike lawful in all the States, old as well as new, North as well as South.

Have we no tendency to the latter condition? Let any one who doubts, carefully contemplate that now almost complete legal combination—piece of machinery, so to speak—compounded of the Nebraska doctrine and the Dred Scott decision. Let him consider not only what work the machinery is adapted to do, and how well adapted; but also let him study the history of its construction, and trace, if he can, or rather fail, if he can, to trace the evidences of design and concert of action among its chief architects from the beginning.

The new year of 1854 found slavery excluded from more than half the States by State constitutions, and from most of the national territory by congressional prohibition. Four days later commenced the struggle which ended in repealing that congressional prohibition. This opened all the national territory to slavery, and was the first point gained.

But so far, Congress only had acted; and an indorsement by the people, real or apparent, was indispensable to save the point already gained and give chance for more.

This necessity had not been overlooked, but had been provided for, as well as might be, in the notable argument of *Squatter Sovereignty*, otherwise called *sacred right of self-government*, which latter phrase, though expressive of the only rightful basis of any government, was so perverted in this attempted use of it, as to amount to just this: That if any one man choose to enslave another, no third man shall be allowed to object. That argument was incorporated into the Nebraska bill itself, in the language which follows: "It being the true intent and meaning of this act, not to legislate slavery into any Territory or State, nor to exclude it therefrom; but to leave the people thereof perfectly free to form and regulate their domestic institutions in their own way, subject only to the Constitution of the United States." Then opened the roar of loose declamation in favour of *Squatter Sovereignty* and *sacred right of self-government*. "But," said opposition members, "let us amend the bill so as to expressly declare that the people of the Territory may exclude slavery." "Not we," said the friends of the measure, and down they voted the amendment.

While the Nebraska bill was passing through Congress, a *law case*, involving the question of a negro's freedom, by reason of his owner having voluntarily taken him first into a free State and then into a Territory covered by the congressional prohibition, and held him as a slave for a long time in each, was passing through the United States Circuit Court for the District of Missouri; and both Nebraska bill and law-suit were brought to a decision, in the same month of May, 1854. The negro's name was "Dred Scott," which name now designates the decision finally rendered in the case. Before the then next presidential election, the law case came to, and was argued, in the Supreme Court of the United States; but the decision of it was deferred until after the election. Still, before the election, Senator Trumbull, on the floor of the Senate, requested the leading advocate of the Nebraska bill to state *his opinion* whether the people of a Territory can constitutionally exclude slavery from their limits, and the latter answers: "That is a question for the Supreme Court."

The election came. Mr. Buchanan was elected, and the indorsement, such as it was, secured. That was the second point gained. The indorsement, however, fell short of a clear popular majority by nearly four hundred thousand votes, and so, perhaps, was not overwhelmingly reliable and satisfactory. The outgoing President, in his last annual message, as impressively as possible echoed back upon the people the weight and authority of the indorsement. The Supreme Court met again; did not announce their decision, but ordered a reargument. The presidential inauguration came, and still no decision of the Court; but the incoming President in his inaugural address fervently exhorted the people to abide by the forthcoming decision, whatever it might be. Then, in a few days, came the decision.

The reputed author of the Nebraska bill finds an early occasion to make a speech at this capitol, indorsing the Dred Scott decision, and vehemently denouncing all opposition to it. The new President, too, seizes the early occasion of the Silliman letter to indorse and strongly construe that decision, and to express his astonishment that any different view had ever been entertained!

At length a squabble springs up between the President and the author of the Nebraska bill, on the mere question of *fact* whether the Lecompton constitution was, or was not, in any just sense, made by the people of Kansas; and in that quarrel, the latter declares that all he wants is a fair vote for the people, and that he cares not whether slavery be voted *down* or *voted up*. I do not understand his declaration that he cares not whether slavery be voted down or voted up, to be intended by him other than as an apt definition of the policy he would impress upon the public mind,—the principle for which he declares he has suffered so much, and is ready to suffer to the end. And well may he cling to that principle. If he has any parental feeling, well may he cling to it. That principle is the only shred left of his original Nebraska doctrine. Under the Dred Scott decision, "squatter sovereignty" squatted out of existence, tumbled down like temporary scaffolding; like the mould at the foundry, it served through one blast, and fell back into loose sand,—helped to carry an election, and then was kicked to the winds. His late joint struggle with the Republicans against the Lecompton constitution, involves nothing of the original Nebraska doctrine. That struggle was made on a point—the right of the people to make their own constitution—upon which he and the Republicans have never differed.

The several points of the Dred Scott decision in connection with Senator Douglas's "care not" policy, constitute the piece of machinery in its present state of advancement. This was the third point gained. The working points of that machinery are:

First. That no negro slave, imported as such from Africa, and no descendant of such slave, can ever be a citizen of any State, in the sense of that term as used in the Constitution of the United States. This point is made in order to deprive the negro, in every possible event, of the benefit of that provision of the United States Constitution which declares that "citizens of each State shall be entitled to all privileges and immunities of citizens in the several States."

Secondly. That "subject to the Constitution of the United States," neither Congress nor a territorial legislature can exclude slavery from any United States Territory. This point is made in order that individual men may fill up the Territories with slaves, without danger of losing them as property, and thus enhance the chances of permanency to the institution through all the future.

Thirdly. That whether the holding a negro in actual slavery in a free State makes him free as against the holder, the United States Courts will not decide, but will leave to be decided by the courts of any slave State the negro may be forced into by the master. This point is made, not to be pressed immediately; but if acquiesced in for a while, and apparently indorsed by the people at an election, then to sustain the logical conclusion that what Dred Scott's master might lawfully do with Dred Scott in the free State of Illinois, every other master may lawfully do, with any other one, or one thousand slaves in Illinois, or in any other free State.

Auxiliary to all this, and working hand-in-hand with it, the Nebraska doctrine, or what is left of it, is to educate and mould public opinion not to care whether slavery is voted down or voted up. This shows exactly where we now are, and partially, also, whither we are tending.

It will throw additional light on the latter, to go back, and run the mind over the string of historical facts already stated. Several things will now appear less dark and mysterious than they did when they were transpiring. The people were to be left "perfectly free," "subject only to the Constitution." What the Constitution had to do with it, outsiders could not then see. Plainly enough now: it was an exactly fitted niche for the Dred Scott decision to afterwards come in, and declare the perfect freedom of the people to be just no freedom at all. Why was the amendment expressly declaring the right of the people voted down? Plainly enough now: the adoption of it would have spoiled the niche for the Dred Scott decision. Why was the Court decision held up? Why even a Senator's individual opinion withheld till after the presidential election? Plainly enough now: the speaking out then would have damaged the perfectly free argument upon which the election was to be carried. Why the outgoing President's felicitation on the indorsement? Why the delay of a reargument? Why the incoming President's advance exhortation in favour of the decision? These things look like the cautious patting and petting of a spirited horse, preparatory to mounting him, when it is dreaded that he may give the rider a fall. And why the hasty after-indorsement of the decision by the President and others?

We cannot absolutely know that all these adaptations are the result of preconcert. But when we see a lot of framed timbers, different portions of which we know have been gotten out at different times and places, and by different workmen—Stephen, Franklin, Roger, and James, for instance (Douglas, Pierce, Taney, Buchanan),—and when we see those timbers joined together, and see they exactly make the frame of a house or a mill, all the tenons and mortices exactly fitting, and all the lengths and proportions of the different pieces exactly adapted to their respective places, and not a piece too many or too few, not omitting even scaffolding—or if a single piece be lacking, we see the place in the frame exactly fitted and prepared yet to bring such piece in,—in such a case, we find it impossible not to believe that Stephen and Franklin and Roger and James all understood one another from the beginning, and all worked upon a common plan or draft, drawn up before the first blow was struck.

It should not be overlooked that by the Nebraska bill the people of a State as well as Territory were to be left "perfectly free," "subject only to the Constitution." Why mention a State? They were legislating for Territories, and not for or about States. Certainly the people of a State are and ought to be subject to the Constitution of the United States; but why is mention of this lugged into this merely territorial law? Why are the people of a Territory and the people of a State therein lumped together, and their relation to the Constitution therein treated as being precisely the same? While the opinion of the Court by Chief Justice Taney, in the Dred Scott case, and the separate opinions of all the concurring judges, expressly declare that the Constitution of the United States neither permits Congress nor a territorial legislature to exclude slavery from any United States Territory, they all omit to declare whether or not the same Constitution permits a State or the people of a State to exclude it. *Possibly* this is a mere omission; but who can be quite sure if McLean or Curtis had sought to get into the opinion a declaration of unlimited power in the people of a State to exclude slavery from their limits,—just as Chase and Mace sought to get such declaration in behalf of the people of a Territory, into the Nebraska Bill,—I ask, who can be quite sure that it would not have been voted down in the one case as it had been in the other? The nearest approach to the point of declaring the power of a State over slavery is made by Judge Nelson. He approaches it more than once, using the precise idea, and almost the language too, of the Nebraska act. On one occasion his exact language is "except in cases where the power is restrained by the Constitution of the United States, the law of the State is supreme over the subject of slavery within its jurisdiction." In what cases the power of the State is so restrained by the United States Constitution is left an open question, precisely as the same question, as to the restraint on the power of the Territories, was left open in the Nebraska act. Put this and that together, and we have another nice little niche, which we may, ere long, see filled with another Supreme Court decision, declaring that the Constitution of the United States does not permit *a State* to exclude slavery from its limits. And this may especially be expected if the doctrine of "care not whether slavery be voted down or voted up" shall gain upon the public mind sufficiently to give promise that such a decision can be maintained when made.

Such a decision is all that slavery now lacks of being alike lawful in all the States. Welcome or unwelcome, such decision is probably coming, and will soon be upon us, unless the power of the present political dynasty shall be met and overthrown. We shall lie down, pleasantly dreaming that the people of Missouri are on the verge of making their State free, and we shall awake to the reality instead, that the Supreme Court has made Illinois a slave State. To meet and overthrow the power of that dynasty is the work now before all those who would prevent that consummation. That is what we have to do. How can we best do it?

There are those who denounce us openly to their own friends, and yet whisper to us softly that Senator Douglas is the aptest instrument there is with which to effect that object. They wish us to *infer* all from the fact that he now has a little quarrel with the present head of that dynasty, and that he has regularly voted with us on a single point, upon which he and we have never differed. They remind us that he is a great man and that the largest of us are very small ones. Let this be granted. But "a living dog is better than a dead lion." Judge Douglas, if not a dead lion, for this work is at least a caged and toothless one. How can he oppose the advances of slavery? He don't care anything about it. His avowed mission is impressing the "public heart" to *care nothing about it*. A leading Douglas Democratic newspaper thinks Douglas's superior talent will be needed to resist the revival of the African slave-trade. Does Douglas believe an effort to revive that trade is approaching? He has not said so. Does he really think so? But if it is, how can he resist it? For years he has laboured to prove it a sacred right of white men to take negro slaves into the new territories. Can he possibly show that it is a less sacred right to buy them where they can be bought cheapest? And unquestionably they can be bought cheaper in Africa than in Virginia. He has done all in his power to reduce the whole question of slavery to one of a mere right of property: and, as such, how can he oppose the foreign slave-trade?—how can he refuse that trade in that property shall be "perfectly free," unless he does it as a protection to home production? And as the home producers will probably not ask the protection, he will be wholly without a ground of opposition.

Senator Douglas holds, we know, that a man may rightfully be wiser to-day than he was yesterday—that he may rightfully change when he finds himself wrong. But can we, for that reason, run ahead, and infer that he will make any particular change, of which he himself has given no intimation? Can we safely base our action upon any such vague inference?

Now, as ever, I wish not to misrepresent Judge Douglas's position, question his motives, or do aught that can be personally offensive to him. Whenever, if ever, he and we can come together on principle, so that our cause may have assistance from his great ability, I hope to have interposed no adventitious obstacle. But, clearly, he is not now with us—he does not pretend to be—he does not promise ever to be.

Our cause, then, must be intrusted to, and conducted by, its own undoubted friends—those whose hands are free, whose hearts are in the work, who do care for the result. Two years ago the Republicans of the nation mustered over thirteen hundred thousand strong. We did this under the single impulse of resistance to a common danger, with every external circumstance against us. Of strange, discordant, and even hostile elements, we gathered from the four winds, and formed and fought the battle through, under the constant hot fire of a disciplined, proud, and pampered enemy. Did we brave all then to falter now?—now, when that same enemy is wavering, dissevered, and belligerent? The result is not doubtful. We shall not fail. If we stand firm, we shall not fail. Wise counsels may accelerate or mistakes delay it; but sooner or later the victory is sure to come.

Lincoln's Reply to Judge Douglas at Chicago on Popular Sovereignty, the Nebraska Bill, etc. July 10, 1858

... Popular sovereignty! everlasting popular sovereignty! Let us for a moment inquire into this vast matter of popular sovereignty. What is popular sovereignty? We recollect that at an early period in the history of this struggle, there was another name for the same thing,—*squatter sovereignty*. It was not exactly popular sovereignty, but squatter sovereignty. What do these terms mean? What do those terms mean when used now? And vast credit is taken by our friend, the Judge, in regard to his support of it, when he declares the last years of his life have been, and all the future years of his life shall be, devoted to this matter of popular sovereignty. What is it? Why, it is the sovereignty of the people! What was squatter sovereignty? I suppose, if it had any signification at all, it was the right of the people to govern themselves, to be sovereign in their own affairs, while they were squatted down in a country not their own,—while they had squatted on a territory that did not belong to them, in the sense that a State belongs to the people who inhabit it,—when it belonged to the nation; such right to govern themselves was called "squatter sovereignty."

Now, I wish you to mark, What has become of that squatter sovereignty? What has become of it? Can you get anybody to tell you now that the people of a Territory have any authority to govern themselves, in regard to this mooted question of slavery, before they form a State constitution? No such thing at all, although there is a general running fire, and although there has been a hurrah made in every speech on that side, assuming that policy had given to the people of a Territory the right to govern themselves upon this question; yet the point is dodged. To-day it has been decided—no more than a year ago it was decided by the Supreme Court of the United States, and is insisted upon to-day—that the people of a Territory have no right to exclude slavery from a Territory; that if any one man chooses to take slaves into a Territory, all the rest of the people have no right to keep them out. This being so, and this decision being made, one of the points that the Judge approved, and one in the approval of which he says he means to keep me down,—*put* me down I should not say, for I have never been up! He says he is in favour of it, and sticks to it, and expects to win his battle on that decision, which says that there is no such thing as squatter sovereignty, but that any one man may take slaves into a Territory, and all the other men in the Territory may be opposed to it, and yet by reason of the Constitution they cannot prohibit it. When that is so, how much is left of this vast matter of squatter sovereignty, I should like to know?

When we get back, we get to the point of the right of the people to make a constitution. Kansas was settled, for example, in 1854. It was a Territory yet, without having formed a constitution, in a very regular way, for three years. All this time negro slavery could be taken in by any few individuals, and by that decision of the Supreme Court, which the Judge approves, all the rest of the people cannot keep it out; but when they come to make a constitution they may say they will not have slavery. But it is there; they are obliged to tolerate it in some way, and all experience shows it will be so,—for they will not take the negro slaves and absolutely deprive the owners of them. All experience shows this to be so. All that space of time that runs from the beginning of the settlement of the Territory until there is a sufficiency of people to make a State constitution,—all that portion of time popular sovereignty is given up. The seal is absolutely put down upon it by the court decision, and Judge Douglas puts his own upon the top of that; yet he is appealing to the people to give him vast credit for his devotion to popular sovereignty.

Again, when we get to the question of the right of the people to form a State constitution as they please, to form it with slavery or without slavery,—if that is anything new I confess I don't know it. Has there ever been a time when anybody said that any other than the people of a Territory itself should form a constitution? What is now in it that Judge Douglas should have fought several years of his life, and pledge himself to fight all the remaining years of his life for? Can Judge Douglas find anybody on earth that said that anybody else should form a constitution for a people?... It is enough for my purpose to ask, whenever a Republican said anything against it? They never said anything against it, but they have constantly spoken for it; and whosoever will undertake to examine the platform and the speeches of responsible men of the party, and of irresponsible men, too, if you please, will be unable to find one word from anybody in the Republican ranks opposed to that popular sovereignty which Judge Douglas thinks he has invented. I suppose that Judge Douglas will claim in a little while that he is the inventor of the idea that the people should govern themselves; that nobody ever thought of such a thing until he brought it forward. We do not remember that in that old Declaration of Independence it is said that "We hold these truths to be self-evident, that all men are created equal; that they are endowed by their Creator with certain inalienable rights; that among these are life, liberty, and the pursuit of happiness; that to secure these rights, governments are instituted among men, deriving their just powers from the consent of the governed." There is the origin of popular sovereignty. Who, then, shall come in at this day and claim that he invented it? The Lecompton constitution connects itself with this question, for it is in this matter of the Lecompton constitution that our friend Judge Douglas claims such vast credit. I agree that in opposing the Lecompton constitution, so far as I can perceive, he was right. I do not deny that at all; and, gentlemen, you will readily see why I could not deny it, even if I wanted to. But I do not wish to, for all the Republicans in the nation opposed it, and they would have opposed it just as much without Judge Douglas's aid as with it. They had all taken ground against it long before he did. Why, the reason that he urges against that constitution I urged against him a year before. I have the printed speech in my hand. The argument that he makes why that constitution should not be adopted, that the people were not fairly represented nor allowed to vote, I pointed out in a speech a year ago, which I hold in my hand now, that no fair chance was to be given to the people.

... A little more now as to this matter of popular sovereignty and the Lecompton constitution. The Lecompton constitution, as the Judge tells us, was defeated. The defeat of it was a good thing, or it was not. He thinks the defeat of it was a good thing, and so do I; and we agree in that. Who defeated it? [A voice: "Judge Douglas."] Yes, he furnished himself; and if you suppose he controlled the other Democrats that went with him, he furnished three votes, while the Republicans furnished twenty.

That is what he did to defeat it. In the House of Representatives he and his friends furnished some twenty votes, and the Republicans furnished ninety odd. Now, who was it that did the work? [A voice: "Douglas."] Why, yes, Douglas did it? To be sure he did!

Let us, however, put that proposition another way. The Republicans could not have done it without Judge Douglas. Could he have done it without them? Which could have come the nearest to doing it without the other? Ground was taken against it by the Republicans long before Douglas did it. The proposition of opposition to that measure is about five to one. [A voice: "Why don't they come out on it?"] You don't know what you are talking about, my friend; I am quite willing to answer any gentleman in the crowd who asks an intelligent question.

Now, who in all this country has ever found any of our friends of Judge Douglas's way of thinking, and who have acted upon this main question, that have ever thought of uttering a word in behalf of Judge Trumbull? I defy you to show a printed resolution passed in a Democratic meeting. I take it upon myself to defy any man to show a printed resolution, large or small, of a Democratic meeting in favour of Judge Trumbull, or any of the five to one Republicans who beat that bill. Everything must be for the Democrats! They did everything, and the five to the one that really did the thing, they snub over, and they do not seem to remember that they have an existence upon the face of the earth.

Gentlemen, I fear that I shall become tedious. I leave this branch of the subject to take hold of another. I take up that part of Judge Douglas's speech in which he respectfully attended to me.

Judge Douglas made two points upon my recent speech at Springfield. He says they are to be the issues of this campaign. The first one of these points he bases upon the language in a speech which I delivered at Springfield, which I believe I can quote correctly from memory. I said that "we are now far into the fifth year since a policy was instituted for the avowed object and with the confident promise of putting an end to slavery agitation; under the operation of that policy, that agitation has not only not ceased, but has constantly augmented. I believe it will not cease until a crisis shall have been reached and passed. 'A house divided against itself cannot stand.' I believe this government cannot endure permanently half slave and half free. I do not expect the Union to be dissolved,"—I am quoting from my speech,—"I do not expect the house to fall, but I do expect it will cease to be divided. It will become all one thing or all the other. Either the opponents of slavery will arrest the further spread of it, and place it where the public mind shall rest in the belief that it is in the course of ultimate extinction, or its advocates will push it forward until it shall become alike lawful in all the States, old as well as new; North as well as South."

That is the paragraph! In this paragraph which I have quoted in your hearing, and to which I ask the attention of all, Judge Douglas thinks he discovers great political heresy. I want your attention particularly to what he has inferred from it. He says I am in favour of making all the States of this Union uniform in all their internal regulations; that in all their domestic concerns I am in favour of making them entirely uniform. He draws this inference from the language I have quoted to you. He says that I am in favour of making war by the North upon the South for the extinction of slavery; that I am also in favour of inviting (as he expresses it) the South to a war upon the North for the purpose of nationalizing slavery. Now, it is singular enough, if you will carefully read that passage over, that I did not say that I was in favour of anything in it. I only said what I expected would take place. I made a prediction only,—it may have been a foolish one, perhaps. I did not even say that I desired that slavery should be put in course of ultimate extinction. I do say so now, however; so there need be no longer any difficulty about that. It may be written down in the great speech.

Gentlemen, Judge Douglas informed you that this speech of mine was probably carefully prepared. I admit that it was. I am not master of language; I have not a fine education; I am not capable of entering into a disquisition upon dialectics, as I believe you call it; but I do not believe the language I employed bears any such construction as Judge Douglas puts upon it. But I don't care about a quibble in regard to words. I know what I meant, and I will not leave this crowd in doubt, if I can explain it to them, what I really meant in the use of that paragraph.

I am not, in the first place, unaware that this government has endured eighty-two years, half slave and half free. I know that. I am tolerably well acquainted with the history of the country, and I know that it has endured eighty-two years, half slave and half free. I believe—and that is what I meant to allude to there—I believe it has endured, because, during all that time, until the introduction of the Nebraska bill, the public mind did rest all the time in the belief that slavery was in course of ultimate extinction. That was what gave us the rest that we had through that period of eighty-two years; at least, so I believe. I have always hated slavery, I think, as much as any Abolitionist,—I have been an old-line Whig,—I have always hated it, but I have always been quiet about it until this new era of the introduction of the Nebraska bill began. I always believed that everybody was against it, and that it was in course of ultimate extinction.... They had reason so to believe.

The adoption of the Constitution and its attendant history led the people to believe so, and that such was the belief of the framers of the Constitution itself. Why did those old men, about the time of the adoption of the Constitution, decree that slavery should not go into the new Territory where it had not already gone? Why declare that within twenty years the African slave-trade, by which slaves are supplied, might be cut off by Congress? Why were all these acts? I might enumerate more of these acts; but enough. What were they but a clear indication that the framers of the Constitution intended and expected the ultimate extinction of that institution? And now when I say,—as I said in my speech that Judge Douglas has quoted from,—when I say that I think the opponents of slavery will resist the further spread of it, and place it where the public mind shall rest in the belief that it is in the course of ultimate extinction, I only mean to say that they will place it where the founders of this government originally placed it.

I have said a hundred times, and I have now no inclination to take it back, that I believe there is no right, and ought to be no inclination in the people of the free States, to enter into the slave States and interfere with the question of slavery at all. I have said that always; Judge Douglas has heard me say it. And when it is said that I am in favour of interfering with slavery where it exists, I know it is unwarranted by anything I have ever intended, and, as I believe, by anything I have ever said. If by any means I have ever used language which could fairly be so construed (as, however, I believe I never have), I now correct it.

So much, then, for the inference that Judge Douglas draws, that I am in favour of setting the sections at war with one another. I know that I never meant any such thing, and I believe that no fair mind can infer any such thing from anything I have said.

Now, in relation to his inference that I am in favour of a general consolidation of all the local institutions of the various States.... I have said very many times in Judge Douglas's hearing that no man believed more than I in the principle of self-government; that it lies at the bottom of all my ideas of just government from beginning to end. I have denied that his use of that term applies properly. But for the thing itself I deny that any man has ever gone ahead of me in his devotion to the principle, whatever he may have done in efficiency in advocating it. I think that I have said it in your hearing, that I believe each individual is naturally entitled to do as he pleases with himself and the fruit of his labour, so far as it in no wise interferes with any other man's rights; that each community, as a State, has a right to do exactly as it pleases with all the concerns within that State that interfere with the right of no other State; and that the general government upon principle has no right to interfere with anything other than that general class of things that does concern the whole. I have said that at all times; I have said as illustrations that I do not believe in the right of Illinois to interfere with the cranberry laws of Indiana, the oyster laws of Virginia, or the liquor laws of Maine.

How is it, then, that Judge Douglas infers, because I hope to see slavery put where the public mind shall rest in the belief that it is in the course of ultimate extinction, that I am in favour of Illinois going over and interfering with the cranberry laws of Indiana? What can authorize him to draw any such inference? I suppose there might be one thing that at least enabled him to draw such an inference, that would not be true with me or many others; that is, because he looks upon all this matter of slavery as an exceedingly little thing,—this matter of keeping one-sixth of the population of the whole nation in a state of oppression and tyranny unequalled in the world. He looks upon it as being an exceedingly little thing, only equal to the question of the cranberry laws of Indiana; as something having no moral question in it; as something on a par with the question of whether a man shall pasture his land with cattle or plant it with tobacco; so little and so small a thing that he concludes, if I could desire that anything should be done to bring about the ultimate extinction of that little thing, I must be in favour of bringing about an amalgamation of all the other little things in the Union. Now, it so happens—and there, I presume, is the foundation of this mistake—that the Judge thinks thus; and it so happens that there is a vast portion of the American people that do not look upon that matter as being this very little thing. They look upon it as a vast moral evil; they can prove it as such by the writings of those who gave us the blessings of liberty which we enjoy, and that they so looked upon it, and not as an evil merely confining itself to the States where it is situated; and while we agree that by the Constitution we assented to, in the States where it exists we have no right to interfere with it, because it is in the Constitution, we are both by duty and inclination to stick by that Constitution in all its letter and spirit from beginning to end.

So much, then, as to my disposition, my wish, to have all the State legislatures blotted out and to have one consolidated government and a uniformity of domestic regulations in all the States; by which I suppose it is meant, if we raise corn here we must make sugar-cane grow here too, and we must make those things which grow North grow in the South. All this I suppose he understands I am in favour of doing. Now, so much for all this nonsense—for I must call it so. The Judge can have no issue with me on a question of establishing uniformity in the domestic regulations of the States.

A little now on the other point,—the Dred Scott decision. Another of the issues, he says, that is to be made with me is upon his devotion to the Dred Scott decision and my opposition to it.

I have expressed heretofore, and I now repeat, my opposition to the Dred Scott decision; but I should be allowed to state the nature of that opposition, and I ask your indulgence while I do so. What is fairly implied by the term Judge Douglas has used, "resistance to the decision"? I do not resist it. If I wanted to take Dred Scott from his master I would be interfering with property, and that terrible difficulty that Judge Douglas speaks of, of interfering with property, would arise. But I am doing no such thing as that; all that I am doing is refusing to obey it as a political rule. If I were in Congress, and a vote should come up on a question whether slavery should be prohibited in a new Territory, in spite of the Dred Scott decision, I would vote that it should.

That is what I would do. Judge Douglas said last night that before the decision he might advance his opinion, and it might be contrary to the decision when it was made; but after it was made he would abide by it until it was reversed. Just so! We let this property abide by the decision, but we will try to reverse that decision. We will try to put it where Judge Douglas would not object, for he says he will obey it until it is reversed. Somebody has to reverse that decision, since it is made; and we mean to reverse it, and we mean to do it peaceably.

What are the uses of decisions of courts? They have two uses. First, they decide upon the question before the court. They decide in this case that Dred Scott is a slave. Nobody resists that.

Not only that, but they say to everybody else that persons standing just as Dred Scott stands are as he is. That is, they say that when a question comes up upon another person it will be so decided again, unless the court decides another way, unless the court overrules its decision. Well, we mean to do what we can to have the court decide the other way. That is one thing we mean to try to do.

The sacredness that Judge Douglas throws around this decision is a degree of sacredness that has never been before thrown around any other decision. I have never heard of such a thing. Why, decisions apparently contrary to that decision, or that good lawyers thought were contrary to that decision, have been made by that very court before. It is the first of its kind; it is an astonisher in legal history; it is a new wonder of the world; it is based upon falsehood in the main as to the facts,—allegations of facts upon which it stands are not facts at all in many instances,—and no decision made on any question—the first instance of a decision made under so many unfavourable circumstances—thus placed, has ever been held by the profession as law, and it has always needed confirmation before the lawyers regarded it as settled law; but Judge Douglas will have it that all hands must take this extraordinary decision made under these extraordinary circumstances and give their vote in Congress in accordance with it, yield to it, and obey it in every possible sense. Circumstances alter cases. Do not gentlemen here remember the case of that same Supreme Court some twenty-five or thirty years ago, deciding that a national bank was constitutional? I ask if somebody does not remember that a national bank was declared to be constitutional? Such is the truth, whether it be remembered or not. The bank charter ran out, and a re-charter was granted by Congress. That re-charter was laid before General Jackson. It was urged upon him, when he denied the constitutionality of the bank, that the Supreme Court had decided that it was constitutional; and General Jackson then said that the Supreme Court had no right to lay down a rule to govern a coordinate branch of the government, the members of which had sworn to support the Constitution,—that each member had sworn to support the Constitution as he understood it. I will venture here to say that I have heard Judge Douglas say that he approved of General Jackson for that act. What has now become of all his tirade against "resistance to the Supreme Court"?

My fellow-citizens, getting back a little,—for I pass from these points,—when Judge Douglas makes his threat of annihilation upon the "alliance," he is cautious to say that that warfare of his is to fall upon the leaders of the Republican party. Almost every word he utters and every distinction he makes has its significance. He means for the Republicans who do not count themselves as leaders to be his friends; he makes no fuss over them, it is the leaders that he is making war upon. He wants it understood that the mass of the Republican party are really his friends. It is only the leaders that are doing something, that are intolerant, and require extermination at his hands. As this is clearly and unquestionably the light in which he presents that matter, I want to ask your attention, addressing myself to Republicans here, that I may ask you some questions as to where you, as the Republican party, would be placed if you sustained Judge Douglas in his present position by a re-election? I do not claim, gentlemen, to be unselfish;

I do not pretend that I would not like to go to the United States Senate,—I make no such hypocritical pretence; but I do say to you, that in this mighty issue it is nothing to you, nothing to the mass of the people of the nation, whether or not Judge Douglas or myself shall ever be heard of after this night. It may be a trifle to either of us; but in connection with this mighty question, upon which hang the destinies of the nation, perhaps, it is absolutely nothing. But where will you be placed if you reindorse Judge Douglas? Don't you know how apt he is, how exceedingly anxious he is, at all times to seize upon anything and everything to persuade you that something he has done you did yourselves? Why, he tried to persuade you last night that our Illinois Legislature instructed him to introduce the Nebraska bill. There was nobody in that Legislature ever thought of it; but still he fights furiously for the proposition; and that he did it because there was a standing instruction to our senators to be always introducing Nebraska bills. He tells you he is for the Cincinnati platform; he tells you he is for the Dred Scott decision; he tells you—not in his speech last night, but substantially in a former speech—that he cares not if slavery is voted up or down; he tells you the struggle on Lecompton is past,—it may come up again or not, and if it does, he stands where he stood when, in spite of him and his opposition, you built up the Republican party. If you indorse him, you tell him you do not care whether slavery be voted up or down, and he will close, or try to close, your mouths with his declaration, repeated by the day, the week, the month, and the year. I think, in the position in which Judge Douglas stood in opposing the Lecompton constitution, he was right; he does not know that it will return, but if it does we may know where to find him; and if it does not, we may know where to look for him, and that is on the Cincinnati platform. Now, I could ask the Republican party, after all the hard names Judge Douglas has called them by, ... all his declarations of Black Republicanism—(by the way, we are improving, the black has got rubbed off), but with all that, if he be indorsed by Republican votes, where do you stand? Plainly, you stand ready saddled, bridled, and harnessed, and waiting to be driven over to the slavery-extension camp of the nation,—just ready to be driven over, tied together in a lot,—to be driven over, every man with a rope around his neck, that halter being held by Judge Douglas. That is the question. If Republican men have been in earnest in what they have done, I think they had better not do it; but I think the Republican party is made up of those who, as far as they can peaceably, will oppose the extension of slavery, and who will hope for its ultimate extinction. If they believe it is wrong in grasping up the new lands of the continent, and keeping them from the settlement of free white labourers, who want the land to bring up their families upon; if they are in earnest,—although they may make a mistake, they will grow restless, and the time will come when they will come back again and reorganize, if not by the same name, at least upon the same principles as their party now has. It is better, then, to save the work while it is begun. You have done the labour; maintain it, keep it. If men choose to serve you, go with them; but as you have made up your organization upon principle, stand by it; for, as surely as God reigns over you, and has inspired your minds and given you a sense of propriety and continues to give you hope, so surely will you still cling to these ideas, and you will at last come back again after your wanderings, merely to do your work over again.

We were often,—more than once, at least,—in the course of Judge Douglas's speech last night, reminded that this government was made for white men,—that he believed it was made for white men. Well, that is putting it into a shape in which no one wants to deny it; but the Judge then goes into his passion for drawing inferences that are not warranted. I protest, now and for ever, against that counterfeit logic which presumes that, because I do not want a negro woman for a slave, I do necessarily want her for a wife. My understanding is, that I need not have her for either; but, as God made us separate, we can leave one another alone, and do one another much good thereby. There are white men enough to marry all the white women, and enough black men to marry all the black women; and in God's name let them be so married. The Judge regales us with the terrible enormities that take place by the mixture of races; that the inferior race bears the superior down. Why, Judge, if we do not let them get together in the Territories, they won't mix there. I should say at least that that was a self-evident truth.

Now, it happens that we meet together once every year, somewhere about the 4th of July, for some reason or other. These 4th of July gatherings, I suppose, have their uses. If you will indulge me, I will state what I suppose to be some of them.

We are now a mighty nation: we are thirty, or about thirty, millions of people, and we own and inhabit about one-fifteenth part of the dry land of the whole earth. We run our memory back over the pages of history for about eighty-two years, and we discover that we were then a very small people in point of numbers, vastly inferior to what we are now, with a vastly less extent of country, with vastly less of everything we deem desirable among men. We look upon the change as exceedingly advantageous to us and to our posterity, and we fix upon something that happened away back, as in some way or other being connected with this rise of prosperity. We find a race of men living in that day whom we claim as our fathers and grandfathers; they were iron men; they fought for the principle that they were contending for, and we understand that by what they then did, it has followed that the degree of prosperity which we now enjoy has come to us. We hold this annual celebration to remind ourselves of all the good done in this process of time,—of how it was done, and who did it, and how we are historically connected with it; and we go from these meetings in better humour with ourselves,—we feel more attached the one to the other, and more firmly bound to the country we inhabit. In every way we are better men, in the age and race and country in which we live, for these celebrations. But after we have done all this, we have not yet reached the whole. There is something else connected with it. We have, besides these men—descended by blood from our ancestors—among us, perhaps half our people who are not descendants at all of these men; they are men who have come from Europe,—German, Irish, French, and Scandinavian,—men that have come from Europe themselves, or whose ancestors have come hither and settled here, finding themselves our equal in all things. If they look back through this history, to trace their connection with those days by blood, they find they have none: they cannot carry themselves back into that glorious epoch and make themselves feel that they are part of us; but when they look through that old Declaration of Independence, they find that those old men say that "we hold these truths to be self-evident, that all men are created equal," and then they feel that that moral sentiment taught in that day evidences their relation to those men, that it is the father of all moral principle in them, and that they have a right to claim it as though they were blood of the blood, and flesh of the flesh, of the men who wrote that Declaration; and so they are. That is the electric cord in that Declaration that links the hearts of patriotic and liberty-loving men together; that will link those patriotic hearts as long as the love of freedom exists in the minds of men throughout the world.

Now, sirs, for the purpose of squaring things with this idea of "don't care if slavery is voted up or voted down"; for sustaining the Dred Scott decision; for holding that the Declaration of Independence did not mean anything at all,—we have Judge Douglas giving his exposition of what the Declaration of Independence means, and we have him saying that the people of America are equal to the people of England. According to his construction, you Germans are not connected with it. Now, I ask you in all soberness, if all these things, if indulged in, if ratified, if confirmed and indorsed, if taught to our children and repeated to them, do not tend to rub out the sentiment of liberty in the country, and to transform this government into a government of some other form? Those arguments that are made, that the inferior race are to be treated with as much allowance as they are capable of enjoying; that as much is to be done for them as their condition will allow,—what are these arguments? They are the arguments that kings have made for enslaving the people in all ages of the world. You will find that all the arguments in favour of kingcraft were of this class; they always bestrode the necks of the people,—not that they wanted to do it, but because the people were better off for being ridden. That is their argument; and this argument of the Judge is the same old serpent, that says, "You work, and I eat; you toil, and I will enjoy the fruits of it." Turn in whatever way you will,—whether it come from the mouth of a king, an excuse for enslaving the people of his country, or from the mouth of men of one race as a reason for enslaving the men of another race,—it is all the same old serpent; and I hold, if that course of argumentation that is made for the purpose of convincing the public mind that we should not care about this, should be granted, it does not stop with the negro. I should like to know—taking this old Declaration of Independence, which declares that all men are equal, upon principle, and making exceptions to it—where will it stop? If one man says it does not mean a negro, why not another say it does not mean some other man? If that Declaration is not the truth, let us get the statute-book in which we find it, and tear it out! Who is so bold as to do it? If it is not true, let us tear it out. [Cries of "No! No!"] Let us stick to it, then; let us stand firmly by it, then.

It may be argued that there are certain conditions that make necessities and impose them upon us, and to the extent that a necessity is imposed upon a man, he must submit to it. I think that was the condition in which we found ourselves when we established this government. We had slaves among us; we could not get our Constitution unless we permitted them to remain in slavery; we could not secure the good we did secure, if we grasped for more; but, having by necessity submitted to that much, it does not destroy the principle that is the charter of our liberties. Let that charter stand as our standard.

My friend has said to me that I am a poor hand to quote Scripture. I will try it again, however. It is said in one of the admonitions of our Lord, "Be ye [therefore] perfect even as your Father which is in heaven is perfect." The Saviour, I suppose, did not expect that any human creature could be perfect as the Father in heaven; but He said: "As your Father in heaven is perfect, be ye also perfect." He set that up as a standard, and he who did most toward reaching that standard attained the highest degree of moral perfection. So I say in relation to the principle that all men are created equal, let it be as nearly reached as we can. If we cannot give freedom to every creature, let us do nothing that will impose slavery upon any other creature. Let us, then, turn this government back into the channel in which the framers of the Constitution originally placed it. Let us stand firmly by each other. If we do not do so, we are tending in the contrary direction, that our friend Judge Douglas proposes,—not intentionally,—working in the traces that tend to make this one universal slave nation. He is one that runs in that direction, and as such I resist him.

My friends, I have detained you about as long as I desired to do, and I have only to say, let us discard all this quibbling about this man and the other man, this race and that race and the other race being inferior, and therefore they must be placed in an inferior position. Let us discard all these things, and unite as one people throughout this land, until we shall once more stand up declaring that all men are created equal.

My friends, I could not, without launching off upon some new topic, which would detain you too long, continue to-night. I thank you for this most extensive audience that you have furnished me to-night. I leave you, hoping that the lamp of liberty will burn in your bosoms until there shall no longer be a doubt that all men are created free and equal.

From a Speech at Springfield, Illinois. July 17, 1858

... There is still another disadvantage under which we labour, and to which I will ask your attention. It arises out of the relative positions of the two persons who stand before the State as candidates for the Senate. Senator Douglas is of world-wide renown. All the anxious politicians of his party, or who have been of his party for years past, have been looking upon him as certainly, at no distant day, to be the President of the United States. They have seen, in his round, jolly, fruitful face, post-offices, land-offices, marshalships, and cabinet appointments, chargéships and foreign missions, bursting and sprouting out in wonderful exuberance, ready to be laid hold of by their greedy hands. And as they have been gazing upon this attractive picture so long, they cannot, in the little distraction that has taken place in the party, bring themselves to give up the charming hope. But with greedier anxiety they rush about him, sustain him, and give him marches, triumphal entries, and receptions, beyond what, even in the days of his highest prosperity, they could have brought about in his favour. On the contrary, nobody has ever expected me to be President. In my poor, lean, lank face, nobody has ever seen that any cabbages were sprouting out. These are disadvantages, all taken together, that the Republicans labour under. We have to fight this battle upon principle, and upon principle alone. I am in a certain sense made the standard-bearer in behalf of the Republicans. I was made so merely because there had to be some one so placed,—I being in no wise preferable to any other one of the twenty-five, perhaps a hundred, we have in the Republican ranks. Then I say, I wish it to be distinctly understood and borne in mind, that we have to fight this battle without many—perhaps without any—of the external aids which are brought to bear against us. So I hope those with whom I am surrounded have principle enough to nerve themselves for the task, and leave nothing undone that can fairly be done to bring about the right result. As appears by two speeches I have heard him deliver since his arrival in Illinois, he gave special attention to the speech of mine delivered on the sixteenth of June. He says that he carefully read that speech. He told us that at Chicago a week ago last night, and he repeated it at Bloomington last night.... He says it was evidently prepared with great care. I freely admit it was prepared with care.... But I was very careful not to put anything in that speech as a matter of fact, or make any inferences which did not appear to me to be true and fully warrantable. If I had made any mistake I was willing to be corrected; if I had drawn any inference in regard to Judge Douglas or any one else, which was not warranted, I was fully prepared to modify it as soon as discovered. I planted myself upon the truth and the truth only, so far as I knew it, or could be brought to know it.

Having made that speech with the most kindly feelings toward Judge Douglas, as manifested therein, I was gratified when I found that he had carefully examined it, and had detected no error of fact, nor any inference against him, nor any misrepresentations, of which he thought fit to complain.... He seizes upon the doctrines he supposes to be included in that speech, and declares that upon them will turn the issues of the campaign. He then quotes, or attempts to quote, from my speech. I will not say that he wilfully misquotes, but he does fail to quote accurately. His attempt at quoting is from a passage which I believe I can quote accurately from memory. I shall make the quotation now, with some comments upon it, as I have already said, in order that the Judge shall be left entirely without excuse for misrepresenting me. I do so now, as I hope, for the last time. I do this in great caution, in order that if he repeats his misrepresentation, it shall be plain to all that he does so wilfully. If, after all, he still persists, I shall be compelled to reconstruct the course I have marked out for myself, and draw upon such humble resources as I have for a new course, better suited to the real exigencies of the case. I set out in this campaign with the intention of conducting it strictly as a gentleman, in substance at least, if not in the outside polish. The latter I shall never be, but that which constitutes the inside of a gentleman I hope I understand, and am not less inclined to practise than others. It was my purpose and expectation that this canvass would be conducted upon principle, and with fairness on both sides, and it shall not be my fault if this purpose and expectation shall be given up.

He charges, in substance, that I invite a war of sections; that I propose all local institutions of the different States shall become consolidated and uniform. What is there in the language of that speech which expresses such purpose or bears such construction? I have again and again said that I would not enter into any one of the States to disturb the institution of slavery. Judge Douglas said at Bloomington that I used language most able and ingenious for concealing what I really meant; and that while I had protested against entering into the slave States, I nevertheless did mean to go on the banks of the Ohio and throw missiles into Kentucky, to disturb them in their domestic institutions.

... I have said that I do not understand the Declaration to mean that all men were created equal in all respects. The negroes are not our equals in colour; but I suppose it does mean to declare that all men are equal in some respects; they are equal in their right to "life, liberty, and the pursuit of happiness." Certainly the negro is not our equal in colour, perhaps not in many other respects. Still, in the right to put into his mouth the bread that his own hands have earned, he is the equal of every other man, white or black. In pointing out that more has been given you, you cannot be justified in taking away the little which has been given him. All I ask for the negro is, that if you do not like him, let him alone. If God gave him but little, that little let him enjoy.

... One more point on this Springfield speech, which Judge Douglas says he has read so carefully. I expressed my belief in the existence of a conspiracy to perpetuate and nationalize slavery. I did not profess to know it, nor do I now. I showed the part Judge Douglas had played in the string of facts, constituting to my mind the proof of that conspiracy. I showed the parts played by others.

I charged that the people had been deceived into carrying the last presidential election, by the impression that the people of the Territories might exclude slavery if they chose, when it was known in advance by the conspirators that the court was to decide that neither Congress nor the people could so exclude slavery. These charges are more distinctly made than anything else in the speech.

Judge Douglas has carefully read and re-read that speech. He has not, so far as I know, contradicted those charges. In the two speeches which I heard he certainly did not. On his own tacit admission I renew that charge. I charge him with having been a party to that conspiracy and to that deception, for the sole purpose of nationalizing slavery.

From Lincoln's Reply to Douglas in the First Joint Debate at Ottawa, Illinois. August 21, 1858

When a man bears himself somewhat misrepresented, it provokes him—at least, I find it so with myself; but when misrepresentation becomes very gross and palpable, it is more apt to amuse him.... [After stating the charge of an arrangement between himself and Judge Trumbull.]

Now, all I have to say upon that subject is, that I think no man—not even Judge Douglas—can prove it, because it is not true. I have no doubt he is "conscientious" in saying it. As to those resolutions that he took such a length of time to read, as being the platform of the Republican party in 1854, I say I never had anything to do with them, and I think Trumbull never had. Judge Douglas cannot show that either of us ever had anything to do with them....

Now, about this story that Judge Douglas tells of Trumbull bargaining to sell out the old Democratic party, and Lincoln agreeing to sell out the old Whig party, I have the means of knowing about that; Judge Douglas cannot have; and I know there is no substance to it whatever....

A man cannot prove a negative, but he has a right to claim that when a man makes an affirmative charge, he must offer some proof to show the truth of what he says. I certainly cannot introduce testimony to show the negative about things, but I have a right to claim that if a man says he knows a thing, then he must show how he knows it. I always have a right to claim this; and it is not satisfactory to me that he may be "conscientious" on the subject.

... Anything that argues me into his idea of perfect social and political equality with the negro is but a specious and fantastic arrangement of words, by which a man can prove a horse-chestnut to be a chestnut horse. I will say here, while upon this subject, that I have no purpose, either directly or indirectly, to interfere with the institution of slavery in the States where it exists. I believe I have no lawful right to do so, and I have no inclination to do so. I have no purpose to introduce political and social equality between the white and the black races. There is a physical difference between the two, which, in my judgment, will probably for ever forbid their living together upon the footing of perfect equality; and inasmuch as it becomes a necessity that there must be a difference, I, as well as Judge Douglas, am in favour of the race to which I belong having the superior position. I have never said anything to the contrary; but I hold, that, notwithstanding all this, there is no reason in the world why the negro is not entitled to all the natural rights enumerated in the Declaration of Independence,—the right to life, liberty, and the pursuit of happiness. I hold that he is as much entitled to these as the white man. I agree with Judge Douglas, he is not my equal in many respects, certainly not in colour, perhaps not in moral or intellectual endowment. But in the right to eat the bread, without the leave of anybody, which his own hand earns, he is my equal, and the equal of Judge Douglas, and the equal of any living man.

... As I have not used up so much of my time as I had supposed, I will dwell a little longer upon one or two of these minor topics upon which the Judge has spoken. He has read from my speech at Springfield, in which I say that "a house divided against itself cannot stand." Does the Judge say it can stand? I don't know whether he does or not. The Judge does not seem to be attending to me just now, but I would like to know if it is his opinion that a house divided against itself can stand? If he does, then there is a question of veracity, not between him and me, but between the Judge and an authority of a somewhat higher character.

Now, my friends, I ask your attention to this matter for the purpose of saying something seriously, I know that the Judge may readily enough agree with me that the maxim which was put forth by the Saviour is true, but he may allege that I misapply it; and the Judge has a right to urge that in my application I do misapply it, and then I have a right to show that I do not misapply it. When he undertakes to say that because I think this nation, so far as the question of slavery is concerned, will all become one thing or all the other, I am in favour of bringing about a dead uniformity in the various States, in all their institutions, he argues erroneously. The great variety of local institutions in the States, springing from differences in the soil, differences in the face of the country, and in the climate, are bonds of union. They do not make "a house divided against itself," but they make a house united. If they produce in one section of the country what is called for by the wants of another section, and this other section can supply the wants of the first, they are not matters of discord, but bonds of union, true bonds of union. But can this question of slavery be considered as among these varieties in the institutions of the country? I leave it for you to say, whether in the history of our government, this institution of slavery has not always failed to be a bond of union, and, on the contrary, been an apple of discord and an element of division in the house. I ask you to consider whether so long as the moral constitution of men's minds shall continue to be the same, after this generation and assemblage shall sink into the grave, and another race shall arise with the same moral and intellectual development we have—whether, if that institution is standing in the same irritating position in which it now is, it will not continue an element of division?

If so, then I have a right to say that, in regard to this question, the Union is a house divided against itself; and when the Judge reminds me that I have often said to him that the institution of slavery has existed for eighty years in some States, and yet it does not exist in some others, I agree to the fact, and I account for it by looking at the position in which our fathers originally placed it,—restricting it from the new Territories where it had not gone, and legislating to cut off its source by the abrogation of the slave-trade, thus putting the seal of legislation against its spread. The public mind did rest in the belief that it was in the course of ultimate extinction. But lately, I think,—and in this I charge nothing on the Judge's motives,—lately, I think that he and those acting with him have placed that institution on a new basis, which looks to the perpetuity and nationalization of slavery. And while it is placed on this new basis, I say, and I have said, that I believe we shall not have peace upon the question, until the opponents of slavery arrest the further spread of it, and place it where the public mind shall rest in the belief that it is in the course of ultimate extinction; or, on the other hand, that its advocates will push it forward until it shall become alike lawful in all the States, old as well as new, North as well as South. Now, I believe if we could arrest the spread, and place it where Washington and Jefferson and Madison placed it, it would be in the course of ultimate extinction, and the public mind would, as for eighty years past, believe that it was in the course of ultimate extinction. The crisis would be past, and the institution might be let alone for a hundred years—if it should live so long—in the States where it exists, yet it would be going out of existence in the way best for both the black and the white races. [A voice: "Then do you repudiate popular sovereignty?"] Well, then, let us talk about popular sovereignty. What is popular sovereignty? Is it the right of the people to have slavery or not to have it, as they see fit, in the Territories? I will state—and I have an able man to watch me—my understanding is that popular sovereignty, as now applied to the question of slavery, does allow the people of a Territory to have slavery if they want to, but does not allow them not to have it if they do not want it. I do not mean that if this vast concourse of people were in a Territory of the United States, any one of them would be obliged to have a slave if he did not want one; but I do say that, as I understand the Dred Scott decision, if any one man wants slaves, all the rest have no way of keeping that one man from holding them.

When I made my speech at Springfield, of which the Judge complains, and from which he quotes, I really was not thinking of the things which he ascribes to me at all. I had no thought in the world that I was doing anything to bring about a war between the free and slave States. I had no thought in the world that I was doing anything to bring about a political and social equality of the black and white races. It never occurred to me that I was doing anything or favouring anything to reduce to a dead uniformity all the local institutions of the various States. But I must say, in all fairness to him, if he thinks I am doing something which leads to these bad results, it is none the better that I did not mean it. It is just as fatal to the country, if I have any influence in producing it, whether I intend it or not. But can it be true that placing this institution upon the original basis—the basis upon which our fathers placed it—can have any tendency to set the Northern and the Southern States at war with one another, or that it can have any tendency to make the people of Vermont raise sugar-cane, because they raise it in Louisiana, or that it can compel the people of Illinois to cut pine logs on the Grand Prairie, where they will not grow, because they cut pine logs in Maine, where they do grow? The Judge says this is a new principle started in regard to this question. Does the Judge claim that he is working on the plan of the founders of the government? I think he says in some of his speeches—indeed, I have one here now—that he saw evidence of a policy to allow slavery to be south of a certain line, while north of it it should be excluded, and he saw an indisposition on the part of the country to stand upon that policy, and, therefore, he set about studying the subject upon original principles, and upon original principles he got up the Nebraska bill! I am fighting it upon these "original principles"—fighting it in the Jeffersonian, Washingtonian, Madisonian fashion....

If I have brought forward anything not a fact, if he (Judge Douglas) will point it out, it will not even ruffle me to take it back. But if he will not point out anything erroneous in the evidence, is it not rather for him to show by a comparison of the evidence that I have reasoned falsely, than to call the "kind, amiable, intelligent gentleman" a liar?

I want to ask your attention to a portion of the Nebraska bill which Judge Douglas has quoted: "It being the true intent and meaning of this act, not to legislate slavery into any Territory or State, nor to exclude it therefrom, but to leave the people thereof perfectly free to form and regulate their domestic institutions in their own way, subject only to the Constitution of the United States." Thereupon Judge Douglas and others began to argue in favour of "popular sovereignty,"—the right of the people to have slaves if they wanted them, and to exclude slavery if they did not want them. "But," said, in substance, a senator from Ohio (Mr. Chase, I believe), "we more than suspect that you do not mean to allow the people to exclude slavery if they wish to; and if you do mean it, accept an amendment which I propose, expressly authorizing the people to exclude slavery." I believe I have the amendment here before me, which was offered, and under which the people of the Territory, through their proper representatives, might, if they saw fit, prohibit the existence of slavery therein.

And now I state it as a fact, to be taken back if there is any mistake about it, that Judge Douglas and those acting with him voted that amendment down. I now think that those who voted it down had a real reason for doing so. They know what that reason was. It looks to us, since we have seen the Dred Scott decision pronounced, holding that "under the Constitution" the people cannot exclude slavery—I say it looks to outsiders, poor, simple, "amiable, intelligent gentlemen," as though the niche was left as a place to put that Dred Scott decision in, a niche that would have been spoiled by adopting the amendment. And now I say again, if this was not the reason, it will avail the Judge much more to calmly and good-humouredly point out to these people what that other reason was for voting the amendment down, than swelling himself up to vociferate that he may be provoked to call somebody a liar.

Again, there is in that same quotation from the Nebraska bill this clause: "it being the true intent and meaning of this bill not to legislate slavery into any Territory or State." I have always been puzzled to know what business the word "State" had in that connection. Judge Douglas knows—he put it there. He knows what he put it there for. We outsiders cannot say what he put it there for. The law they were passing was not about States, and was not making provision for States. What was it placed there for? After seeing the Dred Scott decision, which holds that the people cannot exclude slavery from a Territory, if another Dred Scott decision shall come, holding that they cannot exclude it from a State, we shall discover that when the word was originally put there, it was in view of something that was to come in due time; we shall see that it was the other half of something. I now say again, if there was any different reason for putting it there, Judge Douglas, in a good-humoured way, without calling anybody a liar, can tell what the reason was....

Now, my friends, ... I ask the attention of the people here assembled, and elsewhere, to the course that Judge Douglas is pursuing every day as bearing upon this question of making slavery national. Not going back to the records, but taking the speeches he makes, the speeches he made yesterday and the day before, and makes constantly, all over the country, I ask your attention to them. In the first place, what is necessary to make the institution national? Not war: there is no danger that the people of Kentucky will shoulder their muskets and ... march into Illinois to force the blacks upon us. There is no danger of our going over there, and making war upon them. Then what is necessary for the nationalization of slavery? It is simply the next Dred Scott decision. It is merely for the Supreme Court to decide that no State under the Constitution can exclude it, just as they have already decided that under the Constitution neither Congress nor the territorial legislature can do it. When that is decided and acquiesced in, the whole thing is done. This being true and this being the way, as I think, that slavery is to be made national, let us consider what Judge Douglas is doing every day to that end. In the first place, let us see what influence he is exerting on public sentiment. In this and like communities, public sentiment is everything. With public sentiment nothing can fail; without it nothing can succeed. Consequently he who moulds public sentiment goes deeper than he who enacts statutes or pronounces decisions. He makes statutes and decisions possible or impossible to be executed. This must be borne in mind, as also the additional fact that Judge Douglas is a man of vast influence, so great that it is enough for many men to profess to believe anything when they once find out that Judge Douglas professes to believe it. Consider also the attitude he occupies at the head of a large party,—a party which he claims has a majority of all the voters in the country.

This man sticks to a decision which forbids the people of a Territory to exclude slavery, and he does so not because he says it is right in itself,—he does not give any opinion on that,—but because it has been decided by the Court, and, being decided by the Court, he is, and you are, bound to take it in your political action as law,—not that he judges at all of its merits, but because a decision of the Court is to him a "Thus saith the Lord." He places it on that ground alone, and you will bear in mind that thus committing himself unreservedly to this decision, commits himself just as firmly to the next one as to this. He did not commit himself on account of the merit or demerit of the decision, but it is a "Thus saith the Lord." The next decision as much as this will be a "Thus saith the Lord." There is nothing that can divert or turn him away from this decision. It is nothing that I point out to him that his great prototype, General Jackson, did not believe in the binding force of decisions. It is nothing to him that Jefferson did not so believe. I have said that I have often heard him approve of Jackson's course in disregarding the decision of the Supreme Court pronouncing a national bank constitutional. He says I did not hear him say so. He denies the accuracy of my recollection. I say he ought to know better than I, but I will make no question about this thing, though it still seems to me that I heard him say it twenty times. I will tell him, though, that he now claims to stand on the Cincinnati platform, which affirms that Congress cannot charter a national bank in the teeth of that old standing decision that Congress can charter a bank. And I remind him of another piece of Illinois history on the question of respect for judicial decisions, and it is a piece of Illinois history belonging to a time when a large party to which Judge Douglas belonged, were displeased with a decision of the Supreme Court of Illinois, because they had decided that a Governor could not remove a secretary of State, and I know that Judge Douglas will not deny that he was then in favour of over-slaughing that decision, by the mode of adding five new Judges, so as to vote down the four old ones. Not only so, but it ended in the Judge's sitting down on the very bench as one of the five new judges to break down the four old ones. It was in this way precisely that he got his title of Judge. Now, when the Judge tells me that men appointed conditionally to sit as members of a Court will have to be catechized beforehand upon some subject, I say, "You know, Judge; you have tried it!" When he says a Court of this kind will lose the confidence of all men, will be prostituted and disgraced by such a proceeding, I say, "You know best, Judge; you have been through the mill."

But I cannot shake Judge Douglas's teeth loose from the Dred Scott decision. Like some obstinate animal (I mean no disrespect) that will hang on when he has once got his teeth fixed—you may cut off a leg, or you may tear away an arm, still he will not relax his hold. And so I may point out to the Judge, and say that he is bespattered all over, from the beginning of his political life to the present time, with attacks upon judicial decisions,—I may cut off limb after limb of his public record, and strive to wrench from him a single dictum of the Court, yet I cannot divert him from it. He hangs to the last to the Dred Scott decision.... Henry Clay, my beau ideal of a statesman, ... once said of a class of men who would repress all tendencies to liberty and ultimate emancipation, that they must, if they would do this, go back to the era of our independence, and muzzle the cannon that thunders its annual joyous return; that they must blow out the moral lights around us; they must penetrate the human soul, and eradicate there the love of liberty; and then, and not till then, could they perpetuate slavery in this country! To my thinking, Judge Douglas is, by his example and vast influence, doing that very thing in this community when he says that the negro has nothing in the Declaration of Independence. Henry Clay plainly understood the contrary. Judge Douglas is going back to the era of our Revolution, and, to the extent of his ability, muzzling the cannon which thunders its annual joyous return. When he invites any people, willing to have slavery, to establish it, he is blowing out the moral lights around us. When he says he "cares not whether slavery is voted down or voted up,"—that it is a sacred right of self-government,—he is, in my judgment, penetrating the human soul and eradicating the light of reason and the love of liberty in this American people. And now I will only say, that when, by all these means and appliances, Judge Douglas shall succeed in bringing public sentiment to an exact accordance with his own views; when these vast assemblages shall echo back all these sentiments; when they shall come to repeat his views and avow his principles, and to say all that he says on these mighty questions,—then it needs only the formality of a second Dred Scott decision, which he indorses in advance, to make slavery alike lawful in all the States, old as well as new, North as well as South.

Lincoln's Reply to Judge Douglas in the Second Joint Debate. Freeport, Illinois. August 27, 1858

... The plain truth is this. At the introduction of the Nebraska policy, we believed there was a new era being introduced in the history of the Republic, which tended to the spread and perpetuation of slavery. But in our opposition to that measure we did not agree with one another in everything. The people in the north end of the State were for stronger measures of opposition than we of the southern and central portions of the State, but we were all opposed to the Nebraska doctrine. We had that one feeling and one sentiment in common. You at the north end met in your conventions, and passed your resolutions. We in the middle of the State and further south did not hold such conventions and pass the same resolutions, although we had in general a common view and a common sentiment. So that these meetings which the Judge has alluded to, and the resolutions he has read from, were local, and did not spread over the whole State. We at last met together in 1856, from all parts of the State, and we agreed upon a common platform. You who held more extreme notions, either yielded those notions, or if not wholly yielding them, agreed to yield them practically, for the sake of embodying the opposition to the measures which the opposite party were pushing forward at that time. We met you then, and if there was anything yielded, it was for practical purposes. We agreed then upon a platform for the party throughout the entire State of Illinois, and now we are all bound as a party to that platform. And I say here to you, if any one expects of me in the case of my election, that I will do anything not signified by our Republican platform and my answers here to-day, I tell you very frankly, that person will be deceived. I do not ask for the vote of any one who supposes that I have secret purposes or pledges that I dare not speak out.... If I should never be elected to any office, I trust I may go down with no stain of falsehood upon my reputation, notwithstanding the hard opinions Judge Douglas chooses to entertain of me.

From Lincoln's Reply at Jonesboro'. September 15, 1858

Ladies and Gentlemen, There is very much in the principles that Judge Douglas has here enunciated that I most cordially approve, and over which I shall have no controversy with him. In so far as he insisted that all the States have the right to do exactly as they please about all their domestic relations, including that of slavery, I agree entirely with him. He places me wrong in spite of all I tell him, though I repeat it again and again, insisting that I have made no difference with him upon this subject. I have made a great many speeches, some of which have been printed, and it will be utterly impossible for him to find anything that I have ever put in print contrary to what I now say on the subject. I hold myself under constitutional obligations to allow the people in all the States, without interference, direct or indirect, to do exactly as they please, and I deny that I have any inclination to interfere with them, even if there were no such constitutional obligation. I can only say again that I am placed improperly—altogether improperly, in spite of all that I can say—when it is insisted that I entertain any other view or purpose in regard to that matter.

While I am upon this subject, I will make some answers briefly to certain propositions that Judge Douglas has put. He says, "Why can't this Union endure permanently half slave and half free?" I have said that I supposed it could not, and I will try, before this new audience, to give briefly some of the reasons for entertaining that opinion. Another form of his question is, "Why can't we let it stand as our fathers placed it?" That is the exact difficulty between us. I say that Judge Douglas and his friends have changed it from the position in which our fathers originally placed it.

I say in the way our fathers originally left the slavery question, the institution was in the course of ultimate extinction. I say when this government was first established, it was the policy of its founders to prohibit the spread of slavery into the new Territories of the United States where it had not existed. But Judge Douglas and his friends have broken up that policy, and placed it upon a new basis, by which it is to become national and perpetual. All I have asked or desired anywhere is that it should be placed back again upon the basis that the fathers of our government originally placed it upon. I have no doubt that it would become extinct for all time to come, if we had but readopted the policy of the fathers by restricting it to the limits it has already covered—restricting it from the new Territories.

I do not wish to dwell on this branch of the subject at great length at this time, but allow me to repeat one thing that I have stated before. Brooks, the man who assaulted Senator Sumner on the floor of the Senate, and who was complimented with dinners and silver pitchers and gold-headed canes, and a good many other things for that feat, in one of his speeches declared that when this government was originally established, nobody expected that the institution of slavery would last until this day. That was but the opinion of one man, but it is such an opinion as we can never get from Judge Douglas or anybody in favour of slavery in the North at all. You can sometimes get it from a Southern man. He said at the same time that the framers of our government did not have the knowledge that experience has taught us—that experience and the invention of the cotton gin have taught us that the perpetuation of slavery is a necessity. He insisted therefore upon its being changed from the basis upon which the fathers of the government left it to the basis of perpetuation and nationalization.

I insist that this is the difference between Judge Douglas and myself—that Judge Douglas is helping the change along. I insist upon this government being placed where our fathers originally placed it.

... When he asks me why we cannot get along with it [slavery] in the attitude where our fathers placed it, he had better clear up the evidences that he has himself changed it from that basis; that he has himself been chiefly instrumental in changing the policy of the fathers. Any one who will read his speech of the twenty-second of March last, will see that he there makes an open confession, showing that he set about fixing the institution upon an altogether different set of principles....

Now, fellow-citizens, in regard to this matter about a contract between myself and Judge Trumbull, and myself and all that long portion of Judge Douglas's speech on this subject. I wish simply to say, what I have said to him before, that he cannot know whether it is true or not, and I do know that there is not a word of truth in it. And I have told him so before. I don't want any harsh language indulged in, but I do not know how to deal with this persistent insisting on a story that I know to be utterly without truth. It used to be the fashion amongst men that when a charge was made, some sort of proof was brought forward to establish it, and if no proof was found to exist, it was dropped. I don't know how to meet this kind of an argument. I don't want to have a fight with Judge Douglas, and I have no way of making an argument up into the consistency of a corn-cob and stopping his mouth with it. All I can do is good-humouredly to say, that from the beginning to the end of all that story about a bargain between Judge Trumbull and myself, there is not a word of truth in it....

When that compromise [of 1850] was made, it did not repeal the old Missouri Compromise. It left a region of United States territory half as large as the present territory of the United States, north of the line of 36° 30', in which slavery was prohibited by act of Congress. This compromise did not repeal that one. It did not affect nor propose to repeal it. But at last it became Judge Douglas's duty, as he thought (and I find no fault with him), as chairman of the Committee on Territories, to bring in a bill for the organization of a territorial government—first of one, then of two Territories north of that line. When he did so, it ended in his inserting a provision substantially repealing the Missouri Compromise. That was because the Compromise of 1850 had not repealed it. And now I ask why he could not have left that compromise alone? We were quiet from the agitation of the slavery question. We were making no fuss about it. All had acquiesced in the compromise measures of 1850. We never had been seriously disturbed by any Abolition agitation before that period.... I close this part of the discussion on my part by asking him the question again, Why, when we had peace under the Missouri Compromise, could you not have let it alone?

He tries to persuade us that there must be a variety in the different institutions of the States of the Union; that that variety necessarily proceeds from the variety of soil, climate, of the face of the country, and the difference of the natural features of the States. I agree to all that. Have these very matters ever produced any difficulty amongst us? Not at all. Have we ever had any quarrel over the fact that they have laws in Louisiana designed to regulate the commerce that springs from the production of sugar, or because we have a different class relative to the production of flour in this State? Have they produced any differences? Not at all. They are the very cements of this Union. They don't make the house a house divided against itself. They are the props that hold up the house and sustain the Union.

But has it been so with this element of slavery? Have we not always had quarrels and difficulties over it? And when will we cease to have quarrels over it? Like causes produce like effects. It is worth while to observe that we have generally had comparative peace upon the slavery question, and that there has been no cause for alarm until it was excited by the effort to spread it into new territory. Whenever it has been limited to its present bounds, and there has been no effort to spread it, there has been peace. All the trouble and convulsion has proceeded from efforts to spread it over more territory. It was thus at the date of the Missouri Compromise. It was so again with the annexation of Texas; so with the territory acquired by the Mexican War; and it is so now. Whenever there has been an effort to spread it, there has been agitation and resistance. Now, I appeal to this audience (very few of whom are my political friends), as rational men, whether we have reason to expect that the agitation in regard to this subject will cease while the causes that tend to reproduce agitation are actively at work? Will not the same cause that produced agitation in 1820, when the Missouri Compromise was formed,—that which produced the agitation upon the annexation of Texas, and at other times,—work out the same results always? Do you think that the nature of man will be changed; that the same causes that produced agitation at one time will not have the same effect at another?

This has been the result so far as my observation of the slavery question and my reading in history extend. What right have we then to hope that the trouble will cease, that the agitation will come to an end, until it shall either be placed back where it originally stood, and where the fathers originally placed it, or, on the other hand, until it shall entirely master all opposition? This is the view I entertain, and this is the reason why I entertained it, as Judge Douglas has read from my Springfield speech.

... At Freeport I answered several interrogatories that had been propounded to me by Judge Douglas at the Ottawa meeting.... At the same time I propounded four interrogatories to him, claiming it as a right that he should answer as many for me as I did for him, and I would reserve myself for a future instalment when I got them ready. The Judge, in answering me upon that occasion, put in what I suppose he intends as answers to all four of my interrogatories. The first one of these I have before me, and it is in these words:

Question 1. If the people of Kansas shall by means entirely unobjectionable in all other respects, adopt a State constitution and ask admission into the Union under it, before they have the requisite number of inhabitants according to the English bill—some 93,000—will you vote to admit them?

As I read the Judge's answer in the newspaper, and as I remember it as pronounced at the time, he does not give any answer which is equivalent to yes or no,—I will or I won't. He answers at very considerable length, rather quarrelling with me for asking the question, and insisting that Judge Trumbull had done something that I ought to say something about; and finally, getting out such statements as induce me to infer that he means to be understood, he will, in that supposed case, vote for the admission of Kansas. I only bring this forward now, for the purpose of saying that, if he chooses to put a different construction upon his answer, he may do it. But if he does not, I shall from this time forward assume that he will vote for the admission of Kansas in disregard of the English bill. He has the right to remove any misunderstanding I may have. I only mention it now, that I may hereafter assume this to have been the true construction of his answer, if he does not now choose to correct me.

The second interrogatory I propounded to him was this:

Question 2. Can the people of a United States Territory in any lawful way, against the wish of any citizen of the United States, exclude slavery from its limits prior to the formation of a State constitution?

To this Judge Douglas answered that they can lawfully exclude slavery from the Territory prior to the formation of a constitution. He goes on to tell us how it can be done. As I understand him, he holds that it can be done by the territorial legislature refusing to make any enactments for the protection of slavery in the Territory, and especially by adopting unfriendly legislation to it. For the sake of clearness, I state it again: that they can exclude slavery from the Territory,—first, by withholding what he assumes to be an indispensable assistance to it in the way of legislation; and second, by unfriendly legislation. If I rightly understand him, I wish to ask your attention for a while to his position.

In the first place, the Supreme Court of the United States has decided that any congressional prohibition of slavery in the Territories is unconstitutional: they have reached this proposition as a conclusion from their former proposition that the Constitution of the United States expressly recognizes property in slaves; and from that other constitutional provision that no person shall be deprived of property without due process of law. Hence they reach the conclusion that as the

Constitution of the United States expressly recognizes property in slaves, and prohibits any person from being deprived of property without due process of law, to pass an act of Congress by which a man who owned a slave on one side of a line would be deprived of him if he took him on the other side, is depriving him of that property without due process of law. That I understand to be the decision of the Supreme Court. I understand also that Judge Douglas adheres most firmly to that decision; and the difficulty is, how is it possible for any power to exclude slavery from the Territory unless in violation of that decision? That is the difficulty.

In the Senate of the United States, in 1856, Judge Trumbull in a speech, substantially if not directly, put the same interrogatory to Judge Douglas, as to whether the people of a Territory had the lawful power to exclude slavery prior to the formation of a constitution? Judge Douglas then answered at considerable length, and his answer will be found in the "Congressional Globe," under date of June 9, 1856. The Judge said that whether the people could exclude slavery prior to the formation of a constitution or not, was a question to be decided by the Supreme Court. He put that proposition, as will be seen by the "Congressional Globe," in a variety of forms, all running to the same thing in substance,—that it was a question for the Supreme Court. I maintain that when he says, after the Supreme Court has decided the question, that the people may yet exclude slavery by any means whatever, he does virtually say that it is not a question for the Supreme Court. He shifts his ground. I appeal to you whether he did not say it was a question for the Supreme Court? Has not the Supreme Court decided that question? When he now says that the people may exclude slavery, does he not make it a question for the people? Does he not virtually shift his ground and say that it is not a question for the court, but for the people? This is a very simple proposition,—a very plain and naked one. It seems to me that there is no difficulty in deciding it. In a variety of ways he said that it was a question for the Supreme Court. He did not stop then to tell us that, whatever the Supreme Court decides, the people can by withholding necessary "police regulations" keep slavery out. He did not make any such answer. I submit to you now, whether the new state of the case has not induced the Judge to sheer away from his original ground? Would not this be the impression of every fair-minded man?

I hold that the proposition that slavery cannot enter a new country without police regulations is historically false. It is not true at all. I hold that the history of this country shows that the institution of slavery was originally planted upon this continent without these "police regulations" which the Judge now thinks necessary for the actual establishment of it. Not only so, but is there not another fact,—how came this Dred Scott decision to be made? It was made upon the case of a negro being taken and actually held in slavery in Minnesota Territory, claiming his freedom because the act of Congress prohibited his being so held there. Will the Judge pretend that Dred Scott was not held there without police regulations? There is at least one matter of record as to his having been held in slavery in the Territory, not only without police regulations, but in the teeth of congressional legislation supposed to be valid at the time. This shows that there is vigour enough in slavery to plant itself in a new country, even against unfriendly legislation. It takes not only law, but the enforcement of law to keep it out. That is the history of this country upon the subject.

I wish to ask one other question. It being understood that the Constitution of the United States guarantees property in slaves in the Territories, if there is any infringement of the right of that property, would not the United States courts, organized for the government of the Territory, apply such remedy as might be necessary in that case? It is a maxim held by the courts that there is no wrong without its remedy; and the courts have a remedy for whatever is acknowledged and treated as a wrong.

Again: I will ask you, my friends, if you were elected members of the legislature, what would be the first thing you would have to do before entering upon your duties? Swear to support the Constitution of the United States. Suppose you believe as Judge Douglas does, that the Constitution of the United States guarantees to your neighbour the right to hold slaves in that Territory,—that they are his property,—how can you clear your oaths unless you give him such legislation as is necessary to enable him to enjoy that property? What do you understand by supporting the Constitution of a State or of the United States? Is it not to give such constitutional helps to the rights established by that Constitution as may be practically needed? Can you, if you swear to support the Constitution and believe that the Constitution establishes a right, clear your oath without giving it support? Do you support the Constitution if, knowing or believing there is a right established under it which needs specific legislation, you withhold that legislation? Do you not violate and disregard your oath? I can conceive of nothing plainer in the world. There can be nothing in the words "support the Constitution," if you may run counter to it by refusing support to any right established under the Constitution. And what I say here will hold with still more force against the Judge's doctrine of "unfriendly legislation." How could you, having sworn to support the Constitution, and believing that it guaranteed the right to hold slaves in the Territories, assist in legislation intended to defeat that right? That would be violating your own view of the Constitution. Not only so, but if you were to do so, how long would it take the courts to hold your votes unconstitutional and void? Not a moment.

Lastly, I would ask, is not Congress itself under obligation to give legislative support to any right that is established under the United States Constitution? I repeat the question, is not Congress itself bound to give legislative support to any right that is established in the United States Constitution? A member of Congress swears to support the Constitution of the United States, and if he sees a right established by that Constitution which needs specific legislative protection, can he clear his oath without giving that protection? Let me ask you why many of us, who are opposed to slavery upon principle, give our acquiescence to a fugitive-slave law? Why do we hold ourselves under obligations to pass such a law, and abide by it when passed? Because the Constitution makes provision that the owners of slaves shall have the right to reclaim them. It gives the right to reclaim slaves; and that right is, as Judge Douglas says, a barren right, unless there is legislation that will enforce it.

The mere declaration, "No person held to service or labour in one State, under the laws thereof, escaping into another, shall, in consequence of any law or regulation therein, be discharged from such service or labour, but shall be delivered up on claim of the party to whom such service or labour may be due," is powerless without specific legislation to enforce it. Now, on what ground would a member of Congress who is opposed to slavery in the abstract, vote for a fugitive law, as I would deem it my duty to do? Because there is a constitutional right which needs legislation to enforce it. And, although it is distasteful to me, I have sworn to support the Constitution; and, having so sworn, I cannot conceive that I do support it if I withhold from that right any necessary legislation to make it practical. And if that is true in regard to a fugitive-slave law, is the right to have fugitive slaves reclaimed any better fixed in the Constitution than the right to hold slaves in the Territories? For this decision is a just exposition of the Constitution, as Judge Douglas thinks. Is the one right any better than the other? If I wished to refuse to give legislative support to slave property in the Territories, if a member of Congress, I could not do it, holding the view that the Constitution establishes that right. If I did it at all, it would be because I deny that this decision properly construes the Constitution. But if I acknowledge with Judge Douglas that this decision properly construes the Constitution, I cannot conceive that I would be less than a perjured man if I should refuse in Congress to give such protection to that property as in its nature it needed....

From Lincoln's Reply to Judge Douglas at Charleston, Illinois. September 18, 1858

Judge Douglas has said to you that he has not been able to get from me an answer to the question whether I am in favour of negro citizenship. So far as I know, the Judge never asked me the question before. He shall have no occasion ever to ask it again, for I tell him very frankly that I am not in favour of negro citizenship.... Now my opinion is, that the different States have the power to make a negro a citizen under the Constitution of the United States, if they choose. The Dred Scott decision decides that they have not that power. If the State of Illinois had that power, I should be opposed to the exercise of it. That is all I have to say about it.

Judge Douglas has told me that he heard my speeches north and my speeches south, ... and there was a very different cast of sentiment in the speeches made at the different points. I will not charge upon Judge Douglas that he wilfully misrepresents me, but I call upon every fair-minded man to take these speeches and read them, and I dare him to point out any difference between my speeches north and south. While I am here, perhaps I ought to say a word, if I have the time, in regard to the latter portion of the Judge's speech, which was a sort of declamation in reference to my having said that I entertained the belief that this government would not endure, half slave and half free. I have said so, and I did not say it without what seemed to me good reasons. It perhaps would require more time than I have now to set forth those reasons in detail; but let me ask you a few questions. Have we ever had any peace on this slavery question? When are we to have peace upon it if it is kept in the position it now occupies? How are we ever to have peace upon it? That is an important question. To be sure, if we will all stop and allow Judge Douglas and his friends to march on in their present career until they plant the institution all over the nation, here and wherever else our flag waves, and we acquiesce in it, there will be peace. But let me ask Judge Douglas how he is going to get the people to do that? They have been wrangling over this question for forty years. This was the cause of the agitation resulting in the Missouri Compromise; this produced the troubles at the annexation of Texas, in the acquisition of the territory acquired in the Mexican War. Again, this was the trouble quieted by the Compromise of 1850, when it was settled "for ever," as both the great political parties declared in their national conventions. That "for ever" turned out to be just four years, when Judge Douglas himself reopened it.

When is it likely to come to an end? He introduced the Nebraska bill in 1854, to put another end to the slavery agitation. He promised that it would finish it all up immediately, and he has never made a speech since, until he got into a quarrel with the President about the Lecompton constitution, in which he has not declared that we are just at the end of the slavery agitation. But in one speech, I think last winter, he did say that he didn't quite see when the end of the slavery agitation would come. Now he tells us again that it is all over, and the people of Kansas have voted down the Lecompton constitution. How is it over? That was only one of the attempts to put an end to the slavery agitation,—one of these "final settlements." Is Kansas in the Union? Has she formed a constitution that she is likely to come in under? Is not the slavery agitation still an open question in that Territory?... If Kansas should sink to-day, and leave a great vacant space in the earth's surface, this vexed question would still be among us. I say, then, there is no way of putting an end to the slavery agitation amongst us, but to put it back upon the basis where our fathers placed it; no way but to keep it out of our new Territories,—to restrict it for ever to the old States where it now exists. Then the public mind will rest in the belief that it is in the course of ultimate extinction. That is one way of putting an end to the slavery agitation.

The other way is for us to surrender, and let Judge Douglas and his friends have their way, and plant slavery over all the States,—cease speaking of it as in any way a wrong—regard slavery as one of the common matters of property, and speak of our negroes as we do of our horse and cattle.

From Lincoln's Reply to Judge Douglas at Galesburg, Illinois. October, 1858

... The Judge has alluded to the Declaration of Independence, and insisted that negroes are not included in that Declaration; and that it is a slander on the framers of that instrument to suppose that negroes were meant therein; and he asks you, Is it possible to believe that Mr. Jefferson, who penned that immortal paper, could have supposed himself applying the language of that instrument to the negro race, and yet held a portion of that race in slavery? Would he not at once have freed them? I only have to remark upon this part of his speech (and that too, very briefly, for I shall not detain myself or you upon that point for any great length of time), that I believe the entire records of the world, from the date of the Declaration of Independence up to within three years ago, may be searched in vain for one single affirmation from one single man, that the negro was not included in the Declaration of Independence; I think I may defy Judge Douglas to show that he ever said so, that Washington ever said so, that any President ever said so, that any member of Congress ever said so, or that any living man upon the whole earth ever said so, until the necessities of the present policy of the Democratic party in regard to slavery had to invent that affirmation. And I will remind Judge Douglas and this audience, that while Mr. Jefferson was the owner of slaves, as undoubtedly he was, in speaking on this very subject, he used the strong language that "he trembled for his country when he remembered that God was just;" and I will offer the highest premium in my power to Judge Douglas if he will show that he, in all his life, ever uttered a sentiment at all akin to that of Jefferson.

... I want to call to the Judge's attention an attack he made upon me in the first one of these debates.... In order to fix extreme Abolitionism upon me, Judge Douglas read a set of resolutions which he declared had been passed by a Republican State Convention, in October 1854, held at Springfield, Illinois, and he declared that I had taken a part in that convention. It turned out that although a few men calling themselves an anti-Nebraska State Convention had sat at Springfield about that time, yet neither did I take any part in it, nor did it pass the resolutions or any such resolutions as Judge Douglas read. So apparent had it become that the resolutions that he read had not been passed at Springfield at all, nor by any State Convention in which I had taken part, that seven days later at Freeport ... Judge Douglas declared that he had been misled ... and promised ... that when he went to Springfield he would investigate the matter.... I have waited as I think a sufficient time for the report of that investigation.

... A fraud, an absolute forgery, was committed, and the perpetration of it was traced to the three,—Lanphier, Harris, and Douglas.... Whether it can be narrowed in any way, so as to exonerate any one of them, is what Judge Douglas's report would probably show. The main object of that forgery at that time was to beat Yates and elect Harris to Congress, and that object was known to be exceedingly dear to Judge Douglas at that time.

... The fraud having been apparently successful upon that occasion, both Harris and Douglas have more than once since then been attempting to put it to new uses. As the fisherman's wife, whose drowned husband was brought home with his body full of eels, said, when she was asked what was to be done with him, 'Take out the eels and set him again,' so Harris and Douglas have shown a disposition to take the eels out of that stale fraud by which they gained Harris's election, and set the fraud again, more than once.... And now that it has been discovered publicly to be a fraud, we find that Judge Douglas manifests no surprise at all.... But meanwhile the three are agreed that each is a most honourable man.

Notes for Speeches. October 1858

Suppose it is true that the negro is inferior to the white in the gifts of nature; is it not the exact reverse of justice that the white should for that reason take from the negro any part of the little which he has had given him? "Give to him that is needy" is the Christian rule of charity; but "Take from him that is needy" is the rule of slavery.

The sum of pro-slavery theology seems to be this: "Slavery is not universally right, nor yet universally wrong; it is better for some people to be slaves; and, in such cases, it is the will of God that they be such."

Certainly there is no contending against the will of God; but still there is some difficulty in ascertaining and applying it to particular cases. For instance, we will suppose the Rev. Dr. Ross has a slave named Sambo, and the question is, "Is it the will of God that Sambo shall remain a slave, or be set free?" The Almighty gives no audible answer to the question, and his revelation, the Bible, gives none—or at most none but such as admits of a squabble as to its meaning; no one thinks of asking Sambo's opinion on it. So at last it comes to this, that Dr. Ross is to decide the question; and while he considers it, he sits in the shade, with gloves on his hands, and subsists on the bread that Sambo is earning in the burning sun. If he decides that God wills Sambo to continue a slave, he thereby retains his own comfortable position; but if he decides that God wills Sambo to be free, he thereby has to walk out of the shade, throw off his gloves, and delve for his own bread. Will Dr. Ross be actuated by the perfect impartiality which has ever been considered most favourable to correct decisions?

We have in this nation the element of domestic slavery. It is a matter of absolute certainty that it is a disturbing element. It is the opinion of all the great men who have expressed an opinion upon it, that it is a dangerous element. We keep up a controversy in regard to it. That controversy necessarily springs from difference of opinion, and if we can learn exactly—can reduce to the lowest elements—what that difference of opinion is, we perhaps shall be better prepared for discussing the different systems of policy that we would propose in regard to that disturbing element.

I suggest that the difference of opinion, reduced to its lowest terms, is no other than the difference between the men who think slavery a wrong and those who do not think it wrong. The Republican party think it wrong—we think it is a moral, a social, and a political wrong. We think it is a wrong not confining itself merely to the persons or the States where it exists, but that it is a wrong which in its tendency, to say the least, affects the existence of the whole nation. Because we think it wrong, we propose a course of policy that shall deal with it as a wrong.

We deal with it as with any other wrong, in so far as we can prevent its growing any larger, and so deal with it that in the run of time there may be some promise of an end to it We have a due regard to the actual presence of it amongst us, and the difficulties of getting rid of it in any satisfactory way, and all the constitutional obligations thrown about it. I suppose that in reference both to its actual existence in the nation, and to our constitutional obligations, we have no right at all to disturb it in the States where it exists, and we profess that we have no more inclination to disturb it than we have the right to do it. We go further than that: we don't propose to disturb it where, in one instance, we think the Constitution would permit us. We think the Constitution would permit us to disturb it in the District of Columbia. Still we do not propose to do that, unless it should be in terms which I don't suppose the nation is very likely soon to agree to—the terms of making the emancipation gradual and compensating the unwilling owners. Where we suppose we have the constitutional right, we restrain ourselves in reference to the actual existence of the institution and the difficulties thrown about it. We also oppose it as an evil so far as it seeks to spread itself. We insist on the policy that shall restrict it to its present limits. We don't suppose that in doing this we violate anything due to the actual presence of the institution, or anything due to the constitutional guaranties thrown around it.

We oppose the Dred Scott decision in a certain way, upon which I ought perhaps to address you in a few words. We do not propose that when Dred Scott has been decided to be a slave by the court, we, as a mob, will decide him to be free. We do not propose that, when any other one, or one thousand, shall be decided by that court to be slaves, we will in any violent way disturb the rights of property thus settled; but we nevertheless do oppose that decision as a political rule, which shall be binding on the voter to vote for nobody who thinks it wrong, which shall be binding on the members of Congress or the President to favour no measure that does not actually concur with the principles of that decision. We do not propose to be bound by it as a political rule in that way, because we think it lays the foundation not merely of enlarging and spreading out what we consider an evil, but it lays the foundation for spreading that evil into the States themselves. We propose so resisting it as to have it reversed if we can, and a new judicial rule established upon this subject.

I will add this, that if there be any man who does not believe that slavery is wrong in the three aspects which I have mentioned, or in any one of them, that man is misplaced and ought to leave us. While, on the other hand, if there be any man in the Republican party who is impatient over the necessity springing from its actual presence, and is impatient of the constitutional guaranties thrown around it, and would act in disregard of these, he too is misplaced, standing with us. He will find his place somewhere else; for we have a due regard, so far as we are capable of understanding them, for all these things. This, gentlemen, as well as I can give it, is a plain statement of our principles in all their enormity.

I will say now that there is a sentiment in the country contrary to me—a sentiment which holds that slavery is not wrong, and therefore goes for the policy that does not propose dealing with it as a wrong. That policy is the Democratic policy, and that sentiment is the Democratic sentiment. If there be a doubt in the mind of any one of this vast audience that this is really the central idea of the Democratic party, in relation to this subject, I ask him to bear with me while I state a few things tending, as I think, to prove that proposition.

In the first place, the leading man,—I think I may do my friend Judge Douglas the honour of calling him such,—advocating the present Democratic policy, never himself says it is wrong. He has the high distinction, so far as I know, of never having said slavery is either right or wrong. Almost everybody else says one or the other, but the Judge never does. If there be a man in the Democratic party who thinks it is wrong, and yet clings to that party, I suggest to him in the first place that his leader don't talk as he does, for he never says that it is wrong.

In the second place, I suggest to him that if he will examine the policy proposed to be carried forward, he will find that he carefully excludes the idea that there is anything wrong in it. If you will examine the arguments that are made on it, you will find that every one carefully excludes the idea that there is anything wrong in slavery.

Perhaps that Democrat who says he is as much opposed to slavery as I am will tell me that I am wrong about this. I wish him to examine his own course in regard to this matter a moment, and then see if his opinion will not be changed a little. You say it is wrong; but don't you constantly object to anybody else saying so? Do you not constantly argue that this is not the right place to oppose it? You say it must not be opposed in the free States, because slavery is not there; it must not be opposed in the slave States, because it is there; it must not be opposed in politics, because that will make a fuss; it must not be opposed in the pulpit, because it is not religion. Then where is the place to oppose it? There is no suitable place to oppose it. There is no plan in the country to oppose this evil overspreading the continent, which you say yourself is coming. Frank Blair and Gratz Brown tried to get up a system of gradual emancipation in Missouri, had an election in August, and got beat; and you, Mr. Democrat, threw up your hat and hallooed, "Hurrah for Democracy!"

So I say again, that in regard to the arguments that are made, when Judge Douglas says he "don't care whether slavery is voted up or voted down," whether he means that as an individual expression of sentiment, or only as a sort of statement of his views on national policy, it is alike true to say that he can thus argue logically if he don't see anything wrong in it; but he cannot say so logically if he admits that slavery is wrong. He cannot say that he would as soon see a wrong voted up as voted down. When Judge Douglas says that whoever or whatever community wants slaves, they have a right to have them, he is perfectly logical if there is nothing wrong in the institution; but if you admit that it is wrong, he cannot logically say that anybody has a right to do wrong. When he says that slave property and horse and hog property are alike to be allowed to go into the Territories, upon the principles of equality, he is reasoning truly if there is no difference between them as property; but if the one is property, held rightfully, and the other is wrong, then there is no equality between the right and wrong; so that, turn it in any way you can, in all the arguments sustaining the Democratic policy, and in that policy itself, there is a careful, studied exclusion of the idea that there is anything wrong in slavery.

Let us understand this. I am not, just here, trying to prove that we are right and they are wrong. I have been stating where we and they stand, and trying to show what is the real difference between us; and I now say that whenever we can get the question distinctly stated,—can get all these men who believe that slavery is in some of these respects wrong, to stand and act with us in treating it as a wrong,—then, and not till then, I think, will we in some way come to an end of this slavery agitation.

Mr. Lincoln's Reply to Judge Douglas in the Seventh and Last Debate. Alton, Illinois. October 15, 1858

... But is it true that all the difficulty and agitation we have in regard to this institution of slavery springs from office-seeking,—from the mere ambition of politicians? Is that the truth? How many times have we had danger from this question? Go back to the day of the Missouri Compromise. Go back to the nullification question, at the bottom of which lay this same slavery question. Go back to the time of the annexation of Texas. Go back to the troubles that led to the Compromise of 1850. You will find that every time, with the single exception of the nullification question, they sprung from an endeavour to spread this institution. There never was a party in the history of this country, and there probably never will be, of sufficient strength to disturb the general peace of the country. Parties themselves may be divided and quarrel on minor questions, yet it extends not beyond the parties themselves. But does not this question make a disturbance outside of political circles? Does it not enter into the churches and rend them asunder? What divided the great Methodist Church into two parts, North and South? What has raised this constant disturbance in every Presbyterian General Assembly that meets? What disturbed the Unitarian Church in this very city two years ago? What has jarred and shaken the great American Tract Society recently,—not yet splitting it, but sure to divide it in the end? Is it not this same mighty, deep-seated power, that somehow operates on the minds of men, exciting and stirring them up in every avenue of society, in politics, in religion, in literature, in morals, in all the manifold relations of life? Is this the work of politicians? Is that irresistible power which for fifty years has shaken the government and agitated the people, to be stilled and subdued by pretending that it is an exceedingly simple thing, and we ought not to talk about it? If you will get everybody else to stop talking about it, I assure you that I will quit before they have half done so. But where is the philosophy or statesmanship which assumes that you can quiet that disturbing element in our society, which has disturbed us for more than half a century, which has been the only serious danger that has threatened our institutions? I say where is the philosophy or the statesmanship, based on the assumption that we are to quit talking about it, and that the public mind is all at once to cease being agitated by it? Yet this is the policy here in the North that Douglas is advocating,—that we are to care nothing about it! I ask you if it is not a false philosophy? Is it not a false statesmanship that undertakes to build up a system of policy upon the basis of caring nothing about the very thing that everybody does care the most about,—a thing which all experience has shown we care a very great deal about?

... The Judge alludes very often in the course of his remarks to the exclusive right which the States have to decide the whole thing for themselves. I agree with him very readily.... Our controversy with him is in regard to the new Territories. We agree that when States come in as States they have the right and power to do as they please.... We profess constantly that we have no more inclination than belief in the power of the government to disturb it; yet we are driven constantly to defend ourselves from the assumption that we are warring upon the rights of the

States. What I insist upon is, that the new Territories shall be kept free from it while in the territorial condition ...

... These are false issues, upon which Judge Douglas has tried to force the controversy....

The real issue in this controversy—the one dressing upon every mind—is the sentiment on the part of one class that looks upon the institution of slavery as a wrong, and of another class that does not look upon it as a wrong. The sentiment that contemplates the institution of slavery in this country as a wrong is the sentiment of the Republican party. It is the sentiment around which all their actions, all their arguments, circle; from which all their propositions radiate. They look upon it as being a moral, social, and political wrong; and while they contemplate it as such, they nevertheless have due regard for its actual existence among us, and the difficulties of getting rid of it in any satisfactory way, and to all the constitutional obligations thrown about it. Yet, having a due regard for these, they desire a policy in regard to it that looks to its not creating any more danger. They insist that it, as far as may be, be treated as a wrong; and one of the methods of treating it as a wrong is to make provision that it shall grow no larger. They also desire a policy that looks to a peaceful end of slavery some time, as being a wrong. These are the views they entertain in regard to it, as I understand them; and all their sentiments, all their arguments and propositions are brought within this range, I have said, and I here repeat it, that if there be a man amongst us who does not think that the institution of slavery is wrong in any one of the aspects of which I have spoken, he is misplaced, and ought not to be with us. And if there be a man amongst us who is so impatient of it as a wrong as to disregard its actual presence among us, and the difficulty of getting rid of it suddenly in a satisfactory way, and to disregard the constitutional obligations thrown about it, that man is misplaced if he is on our platform. We disclaim sympathy with him in practical action. He is not placed properly with us.

On this subject of treating it as a wrong and limiting its spread, let me say a word. Has anything ever threatened the existence of this Union save and except this very institution of slavery? What is it that we hold most dear amongst us? Our own liberty and prosperity. What has ever threatened our liberty and prosperity save and except this institution of slavery? If this is true, how do you propose to improve the condition of things by enlarging slavery,—by spreading it out and making it bigger? You may have a wen or a cancer upon your person, and not be able to cut it out lest you bleed to death; but surely it is no way to cure it, to engraft it and spread it over your whole body. That is no proper way of treating what you regard as a wrong. You see this peaceful way of dealing with it as a wrong,—restricting the spread of it, and not allowing it to go into new countries where it has not already existed. That is the peaceful way—the old-fashioned way—the way in which the fathers themselves set us the example.

On the other hand, I have said there is a sentiment which treats it as not being wrong. That is the Democratic sentiment of this day. I do not mean to say that every man who stands within that range positively asserts that it is right. That class will include all who positively assert that it is right, and all who, like Judge Douglas, treat it as indifferent, and do not say it is either right or wrong. These two classes of men fall within the general class of those who do not look upon it as a wrong. And if there be among you anybody who supposes that he, as a Democrat, can consider himself "as much opposed to slavery as anybody," I would like to reason with him. You never treat it *as* a wrong. What other thing that you consider a wrong do you deal with as you deal with that? Perhaps you say it is wrong, but your leader never does, and you quarrel with anybody who says it is wrong. Although you pretend to say so yourself, you can find no fit place to deal with it as a wrong. You must not say anything about it in the free States, because it is not here. You must not say anything about it in the slave States, because it is there. You must not say anything about it in the pulpit, because that is religion, and has nothing to do with it. You must not say anything about it in politics, because that will disturb the security of "my place." There is no place to talk about it as being a wrong, although you say yourself it is a wrong. But, finally, you will screw yourself up to the belief that if the people of the slave States should adopt a system of gradual emancipation on the slavery question, you would be in favour of it. You would be in favour of it! You say that is getting it in the right place, and you would be glad to see it succeed. But you are deceiving yourself. You all know that Frank Blair and Gratz Brown, down there in St. Louis, undertook to introduce that system in Missouri. They fought as valiantly as they could for the system of gradual emancipation, which you pretend you would be glad to see succeed. Now I will bring you to the test. After a hard fight they were beaten; and when the news came over here, you threw up your hats and hurrahed for Democracy! More than that; take all the argument made in favour of the system you have proposed, and it carefully excludes the idea that there is anything wrong in the institution of slavery. The arguments to sustain that policy carefully exclude it. Even here to-day, you heard Judge Douglas quarrel with me, because I uttered a wish that it might sometime come to an end. Although Henry Clay could say he wished every slave in the United States was in the country of his ancestors, I am denounced by those who pretend to respect Henry Clay, for uttering a wish that it might sometime, in some peaceful way, come to an end.

The Democratic policy in regard to that institution will not tolerate the merest breath, the slightest hint, of the least degree of wrong about it. Try it by some of Judge Douglas's arguments. He says he "don't care whether it is voted up or voted down in the Territories." I do not care myself in dealing with that expression whether it is intended to be expressive of his individual sentiments on the subject or only of the national policy he desires to have established.

But no man can logically say it who does see a wrong in it; because no man can logically say he don't care whether a wrong is voted up or voted down.... Any man can say that who does not see anything wrong in slavery.... But if it is a wrong, he cannot say that people have a right to do wrong. He says that, upon the score of equality, slaves should be allowed to go into a new Territory like other property. This is strictly logical if there is no difference between it and other property.... But if you insist that one is wrong and the other right, there is no use to institute a comparison between right and wrong.... The Democratic policy everywhere carefully excludes the idea that there is anything wrong in it.

That is the real issue. That is the issue that will continue in this country when these poor tongues of Judge Douglas and myself shall be silent. It is the eternal struggle between these two principles—right and wrong—throughout the world. They are the two principles that have stood face to face from the beginning of time, and will ever continue to struggle.

The one is the common right of humanity, and the other the divine right of kings. It is the same principle in whatever shape it develops itself. It is the same spirit that says, "You toil and work and earn bread, and I'll eat it." No matter in what shape it comes, whether from the mouth of a king, who seeks to bestride the people of his own nation and live by the fruit of their labour, or from one race of men as an apology for enslaving another race,—it is the same tyrannical principle.... Whenever the issue can be distinctly made, and all extraneous matter thrown out, so that men can fairly see the real difference between the parties, this controversy will soon be settled, and it will be done peaceably, too. There will be no war, no violence. It will be placed again where the wisest and best men of the world placed it.

From a Speech at Columbus, Ohio, on the Slave Trade, Popular Sovereignty, etc. September 16, 1859

... The Republican party, as I understand its principles and policy, believes that there is great danger of the institution of slavery being spread out and extended, until it is ultimately made alike lawful in all the States of this Union; so believing, to prevent that incidental and ultimate consummation is the original and chief purpose of the Republican organization.

I say "chief purpose" of the Republican organization; for it is certainly true that if the national House shall fall into the hands of the Republicans, they will have to attend to all the matters of national house-keeping as well as this. The chief and real purpose of the Republican party is eminently conservative. It proposes nothing save and except to restore this Government to its original tone in regard to this element of slavery, and there to maintain it, looking for no further change in reference to it than that which the original framers of the Government themselves expected and looked forward to.

The chief danger to this purpose of the Republican party is not just now the revival of the African slave-trade, or the passage of a Congressional slave-code ... but the most imminent danger that now threatens that purpose is that insidious Douglas popular sovereignty. This is the miner and sapper. While it does not propose to revive the African slave-trade, nor to pass a slave-code, nor to make a second Dred Scott decision, it is preparing us for the onslaught and charge of these ultimate enemies when they shall be ready to come on, and the word of command for them to advance shall be given. I say this *Douglas* popular sovereignty—for there is a broad distinction, as I now understand it, between that article and a genuine popular sovereignty.

I believe there is a genuine popular sovereignty. I think a definition of genuine popular sovereignty in the abstract would be about this: that each man shall do precisely as he pleases with himself, and with all those things which exclusively concern him. Applied to governments, this principle would be, that a general government shall do all those things which pertain to it; and all the local governments shall do precisely as they please in respect to those matters which exclusively concern them. I understand that this government of the United States under which we live, is based upon this principle; and I am misunderstood if it is supposed that I have any war to make upon that principle.

Now, what is Judge Douglas's popular sovereignty? It is, as a principle, no other than that if one man chooses to make a slave of another man, neither that other man nor anybody else has a right to object. Applied in government, as he seeks to apply it, it is this: If, in a new Territory into which a few people are beginning to enter for the purpose of making their homes, they choose to either exclude slavery from their limits or to establish it there, however one or the other may affect the persons to be enslaved, or the infinitely greater number of persons who are afterward to inhabit that Territory, or the other members of the families of communities of which they are but an incipient member, or the general head of the family of States as parent of all,— however their action may affect one or the other of these, there is no power or right to interfere. That is Douglas popular sovereignty applied.

... I cannot but express my gratitude that this true view of this element of discord among us, as I believe it is, is attracting more and more attention. I do not believe that Governor Seward uttered that sentiment because I had done so before, but because he reflected upon this subject, and saw the truth of it. Nor do I believe, because Governor Seward or I uttered it, that Mr. Hickman of Pennsylvania, in different language, since that time, has declared his belief in the utter antagonism which exists between the principles of liberty and slavery. You see we are multiplying. Now, while I am speaking of Hickman, let me say, I know but little about him. I have never seen him, and know scarcely anything about the man; but I will say this much about him: of all the anti-Lecompton Democracy that have been brought to my notice, he alone has the true, genuine ring of the metal.

... Judge Douglas ... proceeds to assume, without proving it, that slavery is one of those little, unimportant, trivial matters which are of just about as much consequence as the question would be to me, whether my neighbour should raise horned cattle or plant tobacco; that there is no moral question about it, but that it is altogether a matter of dollars and cents; that when a new Territory is opened for settlement, the first man who goes into it may plant there a thing which, like the Canada thistle or some other of those pests of the soil, cannot be dug out by the millions of men who will come thereafter; that it is one of those little things that is so trivial in its nature that it has no effect upon anybody save the few men who first plant upon the soil; that it is not a thing which in any way affects the family of communities composing these States, nor any way endangers the general government. Judge Douglas ignores altogether the very well-known fact that we have never had a serious menace to our political existence except it sprang from this thing, which he chooses to regard as only upon a par with onions and potatoes.

... Did you ever, five years ago, hear of anybody in the world saying that the negro had no share in the Declaration of National Independence; that it did not mean negroes at all; and when "all men" were spoken of, negroes were not included?

... Then I suppose that all now express the belief that the Declaration of Independence never did mean negroes. I call upon one of them to say that he said it five years ago. If you think that now, and did not think it then, the next thing that strikes me is to remark that there has been a *change* wrought in you, and a very significant change it is, being no less than changing the negro, in your estimation, from the rank of a man to that of a brute....

Is not this change wrought in your minds a very important change? Public opinion in this country is everything. In a nation like ours this popular sovereignty and squatter sovereignty have already wrought a change in the public mind to the extent I have stated....

... Now, if you are opposed to slavery honestly, I ask you to note that fact (the popular-sovereignty of Judge Douglas), and the like of which is to follow, to be plastered on, layer after layer, until very soon you are prepared to deal with the negro everywhere as with the brute. If public sentiment has not been debauched already to this point, a new turn of the screw in that direction is all that is wanting; and this is constantly being done by the teachers of this insidious popular sovereignty. You need but one or two turns further, until your minds, now ripening under these teachings, will be ready for all these things, and you will receive and support or submit to the slave-trade, revived with all its horrors,—a slave-code enforced in our Territories,—and a new Dred Scott decision to bring slavery up into the very heart of the free North.

... I ask attention to the fact that in a pre-eminent degree these popular sovereigns are at this work: blowing out the moral lights around us; teaching that the negro is no longer a man, but a brute; that the Declaration has nothing to do with him; that he ranks with the crocodile and the reptile; that man with body and soul is a matter of dollars and cents. I suggest to this portion of the Ohio Republicans, or Democrats, if there be any present, the serious consideration of this fact, that there is now going on among you a steady process of debauching public opinion on this subject. With this, my friends, I bid you adieu.

From a Speech at Cincinnati, Ohio, on the Intentions of "Black Republicans," the Relation of Labour and Capital, etc. September 17, 1859

... I say, then, in the first place to the Kentuckians that I am what they call, as I understand it, a "Black Republican." I think slavery is wrong, morally and politically. I desire that it should be no further spread in these United States, and I should not object if it should gradually terminate in the whole Union. While I say this for myself, I say to you, Kentuckians, that I understand you differ radically with me upon this proposition; that you believe slavery is a good thing; that slavery is right; that it ought to be extended and perpetuated in this Union. Now, there being this broad difference between us, I do not pretend, in addressing myself to you, Kentuckians, to attempt proselyting you. That would be a vain effort. I do not enter upon it. I only propose to try to show you that you ought to nominate for the next presidency, at Charleston, my distinguished friend, Judge Douglas. In all that, there is no real difference between you and him; I understand he is as sincerely for you, and more wisely for you than you are for yourselves. I will try to demonstrate that proposition.

In Kentucky perhaps—in many of the slave States certainly—you are trying to establish the rightfulness of slavery by reference to the Bible. You are trying to show that slavery existed in the Bible times by Divine ordinance. Now, Douglas is wiser than you, for your own benefit, upon that subject. Douglas knows that whenever you establish that slavery was right by the Bible, it will occur that that slavery was the slavery of the white man,—of men without reference to colour,—and he knows very well that you may entertain that idea in Kentucky as much as you please, but you will never win any Northern support upon it. He makes a wiser argument for you. He makes the argument that the slavery of the black man—the slavery of the man who has a skin of a different colour from your own—is right. He thereby brings to your support Northern voters, who could not for a moment be brought by your own argument of the Bible right of slavery.

... At Memphis he [Judge Douglas] declared that in all contests between the negro and the white man, he was for the white man, but that in all questions between the negro and the crocodile, he was for the negro. He did not make that declaration accidentally ... he made it a great many times.

The first inference seems to be that if you do not enslave the negro, you are wronging the white man in some way or other; and that whoever is opposed to the negro being enslaved is in some way or other against the white man. Is not that a falsehood? If there was a necessary conflict between the white man and the negro, I should be for the white man as much as Judge Douglas; but I say there is no such necessary conflict. I say there is room enough for us all to be free, and that it not only does not wrong the white man that the negro should be free, but it positively wrongs the mass of the white men that the negro should be enslaved,—that the mass of white men are really injured by the effects of slave labour in the vicinity of the fields of their own labour....

There is one other thing that I will say to you in this relation. It is but my opinion; I give it to you without a fee. It is my opinion that it is for you to take him or be defeated; and that if you do take him you may be beaten. You will surely be beaten if you do not take him. We, the Republicans and others forming the opposition of the country, intend "to stand by our guns," to be patient and firm, and in the long run to beat you, whether you take him or not. We know that before we fairly beat you, we have to beat you both together. We know that "you are all of a feather," and that we have to beat you all together, and we expect to do it. We don't intend to be very impatient about it. We mean to be as deliberate and calm about it as it is possible to be, but as firm and resolved as it is possible for men to be. When we do as we say, beat you, you perhaps want to know what we will do with you.

I will tell you, so far as I am authorized to speak for the opposition, what we mean to do with you. We mean to treat you, as near as we possibly can, as Washington, Jefferson, and Madison treated you. We mean to leave you alone, and in no way to interfere with your institution; to abide by all and every compromise of the Constitution, and, in a word, coming back to the original proposition, to treat you, so far as degenerate men (if we have degenerated) may, according to the example of those noble fathers—Washington, Jefferson, and Madison. We mean to remember that you are as good as we; that there is no difference between us other than the difference of circumstances. We mean to recognize and bear in mind always, that you have as good hearts in your bosoms as other people, or as we claim to have, and to treat you accordingly. We mean to marry your girls when we have a chance—the white ones, I mean, and I have the honour to inform you that I once did have a chance in that way.

I have told you what we mean to do. I want to know, now, when that thing takes place, what do you mean to do? I often hear it intimated that you mean to divide the Union whenever a Republican, or anything like it, is elected President of the United States. [A voice: "That is so."] "That is so," one of them says; I wonder if he is a Kentuckian? [A voice: "He is a Douglas man."] Well, then, I want to know what you are going to do with your half of it. Are you going to split the Ohio down through, and push your half off a piece? Or are you going to keep it right alongside of us outrageous fellows? Or are you going to build up a wall some way between your country and ours, by which that movable property of yours can't come over here any more, to the danger of your losing it? Do you think you can better yourselves on that subject by leaving us here under no obligation whatever to return those specimens of your movable property that come hither?

You have divided the Union because we would not do right with you, as you think, upon that subject; when we cease to be under obligation to do anything for you, how much better off do you think you will be? Will you make war upon us and kill us all? Why, gentlemen, I think you are as gallant and as brave men as live; that you can fight as bravely in a good cause, man for man, as any other people living; that you have shown yourselves capable of this upon various occasions; but man for man, you are not better than we are, and there are not so many of you as there are of us. You will never make much of a hand at whipping us. If we were fewer in numbers than you, I think that you could whip us; if we were equal it would likely be a drawn battle; but being inferior in numbers, you will make nothing by attempting to master us....

Labour is the great source from which nearly all, if not all, human comforts and necessities are drawn. There is a difference in opinion about the elements of labour in society. Some men assume that there is a necessary connection between capital and labour, and that connection draws within it the whole of the labour of the community. They assume that nobody works unless capital excites them to work. They begin next to consider what is the best way. They say there are but two ways,—one is to hire men and to allure them to labour by their consent; the other is to buy the men, and drive them to it, and that is slavery. Having assumed that, they proceed to discuss the question of whether the labourers themselves are better off in the condition of slaves or of hired labourers, and they usually decide that they are better off in the condition of slaves.

In the first place, I say the whole thing is a mistake. That there is a certain relation between capital and labour, I admit. That it does exist, and rightfully exist, I think is true. That men who are industrious and sober and honest in the pursuit of their own interests should after a while accumulate capital, and after that should be allowed to enjoy it in peace, and also if they should choose, when they have accumulated it, to use it to save themselves from actual labour, and hire other people to labour for them,—is right. In doing so, they do not wrong the man they employ, for they find men who have not their own land to work upon, or shops to work in, and who are benefited by working for others,—hired labourers, receiving their capital for it. Thus a few men that own capital hire a few others, and these establish the relation of capital and labour rightfully—a relation of which I make no complaint. But I insist that that relation, after all, does not embrace more than one-eighth of the labour of the country.

There are a plenty of men in the slave States that are altogether good enough for me, to be either President or Vice-President, provided they will profess their sympathy with our purpose, and will place themselves on such ground that our men upon principle can vote for them. There are scores of them—good men in their character for intelligence, for talent and integrity. If such an one will place himself upon the right ground, I am for his occupying one place upon the next Republican or opposition ticket. I will go heartily for him. But unless he does so place himself, I think it is perfect nonsense to attempt to bring about a union upon any other basis; that if a union be made, the elements will so scatter that there can be no success for such a ticket. The good old maxims of the Bible are applicable, and truly applicable, to human affairs; and in this, as in other things, we may say that he who is not for us is against us; he who gathereth not with us, scattereth. I should be glad to have some of the many good and able and noble men of the South place themselves where we can confer upon them the high honour of an election upon one or the other end of our ticket. It would do my soul good to do that thing. It would enable us to teach them that inasmuch as we select one of their own number to carry out our principles, we are free from the charge that we mean more than we say....

From a Letter to J.W. Fell. December 20, 1859

I was born February 12, 1809, in Hardin County, Kentucky. My parents were both born in Virginia, of undistinguished families—second families, perhaps I should say. My mother, who died in my tenth year, was of a family of the name of Hanks, some of whom now reside in Adams, and others in Macon County, Illinois. My paternal grandfather, Abraham Lincoln, emigrated from Rockingham County, Virginia, to Kentucky about 1781 or 1782, where a year or two later he was killed by the Indians, not in battle, but by stealth, when he was labouring to open a farm in the forest. His ancestors, who were Quakers, went to Virginia from Berks County, Pennsylvania. An effort to identify them with the New England family of the same name ended in nothing more definite than a similarity of Christian names in both families, such as Enoch, Levi, Mordecai, Solomon, Abraham, and the like.

My father, at the death of his father, was but six years of age, and he grew up literally without education. He removed from Kentucky to what is now Spencer County, Indiana, in my eighth year. We reached our new home about the time the State came into the Union. It was a wild region, with many bears and other wild animals still in the woods. There I grew up. There were some schools, so called, but no qualification was ever required of a teacher beyond "readin', writin', and cipherin'" to the rule of three. If a straggler supposed to understand Latin happened to sojourn in the neighbourhood, he was looked upon as a wizard. There was absolutely nothing to excite ambition for education. Of course, when I came of age I did not know much. Still, somehow, I could read, write, and cipher to the rule of three, but that was all. I have not been to school since. The little advance I now have upon this store of education I have picked up from time to time under the pressure of necessity.

I was raised to farm work, which I continued till I was twenty-two. At twenty-one I came to Illinois, Macon County. Then I got to New Salem, at that time in Sangamon, now in Menard County, where I remained a year as a sort of clerk in a store.

Then came the Black Hawk War; and I was elected a captain of volunteers, a success which gave me more pleasure than any I have had since. I went the campaign, was elated, ran for the legislature the same year (1832), and was beaten—the only time I ever have been beaten by the people. The next and three succeeding biennial elections I was elected to the legislature. I was not a candidate afterward. During this legislative period I had studied law, and removed to Springfield to practise it. In 1846 I was once elected to the lower House of Congress. Was not a candidate for re-election. From 1849 to 1854, both inclusive, practised law more assiduously than ever before. Always a Whig in politics; and generally on the Whig electoral tickets, making active canvasses. I was losing interest in politics when the repeal of the Missouri Compromise aroused me again. What I have done since then is pretty well known.

If any personal description of me is thought desirable, it may be said I am, in height, six feet four inches, nearly; lean in flesh, weighing on an average one hundred and eighty pounds; dark complexion, with coarse black hair and gray eyes. No other marks or brands recollected.

From an Address delivered at Cooper Institute, New York. February 27, 1860

... Now, and hear, let me guard a little against being misunderstood. I do not mean to say we are bound to follow implicitly in whatever our fathers did. To do so, would be to discard all the lights of current experience—to reject all progress, all improvement. What I do say is, that if we would supplant the opinions and policy of our fathers in any case, we should do so on evidence so conclusive, and argument so clear, that even their great authority, fairly considered and weighed, cannot stand; and most surely not in a case whereof we ourselves declare they understood the question better than we.

If any man at this day sincerely believes that the proper division of local from Federal authority, or any part of the Constitution, forbids the Federal Government to control as to slavery in the Federal Territories, he is right to say so, and to enforce his position by all truthful evidence and fair argument he can. But he has no right to mislead others who have less access to history, and less leisure to study it, into the false belief that "our fathers who framed the government under which we live" were of the same opinion—thus substituting falsehood and deception for truthful evidence and fair argument. If any man at this day sincerely believes "our fathers who framed the government under which we live" used and applied principles, in other cases, which ought to have led them to understand that a proper division of local from Federal authority, or some part of the Constitution, forbids the Federal Government to control as to slavery in the Federal Territories, he is right to say so. But he should, at the same time, have the responsibility of declaring that, in his opinion, he understands their principles better than they did themselves; and especially should he not shirk the responsibility by asserting that they understood the question just as well and even better than we do now.

But enough! Let all who believe that "our fathers who framed the government under which we live understood this question just as well, and even better than we do now," speak as they spoke, and act as they acted upon it. This is all Republicans ask, all Republicans desire, in relation to slavery. As those fathers marked it, so let it again be marked, as an evil not to be extended, but to be tolerated and protected only because of and so far as its actual presence among us makes that toleration and protection a necessity. Let all the guaranties those fathers gave it be not grudgingly, but fully and fairly maintained. For this Republicans contend, and with this, so far as I know or believe, they will be content.

And now, if they would listen,—as I suppose they will not,—I would address a few words to the Southern people.

I would say to them: You consider yourselves a reasonable and a just people; and I consider that in the general qualities of reason and justice you are not inferior to any other people. Still, when you speak of us Republicans, you do so only to denounce us as reptiles, or, at the best, as no better than outlaws. You will grant a hearing to pirates or murderers, but nothing like it to

"Black Republicans." In all your contentions with one another, each of you deems an unconditional condemnation of "Black Republicanism" as the first thing to be attended to. Indeed, such condemnation of us seems to be an indispensable prerequisite—license, so to speak—among you to be admitted or permitted to speak at all. Now, can you or not be prevailed upon to pause and to consider whether this is quite just to us, or even to yourselves? Bring forward your charges and specifications, and then be patient long enough to hear us deny or justify.

You say we are sectional. We deny it. That makes an issue; and the burden of proof is upon you. You produce your proof; and what is it? Why, that our party has no existence in your section—gets no votes in your section. The fact is substantially true; but does it prove the issue? If it does, then, in case we should, without change of principle, begin to get votes in your section, we should thereby cease to be sectional. You cannot escape this conclusion; and yet, are you willing to abide by it? If you are, you will probably soon find that we have ceased to be sectional, for we shall get votes in your section this very year. You will then begin to discover, as the truth plainly is, that your proof does not touch the issue. The fact that we get no votes in your section is a fact of your making, and not of ours.

And if there be fault in that fact, that fault is primarily yours, and remains so until you show that we repel you by some wrong principle or practice. If we do repel you by any wrong principle or practice, the fault is ours; but this brings you to where you ought to have started—to a discussion of the right or wrong of our principle. If our principle, put in practice, would wrong your section for the benefit of ours, or for any other object, then our principle, and we with it, are sectional, and are justly opposed and denounced as such. Meet us, then, on the question of whether our principle, put in practice, would wrong your section; and so meet us as if it were possible that something may be said on our side. Do you accept the challenge? No! Then you really believe that the principle which "our fathers who framed the government under which we live" thought so clearly right as to adopt it, and indorse it again and again, upon their official oaths, is in fact so clearly wrong as to demand your condemnation without a moment's consideration.

Some of you delight to flaunt in our faces the warning against sectional parties given by Washington in his Farewell Address. Less than eight years before Washington gave that warning he had, as President of the United States, approved and signed an act of Congress enforcing the prohibition of slavery in the Northwestern Territory, which act embodied the policy of the government upon that subject up to and at the very moment he penned that warning; and about one year after he penned it, he wrote Lafayette that he considered that prohibition a wise measure, expressing in the same connection his hope that we should at some time have a confederacy of free States.

Bearing this in mind, and seeing that sectionalism has since arisen upon this same subject, is that warning a weapon in your hands against us, or in our hands against you? Could Washington himself speak, would he cast the blame of that sectionalism upon us, who sustain his policy, or upon you, who repudiate it? We respect that warning of Washington, and we commend it to you, together with his example pointing to the right application of it.

But you say you are conservative,—eminently conservative,—while we are revolutionary, destructive, or something of the sort.

What is conservatism? Is it not adherence to the old and tried, against the new and untried? We stick to, contend for, the identical old policy on the point in controversy which was adopted by "our fathers who framed the government under which we live"; while you with one accord reject, and scout, and spit upon that old policy, and insist upon substituting something new.

True, you disagree among yourselves as to what that substitute shall be. You are divided on new propositions and plans, but you are unanimous in rejecting and denouncing the old policy of the fathers. Some of you are for reviving the foreign slave-trade; some for a Congressional slave-code for the Territories; some for Congress forbidding the Territories to prohibit slavery within their limits; some for maintaining slavery in the Territories through the judiciary; some for the "gur-reat pur-rinciple" that "if one man would enslave another, no third man should object," fantastically called "popular sovereignty"; but never a man among you is in favour of Federal prohibition of slavery in Federal Territories, according to the practice of "our fathers who framed the government under which we live." Not one of all your various plans can show a precedent or an advocate in the century within which our government originated.

Consider, then, whether your claim for conservatism for yourselves, and your charge of destructiveness against us, are based on the most clear and stable foundations.

Again, you say we have made the slavery question more prominent than it formerly was. We deny it. We admit that it is more prominent, but we deny that we made it so. It was not we, but you, who discarded the old policy of the fathers. We resisted, and still resist, your innovation; and thence comes the greater prominence of the question. Would you have that question reduced to its former proportions? Go back to that old policy. What has been will be again, under the same conditions. If you would have the peace of the old times, readopt the precepts and policy of the old times.

You charge that we stir up insurrections among your slaves. We deny it; and what is your proof? Harper's Ferry! John Brown! John Brown was no Republican; and you have failed to implicate a single Republican in his Harper's Ferry enterprise. If any member of our party is guilty in that matter, you know it, or you do not know it. If you do know it, you are inexcusable for not designating the man and proving the fact. If you do not know it, you are inexcusable for asserting it, and especially for persisting in the assertion after you have tried and failed to make the proof. You need not be told that persisting in a charge which one does not know to be true is simply malicious slander.

Some of you admit that no Republican designedly aided or encouraged the Harper's Ferry affair, but still insist that our doctrines and declarations necessarily lead to such results. We do not believe it. We know we hold no doctrine, and make no declaration, which were not held to and made by "our fathers who framed the government under which we live." You never dealt fairly by us in relation to this affair. When it occurred, some important State elections were near at hand, and you were in evident glee with the belief that, by charging the blame upon us, you could get an advantage of us in those elections. The elections came, and your expectations were not quite fulfilled. Every Republican man knew that, as to himself at least, your charge was a slander, and he was not much inclined by it to cast his vote in your favour. Republican doctrines and declarations are accompanied with a continual protest against any interference whatever with your slaves, or with you about your slaves. Surely this does not encourage them to revolt. True, we do, in common with "our fathers who framed the government under which we live," declare our belief that slavery is wrong; but the slaves do not hear us declare even this. For anything we say or do, the slaves would scarcely know there is a Republican party. I believe they would not, in fact, generally know it but for your misrepresentations of us in their hearing. In your political contests among yourselves, each faction charges the other with sympathy with Black Republicanism; and then, to give point to the charge, defines Black Republicanism to simply be insurrection, blood, and thunder among the slaves.

Slave insurrections are no more common now than they were before the Republican party was organized. What induced the Southampton insurrection, twenty-eight years ago, in which at least three times as many lives were lost as at Harper's Ferry? You can scarcely stretch your very elastic fancy to the conclusion that Southampton was "got up by Black Republicanism." In the present state of things in the United States, I do not think a general, or even a very extensive, slave insurrection is possible. The indispensable concert of action cannot be attained. The slaves have no means of rapid communication; nor can incendiary freemen, black or white, supply it. The explosive materials are everywhere in parcels; but there neither are, nor can be supplied, the indispensable connecting trains.

Much is said by Southern people about the affection of slaves for their masters and mistresses; and a part of it, at least, is true. A plot for an uprising could scarcely be devised and communicated to twenty individuals before some one of them, to save the life of a favourite master or mistress, would divulge it. This is the rule; and the slave revolution in Haiti was not an exception to it, but a case occurring under peculiar circumstances. The Gunpowder Plot of British history, though not connected with slaves, was more in point. In that case, only about twenty were admitted to the secret; and yet one of them, in his anxiety to save a friend, betrayed the plot to that friend, and, by consequence, averted the calamity. Occasional poisonings from the kitchen, and open or stealthy assassinations in the field, and local revolts extending to a score or so, will continue to occur as the natural results of slavery; but no general insurrection of slaves, as I think, can happen in this country for a long time. Whoever much fears, or much hopes, for such an event, will be alike disappointed.

In the language of Mr. Jefferson, uttered many years ago, "It is still in our power to direct the process of emancipation and deportation peaceably, and in such slow degrees as that the evil will wear off insensibly, and their places be, *pari passu,* filled up by free white labourers. If, on the contrary, it is left to force itself on, human nature must shudder at the prospect held up."

Mr. Jefferson did not mean to say, nor do I, that the power of emancipation is in the Federal Government. He spoke of Virginia; and, as to the power of emancipation, I speak of the slaveholding States only. The Federal Government, however, as we insist, has the power of restraining the extension of the institution—the power to insure that a slave insurrection shall never occur on any American soil which is now free from slavery.

John Brown's effort was peculiar. It was not a slave insurrection. It was an attempt by white men to get up a revolt among slaves, in which the slaves refused to participate. In fact, it was so absurd that the slaves, with all their ignorance, saw plainly enough it could not succeed. That affair, in its philosophy, corresponds with the many attempts, related in history, at the assassination of kings and emperors. An enthusiast broods over the oppression of a people till he fancies himself commissioned by Heaven to liberate them. He ventures the attempt, which ends in little else than his own execution. Orsini's attempt on Louis Napoleon, and John Brown's attempt at Harper's Ferry, were, in their philosophy, precisely the same. The eagerness to cast blame on Old England in the one case, and on New England in the other, does not disprove the sameness of the two things.

And how much would it avail you if you could, by the use of John Brown, Helper's book, and the like, break up the Republican organization? Human action can be modified to some extent, but human nature cannot be changed. There is a judgment and a feeling against slavery in this nation, which cast at least a million and a half of votes. You cannot destroy that judgment and feeling—that sentiment—by breaking up the political organization which rallies around it. You can scarcely scatter and disperse an army which has been formed into order in the face of your heaviest fire; but if you could, how much would you gain by forcing the sentiment which created it out of the peaceful channel of the ballot-box into some other channel? What would that other channel probably be? Would the number of John Browns be lessened or enlarged by the operation?

But you will break up the Union rather than submit to a denial of your constitutional rights.

That has a somewhat reckless sound; but it would be palliated, if not fully justified, were we proposing, by the mere force of numbers, to deprive you of some right plainly written down in the Constitution. But we are proposing no such thing.

When you make these declarations you have a specific and well-understood allusion to an assumed constitutional right of yours to take slaves into the Federal Territories, and to hold them there as property. But no such right is specifically written in the Constitution. That instrument is literally silent about any such right. We, on the contrary, deny that such a right has any existence in the Constitution, even by implication.

Your purpose, then, plainly stated, is that you will destroy the government, unless you be allowed to construe and force the Constitution as you please, on all points in dispute between you and us. You will rule or ruin in all events.

This, plainly stated, is your language. Perhaps you will say the Supreme Court has decided the disputed constitutional question in your favour. Not quite so. But waiving the lawyer's distinction between dictum and decision, the court has decided the question for you in a sort of way. The court has substantially said, it is your constitutional right to take slaves into the Federal Territories, and to hold them there as property. When I say the decision was made in a sort of way, I mean it was made in a divided court, by a bare majority of the judges, and they not quite agreeing with one another in the reasons for making it; that it is so made as that its avowed supporters disagree with one another about its meaning, and that it was mainly based upon a mistaken statement of fact—the statement in the opinion that "the right of property in a slave is distinctly and expressly affirmed in the Constitution."

An inspection of the Constitution will show that the right of property in a slave is not "distinctly and expressly affirmed" in it. Bear in mind, the judges do not pledge their judicial opinion that such right is impliedly affirmed in the Constitution; but they pledge their veracity that it is "distinctly and expressly" affirmed there—"distinctly," that is, not mingled with anything else; "expressly," that is, in words meaning just that, without the aid of any inference, and susceptible of no other meaning.

If they had only pledged their judicial opinion that such right is affirmed in the instrument by implication, it would be open to others to show that neither the word "slave" nor "slavery" is to be found in the Constitution, nor the word "property," even, in any connection with language alluding to the things slave or slavery; and that wherever in that instrument the slave is alluded to, he is called a "person"; and wherever his master's legal right in relation to him is alluded to, it is spoken of as "service or labour which may be due"—as a debt payable in service or labour. Also it would be open to show, by contemporaneous history, that this mode of alluding to slaves and slavery, instead of speaking of them, was employed on purpose to exclude from the Constitution the idea that there could be property in man.

To show all this is easy and certain.

When this obvious mistake of the judges shall be brought to their notice, is it not reasonable to expect that they will withdraw the mistaken statement, and reconsider the conclusion based upon it?

And then it is to be remembered that "our fathers who framed the government under which we live"—the men who made the Constitution—decided this same constitutional question in our favour long ago; decided it without division among themselves when making the decision; without division among themselves about the meaning of it after it was made, and, so far as any evidence is left, without basing it upon any mistaken statement of facts.

Under all these circumstances, do you really feel yourselves justified to break up this government unless such a court decision as yours is shall be at once submitted to as a conclusive and final rule of political action? But you will not abide the election of a Republican President! In that supposed event, you say, you will destroy the Union; and then, you say, the great crime of having destroyed it will be upon us! That is cool. A highwayman holds a pistol to my ear, and mutters through his teeth, "Stand and deliver, or I shall kill you, and then you will be a murderer!"

To be sure, what the robber demanded of me—my money—was my own; and I had a clear right to keep it; but it was no more my own than my vote is my own; and the threat of death to me, to extort my money, and the threat of destruction to the Union, to extort my vote, can scarcely be distinguished in principle.

Wrong as we think slavery is, we can yet afford to let it alone where it is, because that much is due to the necessity arising from its actual presence in the nation; but can we, while our votes will prevent it, allow it to spread into the national Territories, and to overrun us here in these free States? If our sense of duty forbids this, then let us stand by our duty fearlessly and effectively. Let us be diverted by none of those sophistical contrivances wherewith we are so industriously plied and belaboured,—contrivances such as groping for some middle ground between the right and the wrong, vain as the search for a man who should be neither a living man nor a dead man; such as a policy of "don't care," on a question about which all true men do care; such as Union appeals beseeching true Union men to yield to disunionists, reversing the Divine rule, and calling not the sinners, but the righteous to repentance; such as invocations to Washington, imploring men to unsay what Washington said, and undo what Washington did.

Neither let us be slandered from our duty by false accusations against us, nor frightened from it by menaces of destruction to the government, nor of dungeons to ourselves. Let us have faith that right makes might, and in that faith let us to the end dare to do our duty as we understand it.

Lincoln's Farewell Address at Springfield, Illinois. February 11, 1861

My Friends, No one not in my situation can appreciate my feeling of sadness at this parting. To this place, and the kindness of these people, I owe everything. Here I have lived a quarter of a century, and have passed from a young to an old man. Here my children have been born, and one is buried. I now leave, not knowing when or whether ever I may return, with a task before me greater than that which rested upon Washington. Without the assistance of that Divine Being who ever attended him I cannot succeed. With that assistance I cannot fail. Trusting in Him, who can go with me and remain with you, and be everywhere for good, let us confidently hope that all will yet be well. To His care commending you, as I hope in your prayers you will commend me, I bid you an affectionate farewell.

A Letter to the Hon. Geo. Ashmun accepting his Nomination for the Presidency. May 23, 1860

I accept the nomination tendered me by the Convention over which you presided, and of which I am formally apprized in the letter of yourself and others, acting as a committee of the Convention for that purpose.

The declaration of principles and sentiments which accompanies your letter, meets my approval; and it shall be my care not to violate or disregard it in any part.

Imploring the assistance of Divine Providence, and with due regard to the views and feelings of all who were represented in the Convention; to the rights of all the States and Territories and people of the nation; to the inviolability of the Constitution; and the perpetual union, harmony, and prosperity of all,—I am most happy to co-operate for the practical success of the principles declared by the Convention.

Your obliged friend and fellow-citizen,
A. LINCOLN.

Letter to Miss Grace Bedell. Springfield, Illinois. October 19, 1860

My dear little Miss, Your very agreeable letter of the 15th is received. I regret the necessity of saying I have no daughter. I have three sons—one seventeen, one nine, and one seven years of age. They, with their mother, constitute my whole family. As to the whiskers, having never worn any, do you not think people would call it a piece of silly affectation if I were to begin it now?

From an Address to the Legislature at Indianapolis, Indiana. February 12, 1861

Fellow-citizens of the State of Indiana, I am here to thank you much for this magnificent welcome, and still more for the generous support given by your State to that political cause which I think is the true and just cause of the whole country and the whole world.

Solomon says "there is a time to keep silence," and when men wrangle by the mouth with no certainty that they mean the same thing while using the same word, it perhaps were as well if they would keep silence.

The words "coercion" and "invasion" are much used in these days, and often with some temper and hot blood. Let us make sure, if we can, that we do not misunderstand the meaning of those who use them. Let us get exact definitions of these words, not from dictionaries, but from the men themselves, who certainly deprecate the things they would represent by the use of words. What then is *coercion*? what is *invasion*? Would the marching of an army into South Carolina, without the consent of her people and with hostile intent towards them, be invasion? I certainly think it would; and it would be coercion also, if the South Carolinians were forced to submit. But if the United States should merely retake and hold its own forts and other property, and collect the duties on foreign importations, or even withhold the mails from places where they were habitually violated, would any or all these things be invasion or coercion? Do our professed lovers of the Union, but who spitefully resolve that they will resist coercion and invasion, understand that such things as these, on the part of the United States, would be coercion or invasion of a State? If so, their idea of means to preserve the object of their affection would seem exceedingly thin and airy. If sick, the little pills of the homoeopathist would be much too large for them to swallow. In their view, the Union as a family relation would seem to be no regular marriage, but a sort of free-love arrangement to be maintained only on *passional attraction*.

By the way, in what consists the special sacredness of a State? I speak not of the position assigned to a State in the Union by the Constitution; for that, by the bond, we all recognize. That position, however, a State cannot carry out of the Union with it. I speak of that assumed primary right of a State to rule all which is *less* than itself, and ruin all which is larger than itself. If a State and a county in a given case should be equal in extent of territory, and equal in number of inhabitants, in what, as a matter of principle, is the State better than the county? Would an exchange of *names* be an exchange of *rights* upon principle? On what rightful principle may a State, being not more than one-fiftieth part of the nation in soil and population, break up the nation, and then coerce a proportionally larger subdivision of itself in the most arbitrary way? What mysterious right to play tyrant is conferred on a district of country, with its people, by merely calling it a State?

Fellow-citizens, I am not asserting anything: I am merely asking questions for you to consider. And now allow me to bid you farewell.

From his Address to the Legislature at Columbus, Ohio. February 13, 1861

It is true, as has been said by the president of the Senate, that a very great responsibility rests upon me in the position to which the votes of the American people have called me. I am deeply sensible of that weighty responsibility. I cannot but know, what you all know, that without a name, perhaps without a reason why I should have a name, there has fallen upon me a task such as did not rest even upon the Father of his Country; and so feeling, I cannot but turn and look for that support without which it will be impossible for me to perform that great task. I turn then, and look to the great American people, and to that God who has never forsaken them. Allusion has been made to the interest felt in relation to the policy of the new Administration. In this I have received from some a degree of credit for having kept silence, and from others, some deprecation. I still think I was right.

In the varying and repeatedly shifting scenes of the present, and without a precedent which could enable me to judge by the past, it has seemed fitting that before speaking upon the difficulties of the country, I should have gained a view of the whole field, being at liberty to modify and change the course of policy as future events may make a change necessary.

I have not maintained silence from any want of real anxiety. It is a good thing that there is no more than anxiety, for there is nothing going wrong. It is a consoling circumstance that when we look out, there is nothing that really hurts anybody. We entertain different views upon political questions, but nobody is suffering anything. This is a most consoling circumstance, and from it we may conclude that all we want is time, patience, and a reliance on that God who has never forsaken this people.

From his Remarks at Pittsburgh, Pennsylvania. February 15, 1861

... The condition of the country is an extraordinary one, and fills the mind of every patriot with anxiety. It is my intention to give this subject all the consideration I possibly can, before specially deciding in regard to it, so that when I do speak, it may be as nearly right as possible. When I do speak, I hope I may say nothing in opposition to the spirit of the Constitution, contrary to the integrity of the Union, or which will prove inimical to the liberties of the people or to the peace of the whole country. And furthermore, when the time arrives for me to speak on this great subject, I hope I may say nothing to disappoint the people generally throughout the country, especially if the expectation has been based upon anything which I have heretofore said.

... If the great American people only keep their temper on both sides of the line, the troubles will come to an end, and the question which now distracts the country will be settled, just as surely as all other difficulties of a like character which have originated in this government have been adjusted. Let the people on both sides keep their self-possession, and just as other clouds have cleared away in due time, so will this great nation continue to prosper as heretofore.

... It is often said that the tariff is the specialty of Pennsylvania. Assuming that direct taxation is not to be adopted, the tariff question must be as durable as the government itself. It is a question of national house-keeping. It is to the government what replenishing the meal-tub is to the family. Ever-varying circumstances will require frequent modifications as to the amount needed and the sources of supply. So far there is little difference of opinion among the people. It is only whether, and how far, duties on imports shall be adjusted to favour home productions. In the home market that controversy begins. One party insists that too much protection oppresses one class for the advantage of another; while the other party argues that, with all its incidents, in the long run all classes are benefited. In the Chicago platform there is a plank upon this subject, which should be a general law to the incoming Administration. We should do neither more nor less than we gave the people reason to believe we would when they gave us their votes. That plank is as I now read:

"That while providing revenue for the support of the general government by duties upon imports, sound policy requires such an adjustment of these imposts as will encourage the development of the industrial interest of the whole country; and we commend that policy of national exchanges which secures to working-men liberal wages, to agriculture remunerating prices, to mechanics and manufacturers adequate reward for their skill, labour, and enterprise, and to the nation commercial prosperity and independence."

... My political education strongly inclines me against a very free use of any of the means by the Executive to control the legislation of the country. As a rule, I think it better that Congress should originate as well as perfect its measures without external bias. I therefore would rather recommend to every gentleman who knows he is to be a member of the next Congress, to take an enlarged view, and post himself thoroughly, so as to contribute his part to such an adjustment of the tariff as shall provide a sufficient revenue, and in its other bearings, so far as possible, be just and equal to all sections of the country and classes of the people.

From his Speech at Trenton to the Senate of New Jersey. February 21, 1861

... I cannot but remember the place that New Jersey holds in our early history. In the early Revolutionary struggle few of the States among the old thirteen had more of the battle-fields of the country within their limits than old New Jersey. May I be pardoned if, upon this occasion, I mention that away back in my childhood, the earliest days of my being able to read, I got hold of a small book, such a one as few of the younger members have ever seen,—"Weems's Life of Washington." I remember all the accounts there given of the battle-fields and struggles for the liberties of the country, and none fixed themselves upon my imagination so deeply as the struggle here at Trenton, New Jersey. The crossing of the river, the contest with the Hessians, the great hardships endured at that time,—all fixed themselves upon my memory more than any single Revolutionary event; and you all know, for you have all been boys, how those early impressions last longer than any others. I recollect thinking then, boy even though I was, that there must have been something more than common that these men struggled for. I am exceedingly anxious that that thing—that something even more than national independence; that something that held out a great promise to all the people of the world for all time to come,—I am exceedingly anxious that this Union, the Constitution, and the liberties of the people shall be perpetuated in accordance with the original idea for which the struggle was made, and I shall be most happy indeed if I shall be an humble instrument in the hands of the Almighty, and of this, His most chosen people, for perpetuating the object of that great struggle.

Address in Independence Hall, Philadelphia. February 22, 1861

I am filled with deep emotion at finding myself standing in this place, where were collected together the wisdom, the patriotism, the devotion to principle, from which sprang the institutions under which we live.

You have kindly suggested to me that in my hands is the task of restoring peace to our distracted country. I can say in return, sir, that all the political sentiments I entertain have been drawn, so far as I have been able to draw them, from the sentiments which originated in and were given to the world from this hall. I have never had a feeling, politically, that did not spring from the sentiments embodied in the Declaration of Independence.

I have often pondered over the dangers which were incurred by the men who assembled here and framed and adopted that Declaration. I have pondered over the toils that were endured by the officers and soldiers of the army who achieved that independence. I have often inquired of myself what great principle or idea it was that kept this Confederacy so long together. It was not the mere matter of separation of the colonies from the motherland, but that sentiment in the Declaration of Independence which gave liberty not alone to the people of this country, but hope to all the world, for all future time. It was that which gave promise that in due time the weights would be lifted from the shoulders of all men, and that all should have an equal chance. This is the sentiment embodied in the Declaration of Independence.

Now, my friends, can this country be saved on that basis? If it can, I will consider myself one of the happiest men in the world if I can help to save it. If it cannot be saved upon that principle, it will be truly awful. But if this country cannot be saved without giving up that principle, I was about to say I would rather be assassinated on this spot than surrender it.

Now, in my view of the present aspect of affairs, there is no need of bloodshed and war. There is no necessity for it. I am not in favour of such a course; and I may say in advance that there will be no bloodshed unless it is forced upon the government. The government will not use force unless force is used against it.

My friends, this is wholly an unprepared speech. I did not expect to be called on to say a word when I came here. I supposed I was merely to do something toward raising a flag. I may, therefore, have said something indiscreet. But I have said nothing but what I am willing to live by, and, if it be the pleasure of Almighty God, to die by.

Reply to the Mayor of Washington, D.C. February 27, 1861

Mr. Mayor, I thank you, and through you the municipal authorities of this city who accompany you, for this welcome. And as it is the first time in my life, since the present phase of politics has presented itself in this country, that I have said anything publicly within a region of country where the institution of slavery exists, I will take this occasion to say that I think very much of the ill-feeling that has existed and still exists between the people in the section from which I came and the people here, is dependent upon a misunderstanding of one another. I therefore avail myself of this opportunity to assure you, Mr. Mayor, and all the gentlemen present, that I have not now, and never have had, any other than as kindly feelings towards you as to the people of my own section. I have not now and never have had any disposition to treat you in any respect otherwise than as my own neighbours. I have not now any purpose to withhold from you any of the benefits of the Constitution under any circumstances, that I would not feel myself constrained to withhold from my own neighbours; and I hope, in a word, that when we become better acquainted,—and I say it with great confidence,—we shall like each other the more. I thank you for the kindness of this reception.

First Inaugural Address. March 4, 1861

Fellow-citizens of the United States, In compliance with a custom as old as the government itself, I appear before you to address you briefly, and to take in your presence the oath prescribed by the Constitution of the United States to be taken by the President "before he enters on the execution of his office."

I do not consider it necessary at present for me to discuss those matters of administration about which there is no special anxiety or excitement.

Apprehension seems to exist among the people of the Southern States that by the accession of a Republican administration their property and their peace and personal security are to be endangered. There has never been any reasonable cause for such apprehension. Indeed, the most ample evidence to the contrary has all the while existed and been open to their inspection. It is found in nearly all the published speeches of him who now addresses you. I do but quote from one of those speeches when I declare that "I have no purpose, directly or indirectly, to interfere with the institution of slavery in the States where it exists. I believe I have no lawful right to do so, and I have no inclination to do so." Those who nominated and elected me did so with full knowledge that I had made this and many similar declarations, and had never recanted them. And, more than this, they placed in the platform for my acceptance, and as a law to themselves and to me, the clear and emphatic resolution which I now read:—

"*Resolved*, That the maintenance inviolate of the rights of the States, and especially the right of each State to order and control its own domestic institutions according to its own judgment exclusively, is essential to that balance of power on which the perfection and endurance of our political fabric depend, and we denounce the lawless invasion by armed force of the soil of any State or Territory, no matter under what pretext, as among the gravest of crimes."

I now reiterate these sentiments; and, in doing so, I only press upon the public attention the most conclusive evidence of which the case is susceptible, that the property, peace, and security of no section are to be in any wise endangered by the now incoming administration. I add, too, that all the protection which, consistently with the Constitution and the laws, can be given, will be cheerfully given to all the States when lawfully demanded, for whatever cause—as cheerfully to one section as to another.

There is much controversy about the delivering up of fugitives from service or labour. The clause I now read is as plainly written in the Constitution as any other of its provisions:—

"No person held to service or labour in one State, under the laws thereof, escaping into another, shall in consequence of any law or regulation therein be discharged from such service or labour, but shall be delivered up on claim of the party to whom such service or labour may be due."

It is scarcely questioned that this provision was intended by those who made it for the reclaiming of what we call fugitive slaves; and the intention of the lawgiver is the law. All members of Congress swear their support to the whole Constitution—to this provision as much as to any other. To the proposition, then, that slaves whose cases come within the terms of this clause "shall be delivered up," their oaths are unanimous. Now, if they would make the effort in good temper, could they not with nearly equal unanimity frame and pass a law by means of which to keep good that unanimous oath?

There is some difference of opinion whether this clause should be enforced by national or by State authority; but surely that difference is not a very material one. If the slave is to be surrendered, it can be of but little consequence to him or to others by which authority it is done. And should any one in any case be content that his oath shall go unkept on a merely unsubstantial controversy as to how it shall be kept?

Again, in any law upon this subject, ought not all the safeguards of liberty known in civilized and humane jurisprudence to be introduced, so that a free man be not, in any case, surrendered as a slave? And might it not be well at the same time to provide by law for the enforcement of that clause in the Constitution which guarantees that "the citizen of each State shall be entitled to all privileges and immunities of citizens in the several States"?

I take the official oath to-day with no mental reservations, and with no purpose to construe the Constitution or laws by any hypercritical rules. And while I do not choose now to specify particular acts of Congress as proper to be enforced, I do suggest that it will be much safer for all, both in official and private stations, to conform to and abide by all those acts which stand unrepealed, than to violate any of them, trusting to find impunity in having them held to be unconstitutional.

It is seventy-two years since the first inauguration of a President under our National Constitution. During that period fifteen different and greatly distinguished citizens have, in succession, administered the executive branch of the government They have conducted it through many perils, and generally with great success. Yet, with all this scope of precedent, I now enter upon the same task for the brief constitutional term of four years under great and peculiar difficulty. A disruption of the Federal Union, heretofore only menaced, is now formidably attempted.

I hold that, in contemplation of universal law and of the Constitution, the Union of these States is perpetual. Perpetuity is implied, if not expressed, in the fundamental law of all national governments. It is safe to assert that no government proper ever had a provision in its organic law for its own termination. Continue to execute all the express provisions of our National Constitution, and the Union will endure for ever—it being impossible to destroy it except by some action not provided for in the instrument itself.

Again, if the United States be not a government proper, but an association of States in the nature of contract merely, can it, as a contract, be peaceably unmade by less than all the parties who made it? One party to a contract may violate it—break it, so to speak; but does it not require all to lawfully rescind it?

Descending from these general principles, we find the proposition that in legal contemplation the Union is perpetual confirmed by the history of the Union itself. The Union is much older than the Constitution. It was formed, in fact, by the Articles of Association in 1774. It was matured and continued by the Declaration of Independence in 1776. It was further matured, and the faith of all the then thirteen States expressly plighted and engaged that it should be perpetual, by the Articles of Confederation in 1778. And, finally, in 1787 one of the declared objects for ordaining and establishing the Constitution was "to form a more perfect Union."

But if the destruction of the Union by one or by a part only of the States be lawfully possible, the Union is less perfect than before the Constitution, having lost the vital element of perpetuity.

It follows from these views that no State upon its own mere motion can lawfully get out of the Union; that resolves and ordinances to that effect are legally void; and that acts of violence, within any State or States, against the authority of the United States, are insurrectionary or revolutionary, according to circumstances.

I therefore consider that, in view of the Constitution and the laws, the Union is unbroken; and to the extent of my ability I shall take care, as the Constitution itself expressly enjoins upon me, that the laws of the Union be faithfully executed in all the States. Doing this I deem to be only a simple duty on my part; and I shall perform it so far as practicable, unless my rightful masters, the American people, shall withhold the requisite means, or in some authoritative manner direct the contrary. I trust this will not be regarded as a menace, but only as the declared purpose of the Union that it will constitutionally defend and maintain itself.

In doing this there needs to be no bloodshed or violence; and there shall be none, unless it be forced upon the national authority. The power confided to me will be used to hold, occupy, and possess the property and places belonging to the government, and to collect the duties and imposts; but beyond what may be necessary for these objects, there will be no invasion, no using of force against or among the people anywhere. Where hostility to the United States, in any interior locality, shall be so great and universal as to prevent competent resident citizens from holding the Federal offices, there will be no attempt to force obnoxious strangers among the people for that object. While the strict legal right may exist in the government to enforce the exercise of these offices, the attempt to do so would be so irritating, and so nearly impracticable withal, that I deem it better to forego for the time the uses of such offices.

The mails, unless repelled, will continue to be furnished in all parts of the Union. So far as possible, the people everywhere shall have that sense of perfect security which is most favourable to calm thought and reflection. The course here indicated will be followed unless current events and experience shall show a modification or change to be proper, and in every case and exigency my best discretion will be exercised according to circumstances actually existing, and with a view and a hope of a peaceful solution of the national troubles and the restoration of fraternal sympathies and affections.

That there are persons in one section or another who seek to destroy the Union at all events, and are glad of any pretext to do it, I will neither affirm nor deny; but if there be such, I need address no word to them. To those, however, who really love the Union may I not speak?

Before entering upon so grave a matter as the destruction of our national fabric, with all its benefits, its memories, and its hopes, would it not be wise to ascertain precisely why we do it? Will you hazard so desperate a step while there is any possibility that any portion of the ills you fly from have no real existence? Will you, while the certain ills you fly to are greater than all the real ones you fly from—will you risk the commission of so fearful a mistake?

All profess to be content in the Union if all constitutional rights can be maintained. Is it true, then, that any right, plainly written in the Constitution, has been denied? I think not. Happily the human mind is so constituted that no party can reach to the audacity of doing this. Think, if you can, of a single instance in which a plainly written provision of the Constitution has ever been denied. If by the mere force of numbers a majority should deprive a minority of any clearly written constitutional right, it might, in a moral point of view, justify revolution—certainly would if such a right were a vital one. But such is not our case. All the vital rights of minorities and of individuals are so plainly assured to them by affirmations and negations, guaranties and prohibitions, in the Constitution, that controversies never arise concerning them. But no organic law can ever be framed with a provision specifically applicable to every question which may occur in practical administration. No foresight can anticipate, nor any document of reasonable length contain, express provisions for all possible questions. Shall fugitives from labour be surrendered by national or by State authority? The Constitution does not expressly say. *May* Congress prohibit slavery in the Territories? The Constitution does not expressly say. *Must* Congress protect slavery in the Territories? The Constitution does not expressly say.

From questions of this class spring all our constitutional controversies, and we divide upon them into majorities and minorities. If the minority will not acquiesce, the majority must, or the government must cease. There is no other alternative; for continuing the government is acquiescence on one side or the other.

If a minority in such case will secede rather than acquiesce, they make a precedent which in turn will divide and ruin them; for a minority of their own will secede from them whenever a majority refuses to be controlled by such minority. For instance, why may not any portion of a new confederacy a year or two hence arbitrarily secede again, precisely as portions of the present Union now claim to secede from it? All who cherish disunion sentiments are now being educated to the exact temper of doing this.

Is there such perfect identity of interests among the States to compose a new Union, as to produce harmony only, and prevent renewed secession?

Plainly, the central idea of secession is the essence of anarchy. A majority held in restraint by constitutional checks and limitations, and always changing easily with deliberate changes of popular opinions and sentiments, is the only true sovereign of a free people. Whoever rejects it does, of necessity, fly to anarchy or to despotism. Unanimity is impossible; the rule of a minority, as a permanent arrangement, is wholly inadmissible; so that, rejecting the majority principle, anarchy or despotism in some form is all that is left.

I do not forget the position, assumed by some, that constitutional questions are to be decided by the Supreme Court; nor do I deny that such decisions must be binding, in any case, upon the parties to a suit, as to the object of that suit, while they are also entitled to very high respect and consideration in all parallel cases by all other departments of the government. And while it is obviously possible that such decision may be erroneous in any given case, still the evil effect following it, being limited to that particular case, with the chance that it may be overruled and never become a precedent for other cases, can better be borne than could the evils of a different practice. At the same time, the candid citizen must confess that if the policy of the government, upon vital questions affecting the whole people, is to be irrevocably fixed by decisions of the Supreme Court, the instant they are made, in ordinary litigation between parties in personal actions, the people will have ceased to be their own rulers, having to that extent practically resigned their government into the hands of that eminent tribunal. Nor is there in this view any assault upon the court or the judges. It is a duty from which they may not shrink to decide cases properly brought before them, and it is no fault of theirs if others seek to turn their decisions to political purposes.

One section of our country believes slavery is right, and ought to be extended, while the other believes it is wrong, and ought not to be extended. This is the only substantial dispute. The fugitive-slave clause of the Constitution, and the law for the suppression of the foreign slave-trade, are each as well enforced, perhaps, as any law can ever be in a community where the moral sense of the people imperfectly supports the law itself. The great body of the people abide by the dry legal obligation in both cases, and a few break over in each. This, I think, cannot be perfectly cured; and it would be worse in both cases after the separation of the sections than before. The foreign slave-trade, now imperfectly suppressed, would be ultimately revived, without restriction, in one section, while fugitive slaves, now only partially surrendered, would not be surrendered at all by the other.

Physically speaking, we cannot separate. We cannot remove our respective sections from each other, nor build an impassable wall between them. A husband and wife may be divorced, and go out of the presence and beyond the reach of each other; but the different parts of our country cannot do this. They cannot but remain face to face, and intercourse, either amicable or hostile, must continue between them. Is it possible, then, to make that intercourse more advantageous or more satisfactory after separation than before? Can aliens make treaties easier than friends can make laws? Can treaties be more faithfully enforced between aliens than laws can among friends? Suppose you go to war, you cannot fight always; and when, after much loss on both sides, and no gain on either, you cease fighting, the identical old questions as to terms of intercourse are again upon you.

This country, with its institutions, belongs to the people who inhabit it. Whenever they shall grow weary of the existing government, they can exercise their constitutional right of amending it, or their revolutionary right to dismember or overthrow it. I cannot be ignorant of the fact that many worthy and patriotic citizens are desirous of having the National Constitution amended. While I make no recommendation of amendments, I fully recognize the rightful authority of the people over the whole subject, to be exercised in either of the modes prescribed in the instrument itself; and I should, under existing circumstances, favour rather than oppose a fair opportunity being afforded the people to act upon it. I will venture to add that to me the convention mode seems preferable, in that it allows amendments to originate with the people themselves, instead of only permitting them to take or reject propositions originated by others not especially chosen for the purpose, and which might not be precisely such as they would wish to either accept or refuse. I understand a proposed amendment to the Constitution—which amendment, however, I have not seen—has passed Congress, to the effect that the Federal Government shall never interfere with the domestic institutions of the States, including that of persons held to service. To avoid misconstruction of what I have said, I depart from my purpose not to speak of particular amendments so far as to say that, holding such a provision to now be implied constitutional law, I have no objection to its being made express and irrevocable.

The chief magistrate derives all his authority from the people, and they have conferred none upon him to fix terms for the separation of the States. The people themselves can do this also if they choose; but the Executive, as such, has nothing to do with it. His duty is to administer the present government, as it came to his hands, and to transmit it, unimpaired by him, to his successor.

Why should there not be a patient confidence in the ultimate justice of the people? Is there any better or equal hope in the world? In our present differences, is either party without faith of being in the right? If the Almighty Ruler of Nations, with his eternal truth and justice, be on your side of the North, or on yours of the South, that truth and that justice will surely prevail by the judgment of this great tribunal of the American people.

By the frame of the government under which we live, this same people have wisely given their public servants but little power for mischief; and have, with equal wisdom, provided for the return of that little to their own hands at very short intervals. While the people retain their virtue and vigilance, no administration, by any extreme of wickedness or folly, can very seriously injure the government in the short space of four years.

My countrymen, one and all, think calmly and well upon this whole subject. Nothing valuable can be lost by taking time. If there be an object to hurry any of you in hot haste to a step which you would never take deliberately, that object will be frustrated by taking time; but no good object can be frustrated by it. Such of you as are now dissatisfied still have the old Constitution unimpaired, and, on the sensitive point, the laws of your own framing under it; while the new administration will have no immediate power, if it would, to change either. If it were admitted that you who are dissatisfied hold the right side in the dispute, there still is no single good reason for precipitate action. Intelligence, patriotism, Christianity, and a firm reliance on Him who has never yet forsaken this favoured land, are still competent to adjust in the best way all our present difficulty.

In your hands, my dissatisfied fellow-countrymen, and not in mine, is the momentous issue of civil war. The government will not assail you. You can have no conflict without being yourselves the aggressors. You have no oath registered in heaven to destroy the government, while I shall have the most solemn one to "preserve, protect, and defend it."

I am loath to close. We are not enemies, but friends. We must not be enemies. Though passion may have strained, it must not break our bonds of affection. The mystic chords of memory, stretching from every battle-field and patriot grave to every living heart and hearthstone all over this broad land, will yet swell the chorus of the Union when again touched, as surely they will be, by the better angels of our nature.

Address at Utica, New York. February 18, 1861

Ladies and Gentlemen, I have no speech to make to you, and no time to speak in. I appear before you that I may see you, and that you may see me; and I am willing to admit, that, so far as the ladies are concerned, I have the best of the bargain, though I wish it to be understood that I do not make the same acknowledgment concerning the men.

From his First Message to Congress, at the Special Session. July 4, 1861

... It is thus seen that the assault upon and reduction of Fort Sumter was in no sense a matter of self-defence on the part of the assailants. They well knew that the garrison in the fort could by no possibility commit aggression upon them. They knew—they were expressly notified—that the giving of bread to the few brave and hungry men of the garrison was all which would on that occasion be attempted, unless themselves, by resisting so much, should provoke more. They knew that this government desired to keep the garrison in the fort, not to assail them, but merely to maintain visible possession, and thus to preserve the Union from actual and immediate dissolution,—trusting, as hereinbefore stated, to time, discussion, and the ballot-box, for final adjustment; and they assailed and reduced the fort for precisely the reverse object,—to drive out the visible authority of the Federal Union, and thus force it to immediate dissolution....

That this was their object the Executive well understood; and having said to them in the inaugural address, "You can have no conflict without being yourselves the aggressors," he took pains not only to keep this declaration good, but also to keep the case so free from the power of ingenious sophistry that the world should not be able to misunderstand it....

By the affair at Fort Sumter, with its surrounding circumstances, that point was reached. Then and thereby the assailants of the government began the conflict of arms, without a gun in sight, or in expectancy to return their fire, save only the few in the fort sent to that harbour years before for their own protection, and still ready to give that protection in whatever was lawful. In this act, discarding all else, they have forced upon the country the distinct issue, "immediate dissolution or blood."

And this issue embraces more than the fate of these United States. It presents to the whole family of man the question whether a constitutional republic or democracy—a government of the people by the same people—can or cannot maintain its territorial integrity against its own domestic foes. It presents the question whether discontented individuals, too few in numbers to control administration according to organic law in any case, can always, upon the pretences made in this case or any other pretences, or arbitrarily without any pretence, break up their government, and thus practically put an end to free government upon the earth. It forces us to ask: "Is there, in all republics, this inherent and fatal weakness?" "Must a government, of necessity, be too strong for the liberties of its own people, or too weak to maintain its own existence?"

So viewing the issue, no choice was left but to call out the war power of the government, and so to resist force employed for its destruction by force for its preservation.

The call was made, and the response of the country was most gratifying, surpassing in unanimity and spirit the most sanguine expectation.

... The people of Virginia have thus allowed this giant insurrection to make its nest within her borders,—and this government has no choice left but to deal with it where it finds it. And it has the less regret, as the loyal citizens have in due form claimed its protection. Those loyal citizens this government is bound to recognize and protect, as being Virginia.

In the border States, so called,—in fact, the Middle States,—there are those who favour a policy which they call "armed neutrality;" that is, an arming of those States to prevent the Union forces passing one way, or the disunion the other, over their soil. This would be disunion completed. Figuratively speaking, it would be the building of an impassable wall along the line of separation,—and yet not quite an impassable one, for under the guise of neutrality, it would tie the hands of Union men, and freely pass supplies from among them to the insurrectionists, which it could not do as an open enemy. At a stroke, it would take all the trouble off the hands of secession, except only what proceeds from the external blockade. It would do for the disunionists that which of all things they most desire,—feed them well and give them disunion without a struggle of their own. It recognizes no fidelity to the Constitution, no obligation to maintain the Union; and while very many who have favoured it are doubtless loyal citizens, it is, nevertheless, very injurious in effect.

... The forbearance of this government had been so extraordinary and so long continued, as to lead some foreign nations to shape their action as if they supposed the early destruction of our National Union was probable. While this, on discovery, gave the Executive some concern, he is now happy to say that the sovereignty and rights of the United States are now everywhere practically respected by foreign powers, and a general sympathy with the country is manifested throughout the world.

... It is now recommended that you give the legal means for making this contest a short and decisive one; that you place at the control of the government for the work, at least four hundred thousand men, and $400,000,000. That number of men is about one-tenth of those of proper ages within the regions where, apparently, all are willing to engage; and the sum is less than a twenty-third part of the money value owned by the men who seem ready to devote the whole.

... A right result at this time, will be worth more to the world than ten times the men and ten times the money. The evidences reaching us from the country leaves no doubt that the material for the work is abundant, and that it needs only the hand of legislation to give it legal sanction, and the hand of the Executive to give it practical shape and efficiency. One of the greatest perplexities of the government is to avoid receiving troops faster than it can provide for them. In a word, the people will save their government, if the government itself will do its part only indifferently well.

It might seem at first thought to be of little difference whether the present movement at the South be called *secession* or *rebellion*. The movers, however, well understand the difference. At the beginning they knew they could never raise their treason to any respectable magnitude by any name which implies violation of law. They knew their people possessed as much of moral sense, as much of devotion to law and order, and as much pride in and reverence for the history and government of their common country as any other civilized and patriotic people. They knew they could make no advancement directly in the teeth of these strong and noble sentiments. Accordingly, they commenced by an insidious debauching of the public mind. They invented an ingenious sophism which, if conceded, was followed by perfectly logical steps, through all the incidents, to the complete destruction of the Union. The sophism itself is that any State of the Union may consistently with the national Constitution, and therefore lawfully and peacefully, withdraw from the Union without the consent of the Union or of any other State. The little disguise that the supposed right is to be exercised only for just cause, themselves to be the sole judges of its justice, is too thin to merit any notice.

With rebellion thus *sugar-coated* they have been drugging the public mind of their section for more than thirty years, and until at length they have brought many good men to a willingness to take up arms against the government the day after some assemblage of men have enacted the farcical pretence of taking their State out of the Union, who could have been brought to no such thing the day before.

This sophism derives much, perhaps the whole of its currency from the assumption that there is some omnipotent and sacred supremacy pertaining to a State—to each State of our Federal Union. Our States have neither more nor less power than that reserved to them in the Union by the Constitution, no one of them ever having been a State out of the Union. The original ones passed into the Union even before they cast off their British colonial dependence, and the new ones each came into the Union directly from a condition of dependence, excepting Texas. And even Texas in its temporary independence was never designated a State. The new ones only took the designation of States on coming into the Union, while that name was first adopted for the old ones in and by the Declaration of Independence. Therein the "United Colonies" were declared to be "free and independent States;" but even then the object plainly was, not to declare their independence of one another or of the Union, but directly the contrary, as their mutual pledges and their mutual action before, at the time, and afterward abundantly show. The express plighting of faith by each and all of the original thirteen in the Articles of Confederation two years later, that the Union shall be perpetual, is most conclusive. Having never been States, either in substance or name, outside of the Union, whence this magical omnipotence of "State-Rights," asserting a claim of power to lawfully destroy the Union itself? Much is said about the "sovereignty" of the States; but the word is not in the National Constitution, nor, as is believed, in any of the State constitutions. What is *sovereignty* in the political sense of the term? Would it be far wrong to define it "a political community without a political superior?" Tested by this, no one of our States, except Texas, ever was a sovereignty. And even Texas gave up the character on coming into the Union, by which act she acknowledged the Constitution of the United States, and the laws and treaties of the United States made in pursuance of the Constitution, to be for her the supreme law of the land. The States have their status in the Union, and they have no other legal status. If they break from this, they can only do so against law and by revolution. The Union, and not themselves separately, procured their independence and their liberty. By conquest or purchase, the Union gave each of them whatever of independence or liberty it has. The Union is older than any of the States, and, in fact, it created them as States. Originally some dependent colonies made the Union, and in turn the Union threw off their old dependence for them, and made them States, such as they are. Not one of them ever had a State constitution independent of the Union. Of course it is not forgotten that all the new States framed their constitutions before they entered the Union,—nevertheless, dependent upon and preparatory to coming into the Union.

Unquestionably the States have the powers and the rights reserved to them in and by the National Constitution; but among these, surely, are not included all conceivable powers, however mischievous or destructive; but, at most, such only as were known in the world at the time, as governmental powers; and, certainly, a power to destroy the government itself had never been known as a governmental—as a merely administrative power. This relative matter of National power and States rights, as a principle, is no other than the principle of generality and locality. Whatever concerns the whole world should be confided to the whole—to the General Government; while whatever concerns only the State should be left exclusively to the State. This is all there is of original principle about it.... What is now combated, is the position that secession is consistent with the Constitution—is lawful and peaceful. It is not contended that there is any express law for it; and nothing should ever be implied as law which leads to unjust or absurd consequences.

The nation purchased with money the countries out of which several of these States were formed; is it just that they shall go off without leave and without refunding? The nation paid very large sums (in the aggregate, I believe, nearly a hundred millions) to relieve Florida of the aboriginal tribes; is it just that she shall now be off without consent, or without making any return? The nation is now in debt for money applied to the benefit of these so-called seceding States in common with the rest; is it just that the creditors shall go unpaid, or the remaining States pay the whole?... Again, if one State may secede, so may another; and when all shall have seceded, none is left to pay the debts. Is this quite just to the creditors? Did we notify them of this sage view of ours when we borrowed their money? If we now recognize this doctrine by allowing the seceders to go in peace, it is difficult to see what we can do if others choose to go, or to extort terms upon which they will promise to remain.

The seceders insist that our Constitution admits of secession. They have assumed to make a national constitution of their own, in which, of necessity, they have either discarded or retained the right of secession, as they insist it exists in ours. If they have discarded it, they thereby admit that, on principle, it ought not to be in ours. If they have retained it, by their own construction of ours, they show that to be consistent they must secede from one another whenever they shall find it the easiest way of settling their debts, or effecting any other or selfish or unjust object. The principle itself is one of disintegration, and upon which no government can stand.

If all the States save one should assert the power to drive that one out of the Union, it is presumed the whole class of seceder politicians would at once deny the power, and denounce the act as the greatest outrage upon State rights. But suppose that precisely the same act, instead of being called "driving the one out," should be called "the seceding of the others from that one," it would be exactly what the seceders claim to do; unless, indeed, they make the point that the one, because it is a minority, may rightfully do what the others, because they are a majority, may not rightfully do....

It may be affirmed without extravagance that the free institutions we enjoy have developed the powers and improved the condition of our whole people, beyond any example in the world. Of this we now have a striking and an impressive illustration. So large an army as the government has now on foot was never before known, without a soldier in it but who has taken his place there of his own free choice. But more than this, there are many single regiments, whose members, one and another, possess full practical knowledge of all the arts, sciences, and professions, and whatever else, whether useful or elegant, is known in the world; and there is scarcely one from which there could not be selected a President, a cabinet, a congress, and perhaps a court, abundantly competent to administer the government itself. Nor do I say that this is not true also in the army of our late friends, now adversaries in this contest; but if it is, so much the better reason why the government which has conferred such benefits on both them and us should not be broken up. Whoever in any section proposes to abandon such a government, would do well to consider in deference to what principle it is that he does it; what better he is likely to get in its stead; whether the substitute will give, or be intended to give, so much of good to the people? There are some foreshadowings on this subject. Our adversaries have adopted some declarations of independence in which, unlike the good old one penned by Jefferson, they omit the words, "all men are created equal." Why? They have adopted a temporary national constitution, in the preamble of which, unlike our good old one signed by Washington, they omit "We, the people," and substitute "We, the deputies of the sovereign and independent States." Why? Why this deliberate pressing out of view the rights of men and the authority of the people?

This is essentially a people's contest. On the side of the Union it is a struggle for maintaining in the world that form and substance of government whose leading object is to elevate the condition of men,—to lift artificial weights from all shoulders, to clear the paths of laudable pursuit for all, to afford all an unfettered start and a fair chance in the race of life. Yielding to partial and temporary departures from necessity, this is the leading object of the government for the existence of which we contend.

I am most happy to believe that the plain people understand and appreciate this. It is worthy of note that while in this, the government's hour of trial, large numbers of those in the army and navy who have been favoured with the offices have resigned and proved false to the hand which had pampered them, not one common soldier or common sailor is known to have deserted his flag.

Our popular government has often been called an experiment. Two points in it our people have already settled,—the successful establishing and the successful administering of it. One still remains,—its successful maintenance against a formidable internal attempt to overthrow it. It is now for them to demonstrate to the world that those who can fairly carry an election can also suppress a rebellion; that ballots are the rightful and peaceful successors of bullets; and that when ballots have fairly and constitutionally decided, there can be no successful appeal back to bullets; that there can be no successful appeal, except to ballots themselves, at succeeding elections. Such will be a great lesson of peace; teaching men that what they cannot take by an election, neither can they take by a war; teaching all the folly of being the beginners of a war.

From his Message to Congress at its Regular Session. December 3, 1861

Fellow-citizens of the Senate and House of Representatives, In the midst of unprecedented political troubles, we have cause of great gratitude to God for unusual good health and abundant harvests.

You will not be surprised to learn that in the peculiar exigencies of the times, our intercourse with foreign nations has been attended with profound solicitude, chiefly turning upon our own domestic affairs.

A disloyal portion of the American people have, during the whole year, been engaged in an attempt to divide and destroy the Union. A nation which endures factious domestic division is exposed to disrespect abroad; and one party, if not both, is sure, sooner or later, to invoke foreign intervention. Nations thus tempted to interfere are not always able to resist the counsels of seeming expediency and ungenerous ambition, although measures adopted under such influences seldom fail to be injurious and unfortunate to those adopting them.

The disloyal citizens of the United States who have offered the ruin of our country in return for the aid and comfort which they have invoked abroad, have received less patronage and encouragement than they probably expected. If it were just to suppose, as the insurgents have seemed to assume, that foreign nations in this case, discarding all moral, social, and treaty obligations, would act solely and selfishly for the most speedy restoration of commerce, including especially the acquisition of cotton, those nations appear as yet not to have seen their way to their object more directly or clearly through the destruction than through the preservation of the Union. If we could dare to believe that foreign nations are actuated by no higher principle than this, I am quite sure a sound argument could be made to show them that they can reach their aim more readily and easily by aiding to crush this rebellion than by giving encouragement to it.

The principal lever relied on by the insurgents for exciting foreign nations to hostility against us, as already intimated, is the embarrassment of commerce. Those nations, however, not improbably saw from the first that it was the Union which made as well our foreign as our domestic commerce. They can scarcely have failed to perceive that the effort for disunion produces the existing difficulty; and that one strong nation promises a more durable peace and a more extensive, valuable, and reliable commerce than can the same nation broken into hostile fragments.

It continues to develop that the insurrection is largely, if not exclusively, a war upon the first principle of popular government,—the rights of the people. Conclusive evidence of this is found in the most grave and maturely considered public documents, as well as in the general tone of the insurgents. In those documents we find the abridgment of the existing right of suffrage, and the denial to the people of all right to participate in the selection of public officers, except the legislative, boldly advocated, with laboured arguments to prove that large control of the people in government is the source of all political evil. Monarchy itself is sometimes hinted at, as a possible refuge from the power of the people.

In my present position, I could scarcely be justified were I to omit raising a warning voice against this approach of returning despotism.

It is not needed nor fitting here that a general argument should be made in favour of popular institutions; but there is one point, with its connections, not so hackneyed as most others, to which I ask a brief attention. It is the effort to place capital on an equal footing with, if not above, labour, in the structure of government. It is assumed that labour is available only in connection with capital; that nobody labours, unless somebody else, owning capital, somehow, by the use of it, induces him to labour. This assumed, it is next considered whether it is best that capital shall hire labourers, and thus induce them to work by their own consent, or buy them and drive them to it without their consent. Having proceeded thus far, it is naturally concluded that all labourers are either hired labourers, or what we call slaves. And further, it is assumed that whoever is once a hired labourer is fixed in that condition for life.

Now, there is no such relation between capital and labour as assumed, nor is there any such thing as a free man being fixed for life in the condition of a hired labourer. Both these assumptions are false, and all inferences from them are groundless.

Labour is prior to and independent of capital. Capital is only the fruit of labour, and could never have existed if labour had not first existed. Labour is the superior of capital, and deserves much the higher consideration. Capital has its rights, which are as worthy of protection as any other rights. Nor is it denied that there is, and probably always will be, a relation between labour and capital, producing mutual benefits. The error is in assuming that the whole labour of the community exists within that relation. A few men own capital, and that few avoid labour themselves, and with their capital hire or buy another few to labour for them. A large majority belong to neither class,—neither work for others, nor have others working for them. In most of the Southern States, a majority of the whole people, of all colours, are neither slaves nor masters; while in the Northern, a majority are neither hirers nor hired. Men with their families—wives, sons, and daughters—work for themselves, on their farms, in their houses, and in their shops, taking the whole product to themselves, and asking no favours of capital on the one hand, nor of hired labourers or slaves on the other. It is not forgotten that a considerable number of persons mingle their own labour with capital—that is, they labour with their own hands, and also buy or hire others to labour for them; but this is only a mixed and not a distinct class. No principle stated is disturbed by the existence of this mixed class.

Again, as has already been said, there is not of necessity any such thing as the free, hired labourer being fixed to that condition for life. Many independent men, everywhere in these

States, a few years back in their lives were hired labourers. The prudent, penniless beginner in the world labours for wages a while, saves a surplus with which to buy tools or land for himself, then labours on his own account another while, and at length hires another new beginner to help him. This is the just and generous and prosperous system which opens the way to all, gives hope to all, and consequent energy and progress and improvement of condition to all. No men living are more worthy to be trusted than those who toil up from poverty, none less inclined to take or touch aught which they have not honestly earned. Let them beware of surrendering a political power which they already possess, and which, if surrendered, will surely be used to close the door of advancement against such as they, and to fix new disabilities and burdens upon them, till all of liberty shall be lost.

Letter to General G.B. McClellan. Washington. February 3, 1862

My dear Sir, You and I have distinct and different plans for a movement of the Army of the Potomac—yours to be down the Chesapeake, up the Rappahannock to Urbana and across land to the terminus of the railroad on the York River; mine to move directly to a point on the railroad southwest of Manassas.

If you will give me satisfactory answers to the following questions, I shall gladly yield my plan to yours.

First. Does not your plan involve a greatly larger expenditure of time and money than mine?

Second. Wherein is a victory more certain by your plan than mine?

Third. Wherein is a victory more valuable by your plan than mine?

Fourth. In fact, would it not be less valuable in this, that it would break no great line of the enemy's communications, while mine would?

Fifth. In case of disaster, would not a retreat be more difficult by your plan than mine?

I have just assisted the Secretary of War in framing part of a despatch to you, relating to army corps, which despatch of course will have reached you long before this will.

I wish to say a few words to you privately on this subject. I ordered the army corps organization, not only on the unanimous opinion of the twelve generals whom you had selected and assigned as generals of division, but also on the unanimous opinion of every *military man* I could get an opinion from (and every modern military book), yourself only excepted. Of course I did not on my own judgment pretend to understand the subject. I now think it indispensable for you to know how your struggle against it is received in quarters which we cannot entirely disregard. It is looked upon as merely an effort to pamper one or two pets and to persecute and degrade their supposed rivals. I have had no word from Sumner, Heintzelman, or Keyes. The commanders of these corps are of course the three highest officers with you, but I am constantly told that you have no consultation or communication with them,—that you consult and communicate with nobody but General Fitz John Porter, and perhaps General Franklin. I do not say these complaints are true or just, but at all events it is proper you should know of their existence. Do the commanders of corps disobey your orders in anything?

... Are you strong enough—are you strong enough, even with my help—to set your foot upon the necks of Sumner, Heintzelman, and Keyes, all at once? This is a practical and a very serious question for you.

Lincoln's Proclamation revoking General Hunter's Order setting the Slaves free. May 19, 1862

... General Hunter nor any other commander or person has been authorized by the Government of the United States to make proclamation declaring the slaves of any State free, and that the supposed proclamation now in question, whether genuine or false, is altogether void so far as respects such declaration.... On the sixth day of March last, by a special Message, I recommended to Congress the adoption of a joint resolution, to be substantially as follows:—
Resolved, That the United States ought to co-operate with any State which may adopt a gradual abolishment of slavery, giving to such State earnest expression to compensate for its inconveniences, public and private, produced by such change of system.

The resolution in the language above quoted was adopted by large majorities in both branches of Congress, and now stands an authentic, definite, and solemn proposal of the nation to the States and people most immediately interested in the subject-matter. To the people of those States I now earnestly appeal. I do not argue—I beseech you to make arguments for yourselves. You cannot, if you would, be blind to the signs of the times. I beg of you a calm and enlarged consideration of them, ranging, if it may be, far above personal and partisan politics. The proposal makes common cause for a common object, casting no reproaches upon any. It acts not the Pharisee. The change it contemplates would come gently as the dews of heaven, not rending or wrecking anything. Will you not embrace it? So much good has not been done by one effort in all past time as in the providence of God it is now your high privilege to do. May the vast future not have to lament that you have neglected it.

Appeal to the Border States in behalf of Compensated Emancipation. July 12, 1862

After the adjournment of Congress, now near, I shall have no opportunity of seeing you for several months. Believing that you of the border States hold more power for good than any other equal number of members, I feel it a duty which I cannot justifiably waive, to make this appeal to you.

I do not speak of emancipation at once, but of a decision at once to emancipate gradually. Room in South America for colonization can be obtained cheaply and in abundance, and when numbers shall be large enough to be company and encouragement for one another, the freed people will not be so reluctant to go.

I am pressed with a difficulty not yet mentioned,—one which threatens division among those who, united, are none too strong. General Hunter is an honest man. He was, and I hope still is, my friend. I valued him none the less for his agreeing with me in the general wish that all men everywhere could be free. He proclaimed all men free within certain States, and I repudiated the proclamation. He expected more good and less harm from the measure than I could believe would follow. Yet in repudiating it, I gave dissatisfaction if not offence to many whose support the country cannot afford to lose. And this is not the end of it. The pressure in this direction is still upon me, and is increasing. By conceding what I now ask, you can relieve me, and, much more, can relieve the country, in this important point.

Upon these considerations I have again begged your attention to the message of March last. Before leaving the Capitol, consider and discuss it among yourselves. You are patriots and statesmen, and as such, I pray you, consider this proposition, and at the least commend it to the consideration of your States and people. As you would perpetuate popular government for the best people in the world, I beseech you that you do in no wise omit this. Our common country is in great peril, demanding the loftiest views and boldest action to bring it speedy relief. Once relieved, its form of government is saved to the world, its beloved history and cherished memories are vindicated, and its happy future fully assured and rendered inconceivably grand.

I intend no reproach or complaint when I assure you that, in my opinion, if you all had voted for the resolution in the gradual-emancipation message of last March, the war would now be substantially ended. And the plan therein proposed is yet one of the most potent and swift means of ending it. Let the States which are in rebellion see, definitely and certainly, that in no event will the States you represent ever join their proposed confederacy, and they cannot much longer maintain the contest. But you cannot divest them of their hope to ultimately have you with them, so long as you show a determination to perpetuate the institution within your own States. Beat them at elections, as you have overwhelmingly done, and, nothing daunted, they still claim you as their own. You and I know what the lever of their power is. Break that lever before their faces, and they can shake you no more for ever.

Most of you have treated me with kindness and consideration, and I trust you will not now think I improperly touch what is exclusively your own, when, for the sake of the whole country, I ask, Can you, for your States, do better than to take the course I urge? Discarding punctilio and maxims adapted to more manageable times, and looking only to the unprecedentedly stern facts of our case, can you do better in any possible event? You prefer that the constitutional relation of the States to the nation shall be practically restored without disturbance of the institution; and if this were done, my whole duty in this respect, under the Constitution and my oath of office, would be performed. But it is not done, and we are trying to accomplish it by war. The incidents of the war cannot be avoided. If the war continues long, as it must if the object be not sooner attained, the institution in your States will be extinguished by mere friction and abrasion,—by the mere incidents of the war. It will be gone, and you will have nothing valuable in lieu of it. Much of its value is gone already. How much better for you and for your people to take the step which at once shortens the war and secures substantial compensation for that which is sure to be wholly lost in any other event? How much better to thus save the money which else we sink for ever in the war! How much better to do it while we can, lest the war ere long render us pecuniarily unable to do it! How much better for you as seller, and the nation as buyer, to sell out and buy out that without which the war could never have been, than to sink both the thing to be sold and the price of it in cutting one another's throats!

From a Letter to Cuthbert Bullitt. July 28, 1862

Now, I think the true remedy is very different from that suggested by Mr. Durant. It does not lie in rounding the rough angles of the war, but in removing the necessity for the war. The people of Louisiana who wish protection to person and property, have but to reach forth their hands and take it. Let them in good faith reinaugurate the national authority, and set up a State government conforming thereto under the Constitution. They know how to do it, and can have the protection of the army while doing it. The army will be withdrawn as soon as such government can dispense with its presence, and the people of the State can then, upon the old constitutional terms, govern themselves to their own liking. This is very simple and easy.

If they will not do this, if they prefer to hazard all for the sake of destroying the government, it is for them to consider whether it is probable that I will surrender the government to save them from losing all. If they decline what I suggest, you will scarcely need to ask what I will do.

What would you do in my position? Would you drop the war where it is, or would you prosecute it in future with elder-stalk squirts charged with rose-water? Would you deal lighter blows rather than heavier ones? Would you give up the contest, leaving any available means untried?

I am in no boastful mood. I shall not do more than I can; but I shall do all I can to save the government, which is my sworn duty as well as my personal inclination. I shall do nothing in malice. What I deal with is too vast for malicious dealing.

Letter to August Belmont. July 31, 1862

Dear Sir, You send to Mr. W—— an extract from a letter written at New Orleans the 9th instant, which is shown to me. You do not give the writer's name; but plainly he is a man of ability, and probably of some note. He says: "The time has arrived when Mr. Lincoln must take a decisive course. Trying to please everybody, he will satisfy nobody. A vacillating policy in matters of importance is the very worst. Now is the time, if ever, for honest men who love their country to rally to its support. Why will not the North say officially that it wishes for the restoration of the Union as it was?"

And so, it seems, this is the point on which the writer thinks I have no policy. Why will he not read and understand what I have said?

The substance of the very declaration he desires is in the inaugural, in each of the two regular messages to Congress, and in many, if not all, the minor documents issued by the Executive since the Inauguration.

Broken eggs cannot be mended; but Louisiana has nothing to do now but to take her place in the Union as it was, barring the already broken eggs. The sooner she does so, the smaller will be the amount of that which will be past mending. This government cannot much longer play a game in which it stakes all, and its enemies stake nothing. Those enemies must understand that they cannot experiment for ten years trying to destroy the government, and if they fail still come back into the Union unhurt. If they expect in any contingency to ever have the Union as it was, I join with the writer in saying, "Now is the time."

How much better it would have been for the writer to have gone at this, under the protection of the army at New Orleans, than to have sat down in a closet writing complaining letters northward.

His Letter to Horace Greeley. August 22, 1862

I have just read yours of the 19th instant, addressed to myself through the "New York Tribune."

If there be in it any statements or assumptions of fact which I may know to be erroneous, I do not now and here controvert them.

If there be in it any inferences which I may believe to be falsely drawn, I do not now and here argue against them.

If there be perceptible in it an impatient and dictatorial tone, I waive it, in deference to an old friend whose heart I have always supposed to be right.

As to the policy I "seem to be pursuing," as you say, I have not meant to leave any one in doubt. I would save the Union. I would save it in the shortest way under the Constitution.

The sooner the national authority can be restored, the nearer the Union will be,—the Union as it was.

If there be those who would not save the Union unless they could at the same time save slavery, I do not agree with them.

If there be those who would not save the Union unless they could at the same time destroy slavery, I do not agree with them.

My paramount object in this struggle is to save the Union, and not either to save or to destroy slavery.

If I could save the Union without freeing any slave, I would do it; if I could save it by freeing all the slaves, I would do it; and if I could save it by freeing some and leaving others alone, I would also do that.

What I do about slavery and the coloured race, I do because I believe it helps to save the Union; and what I forbear, I forbear because I do not believe it would help to save the Union.

I shall do less whenever I shall believe that what I am doing hurts the cause; and I shall do more whenever I shall believe doing more will help the cause.

I shall try to correct errors where shown to be errors, and I shall adopt new views as fast as they shall appear to be true views.

I have here stated my purpose according to my views of official duty, and I intend no modification of my oft-expressed personal wish that all men everywhere could be free.

From his Reply to the Chicago Committee of United Religious Denominations. September 13, 1862

The subject presented in the memorial is one upon which I have thought much for weeks past, and I may even say for months. I am approached with the most opposite opinions and advice, and that by religious men, who are equally certain that they represent the Divine will. I am sure that either the one or the other class is mistaken in that belief, and perhaps, in some respects, both. I hope it will not be irreverent for me to say, that if it is probable that God would reveal His will to others, on a point so connected with my duty, it might be supposed that He would reveal it directly to me; for, unless I am more deceived in myself than I often am, it is my earnest desire to know the will of Providence in this matter. And if I can learn what it is, I will do it. These are not, however, the days of miracles, and I suppose it will be granted that I am not to expect a direct revelation. I must study the plain, physical facts of the case, ascertain what is possible, and learn what appears to be wise and right.

The subject is difficult, and good men do not agree. For instance, four gentlemen of standing and intelligence, from New York, called as a delegation on business connected with the war; but before leaving, two of them earnestly besought me to proclaim general emancipation, upon which the other two at once attacked them. You also know that the last session of Congress had a decided majority of anti-slavery men, yet they could not unite on this policy. And the same is true of the religious people.

Why the rebel soldiers are praying with a great deal more earnestness, I fear, than our own troops, and expecting God to favour their side: for one of our soldiers who had been taken prisoner told Senator Wilson a few days since that he met nothing so discouraging as the evident sincerity of those he was among in their prayers. But we will talk over the merits of the case.

What good would a proclamation of emancipation from me do, especially as we are now situated? I do not want to issue a document that the whole world will see must necessarily be inoperative, like the Pope's bull against the comet! Would my word free the slaves, when I cannot even enforce the Constitution in the rebel States? Is there a single court or magistrate or individual that would be influenced by it there?

And what reason is there to think it would have any greater effect upon the slaves than the late law of Congress, which I approved, and which offers protection and freedom to the slaves of rebel masters who come within our lines? Yet I cannot learn that that law has caused a single slave to come over to us. And suppose they could be induced by a proclamation of freedom from me to throw themselves upon us, what should we do with them? How can we feed and care for such a multitude? General Butler wrote me a few days since that he was issuing more rations to the slaves who have rushed to him than to all the white troops under his command. They eat, and that is all; though it is true General Butler is feeding the whites also by the thousand, for it nearly amounts to a famine there. If now, the pressure of the war should call off our forces from New Orleans to defend some other point, what is to prevent the masters from reducing the blacks to slavery again? For I am told that whenever the rebels take any black prisoners, free or slave, they immediately auction them off! They did so with those they took from a boat that was aground in the Tennessee River a few days ago. And then I am very ungenerously attacked for it. For instance, when, after the late battles at and near Bull Run, an expedition went out from Washington under a flag of truce to bury the dead and bring in the wounded, and the rebels seized the blacks who went along to help, and sent them into slavery, Horace Greeley said in his paper "that the government would probably do nothing about it." What could I do?

Now, then, tell me, if you please, what possible result of good would follow the issuing of such a proclamation as you desire? Understand, I raise no objections against it on legal or constitutional grounds, for, as commander-in-chief of the army and navy, in time of war I suppose I have a right to take any measures which may best subdue the enemy; nor do I urge objections of a moral nature, in view of possible consequences of insurrection and massacre at the South. I view this matter as a practical war-measure, to be decided on according to the advantages or disadvantages it may offer to the suppression of the rebellion.

[The committee had said that emancipation would secure us the sympathy of the world, slavery being the cause of the war. To which the President replied:]

I admit that slavery is at the root of the rebellion, or at least its *sine qua non*. The ambition of politicians may have instigated them to act, but they would have been impotent without slavery as their instrument. I will also concede that emancipation would help us in Europe, and convince them that we are incited by something more than ambition. I grant further, that it would help somewhat at the North, though not so much, I fear, as you and those you represent, imagine. Still, some additional strength would be added in that way to the war,—and then, unquestionably, it would weaken the rebels by drawing off their labourers, which is of great importance; but I am not so sure that we could do much with the blacks. If we were to arm them, I fear that in a few weeks the arms would be in the hands of the rebels; and indeed, thus far, we have not had arms enough to equip our white troops. I will mention another thing, though it meet only your scorn and contempt. There are fifty thousand bayonets in the Union armies from the border slave States. It would be a serious matter if, in consequence of a proclamation such as you desire, they should go over to the rebels. I do not think they all would,—not so many indeed, as a year ago, nor as six months ago; not so many to-day as yesterday. Every day increases their Union feeling. They are also getting their pride enlisted, and want to beat the rebels. Let me say one thing more: I think you should admit that we already have an important principle to rally and unite the people, in the fact that constitutional government is at stake. This is a fundamental idea, going down about as deep as anything.

Do not misunderstand me because I have mentioned these objections. They indicate the difficulties that have thus far prevented my action in some such way as you desire. I have not decided against a proclamation of liberty to the slaves, but hold the matter under advisement. And I can assure you that the subject is on my mind by day and night, more than any other. Whatever shall appear to be God's will, I will do. I trust that in the freedom with which I have canvassed your views, I have not in any respect injured your feelings.

From the Annual Message to Congress. December 1, 1862

Since your last annual assembling, another year of health and bountiful harvests has passed; and while it has not pleased the Almighty to bless us with a return of peace, we can but press on, guided by the best light He gives us, trusting that in His own good time and wise way, all will yet be well.

The correspondence, touching foreign affairs, which has taken place during the last year, is herewith submitted, in virtual compliance with a request to that effect made by the House of Representatives near the close of the last session of Congress.

If the condition of our relations with other nations is less gratifying than it has usually been at former periods, it is certainly more satisfactory than a nation so unhappily distracted as we are, might reasonably have apprehended. In the month of June last, there were some grounds to expect that the maritime powers, which, at the beginning of our domestic difficulties, so unwisely and unnecessarily, as we think, recognized the insurgents as a belligerent, would soon recede from that position, which has proved only less injurious to themselves than to our own country. But the temporary reverses which afterward befell the national arms, and which were exaggerated by our own disloyal citizens abroad, have hitherto delayed that act of simple justice.

The Civil War, which has so radically changed for the moment the occupations and habits of the American people, has necessarily disturbed the social condition and affected very deeply the prosperity of the nations with which we have carried on a commerce that has been steadily increasing throughout a period of half a century. It has, at the same time, excited political ambitions and apprehensions which have produced a profound agitation throughout the civilized world. In this unusual agitation we have forborne from taking part in any controversy between foreign States, and between parties or factions in such States. We have attempted no propagandism and acknowledged no revolution. But we have left to every nation the exclusive conduct and management of its own affairs. Our struggle has been, of course, contemplated by foreign nations with reference less to its own merits than to its supposed and often exaggerated effects and consequences resulting to those nations themselves. Nevertheless, complaint on the part of this government, even if it were just, would certainly be unwise....

There is no line, straight or crooked, suitable for a national boundary, upon which to divide. Trace through from east to west upon the line between the free and the slave country, and we shall find a little more than one-third of its length are rivers, easy to be crossed, and populated, or soon to be populated, thickly upon both sides; while nearly all its remaining length are merely surveyors' lines, over which people may walk back and forth without any consciousness of their presence. No part of this line can be made any more difficult to pass, by writing it down on paper or parchment as a national boundary. The fact of separation, if it comes, gives up, on the part of the seceding section, the fugitive-slave clause, along with all other constitutional obligations upon the section seceded from, while I should expect no treaty stipulation would be ever made to take its place.

But there is another difficulty. The great interior region bounded east by the Alleghanies, north by the British dominions, west by the Rocky Mountains, and south by the line along which the culture of corn and cotton meets, ... already has above ten millions of people, and will have fifty millions within fifty years, if not prevented by any political folly or mistake. It contains more than one-third of the country owned by the United States,—certainly more than one million of square miles. Once half as populous as Massachusetts already is, and it would have more than seventy-five millions of people. A glance at the map shows that, territorially speaking, it is the great body of the republic. The other parts are but marginal borders to it, the magnificent region sloping west from the Rocky Mountains to the Pacific being the deepest, and also the richest, in undeveloped resources. In the production of provisions, grains, grasses, and all which proceed from them, this great interior region is naturally one of the most important in the world. Ascertain from the statistics the small proportion of the region which has, as yet, been brought into cultivation, and also the large and rapidly increasing amount of its products, and we shall be overwhelmed with the magnitude of the prospect presented. And yet this region has no sea-coast, touches no ocean anywhere. As part of one nation, its people now find, and may for ever find, their way to Europe by New York, to South America and Africa by New Orleans, and to Asia by San Francisco. But separate our common country into two nations, as designed by the present rebellion, and every man of this great interior region is thereby cut off from one or more of these outlets,—not perhaps by a physical barrier, but by embarrassing and onerous trade regulations.

And this is true, wherever a dividing or boundary line may be fixed. Place it between the now free and slave country, or place it south of Kentucky, or north of Ohio, and still the truth remains that none south of it can trade to any port or place north of it, except upon terms dictated by a government foreign to them. These outlets, east, west, and south, are indispensable to the well-being of the people inhabiting, and to inhabit, this vast interior region. Which of the three may be the best, is no proper question. All are better than either; and all of right belong to that people and their successors for ever. True to themselves, they will not ask where a line of separation shall be, but will vow rather that there shall be no such line. Nor are the marginal regions less interested in these communications to and through them to the great outside world. They too, and each of them, must have access to this Egypt of the west, without paying toll at the crossing of any national boundary.

Our national strife springs not from our permanent part, not from the land we inhabit, not from our national homestead. There is no possible severing of this but would multiply and not mitigate evils among us. In all its adaptations and aptitudes, it demands union and abhors separation. In fact, it would ere long force reunion, however much of blood and treasure the separation might have cost....

Fellow-citizens, we cannot escape history. We of this Congress and this Administration will be remembered in spite of ourselves. No personal significance or insignificance can spare one or another of us. The fiery trial through which we pass will light us down, in honour or dishonour, to the latest generation. We say we are for the Union. The world will not forget that we say this. We know how to save the Union. The world knows we do know how to save it.

We, even we here, hold the power and bear the responsibility. In giving freedom to the slave, we assure freedom to the free,—honourable alike in what we give and what we preserve. We shall nobly save or meanly lose the last, best hope of earth. Other means may succeed; this could not fail. The way is plain, peaceful, generous, just,—a way which, if followed, the world will for ever applaud, and God must for ever bless.

Emancipation Proclamation. January 1, 1863

Whereas, on the twenty-second day of September, in the year of our Lord one thousand eight hundred and sixty-two, a proclamation was issued by the President of the United States, containing, among other things, the following, to wit:

"That on the first day of January, in the year of our Lord one thousand eight hundred and sixty-three, all persons held as slaves within any State, or designated part of a State, the people whereof shall then be in rebellion against the United States, shall be then, thenceforward, and for ever free; and the Executive Government of the United States, including the military and naval authority thereof, will recognize and maintain the freedom of such persons, and will do no act or acts to repress such persons, or any of them, in any efforts they may make for their actual freedom.

"That the Executive will, on the first day of January aforesaid, by proclamation, designate the States and parts of States, if any, in which the people thereof respectively shall then be in rebellion against the United States; and the fact that any State, or the people thereof, shall on that day be in good faith represented in the Congress of the United States by members chosen thereto at elections wherein a majority of the qualified voters of such State shall have participated, shall in the absence of strong countervailing testimony be deemed conclusive evidence that such State and the people thereof are not then in rebellion against the United States."

Now, therefore, I, Abraham Lincoln, President of the United States, by virtue of the power in me vested as commander-in-chief of the army and navy of the United States, in time of actual armed rebellion against the authority and government of the United States, and as a fit and necessary war measure for suppressing said rebellion, do, on this first day of January, in the year of our Lord one thousand eight hundred and sixty-three, and in accordance with my purpose so to do, publicly proclaimed for the full period of one hundred days from the day first above mentioned, order and designate as the States and parts of States wherein the people thereof, respectively, are this day in rebellion against the United States, the following, to wit:

Arkansas, Texas, Louisiana (except the parishes of St. Bernard, Plaquemines, Jefferson, St. John, St. Charles, St. James, Ascension, Assumption, Terrebonne, Lafourche, St. Mary, St. Martin, and Orleans, including the city of New Orleans), Mississippi, Alabama, Florida, Georgia, South Carolina, North Carolina, and Virginia (except the forty-eight counties designated as West Virginia, and also the counties of Berkeley, Accomac, Northampton, Elizabeth City, York, Princess Anne, and Norfolk, including the cities of Norfolk and Portsmouth), and which excepted parts are for the present left precisely as if this proclamation were not issued.

And by virtue of the power and for the purpose aforesaid, I do order and declare that all persons held as slaves within said designated States and parts of States are, and henceforward shall be, free; and that the Executive Government of the United States, including the military and naval authorities thereof, will recognize and maintain the freedom of said persons.

And I hereby enjoin upon the people so declared to be free to abstain from all violence, unless in necessary self-defence; and I recommend to them that, in all cases when allowed, they labour faithfully for reasonable wages.

And I further declare and make known that such persons of suitable condition will be received into the armed service of the United States to garrison forts, positions, stations, and other places, and to man vessels of all sorts in said service.

And upon this act, sincerely believed to be an act of justice, warranted by the Constitution upon military necessity, I invoke the considerate judgment of mankind and the gracious favour of Almighty God.

In witness whereof, I have hereunto set my hand, and caused the seal of the United States to be affixed.

[L.S.]

Done at the city of Washington, this first day of January, in the year of our Lord one thousand eight hundred and sixty-three, and of the independence of the United States of America the eighty-seventh.

ABRAHAM LINCOLN.

By the President:
WILLIAM H. SEWARD,
Secretary of State.

Letter to General Grant. July 13, 1863

My dear General, I do not remember that you and I ever met personally. I write this now as a grateful acknowledgment for the almost inestimable service you have done the country. I wish to say a word further. When you first reached the vicinity of Vicksburg, I thought you should do what you finally did—march the troops across the neck, run the batteries with the transports, and thus go below; and I never had any faith, except a general hope that you knew better than I, that the Yazoo Pass expedition and the like could succeed. When you got below and took Port Gibson, Grand Gulf, and vicinity, I thought you should go down the river and join General Banks, and when you turned northward, east of the Big Black, I feared it was a mistake. I now wish to make the personal acknowledgment that you were right and I was wrong.

Yours very truly,
A. LINCOLN.

Letter to —— Moulton. Washington. July 31, 1863

My dear Sir, There has been a good deal of complaint against you by your superior officers of the Provost-Marshal-General's Department, and your removal has been strongly urged on the ground of "persistent disobedience of orders and neglect of duty." Firmly convinced, as I am, of the patriotism of your motives, I am unwilling to do anything in your case which may seem unnecessarily harsh or at variance with the feelings of personal respect and esteem with which I have always regarded you. I consider your services in your district valuable, and should be sorry to lose them. It is unnecessary for me to state, however, that when differences of opinion arise between officers of the government, the ranking officer must be obeyed. You of course recognize as clearly as I do the importance of this rule. I hope you will conclude to go on in your present position under the regulations of the department. I wish you would write to me.

Letter to Mrs. Lincoln. Washington. August 8, 1863

My dear Wife, All as well as usual, and no particular trouble anyway. I put the money into the Treasury at five per cent., with the privilege of withdrawing it any time upon thirty days' notice. I suppose you are glad to learn this. Tell dear Tad poor "Nanny Goat" is lost, and Mrs. Cuthbert and I are in distress about it. The day you left Nanny was found resting herself and chewing her little cud on the middle of Tad's bed; but now she's gone! The gardener kept complaining that she destroyed the flowers, till it was concluded to bring her down to the White House. This was done, and the second day she had disappeared and has not been heard of since. This is the last we know of poor "Nanny."

Letter to James H. Hackett. Washington. August 17, 1863

My dear Sir, Months ago I should have acknowledged the receipt of your book and accompanying kind note; and I now have to beg your pardon for not having done so.

For one of my age I have seen very little of the drama. The first presentation of Falstaff I ever saw was yours here, last winter or spring. Perhaps the best compliment I can pay is to say, as I truly can, I am very anxious to see it again. Some of Shakespeare's plays I have never read; while others I have gone over perhaps as frequently as any unprofessional reader. Among the latter are *Lear*, *Richard III.*, *Henry VIII.*, *Hamlet*, and especially *Macbeth*. I think nothing equals *Macbeth*. It is wonderful.

Unlike you gentlemen of the profession, I think the soliloquy in *Hamlet* commencing "Oh, my offence is rank," surpasses that commencing "To be or not to be." But pardon this small attempt at criticism. I should like to hear you pronounce the opening speech of Richard III. Will you not soon visit Washington again? If you do, please call and let me make your personal acquaintance.

Note to Secretary Stanton. Washington. November 11, 1863

Dear Sir, I personally wish Jacob Freese, of New Jersey, to be appointed Colonel of a coloured regiment, and this regardless of whether he can tell the exact shade of Julius Cæsar's hair.

The Letter to James C. Conkling. August 26, 1863

Your letter inviting me to attend a mass meeting of unconditional Union men, to be held at the capital of Illinois on the third day of September, has been received. It would be very agreeable to me to thus meet my old friends at my own home, but I cannot just now be absent from here so long as a visit there would require.

The meeting is to be of all those who maintain unconditional devotion to the Union; and I am sure my old political friends will thank me for tendering, as I do, the nation's gratitude to those and other noble men whom no partisan malice or partisan hope can make false to the nation's life.

There are those who are dissatisfied with me. To such I would say: You desire peace, and you blame me that we do not have it. But how can we attain it? There are but three conceivable ways. First, to suppress the rebellion by force of arms. This I am trying to do. Are you for it? If you are, so far we are agreed. If you are not for it, a second way is to give up the Union. I am against this. Are you for it? If you are, you should say so plainly. If you are not for force, nor yet for dissolution, there only remains some imaginable compromise. I do not believe any compromise embracing the maintenance of the Union is now possible. All I learn leads to a directly opposite belief. The strength of the rebellion is its military, its army. That army dominates all the country and all the people within its range. Any offer of terms made by any man or men within that range, in opposition to that army, is simply nothing for the present, because such man or men have no power whatever to enforce their side of a compromise, if one were made with them.

To illustrate: Suppose refugees from the South and peace men of the North get together in convention, and frame and proclaim a compromise embracing a restoration of the Union. In what way can that compromise be used to keep Lee's army out of Pennsylvania? Meade's army can keep Lee's out of Pennsylvania, and, I think, can ultimately drive it out of existence. But no paper compromise, to which the controllers of Lee's army are not agreed, can at all affect that army. In an effort at such compromise we should waste time which the enemy would improve to our disadvantage; and that would be all. A compromise, to be effective, must be made either with those who control the rebel army, or with the people first liberated from the domination of that army by the success of our own army. Now, allow me to assure you that no word or intimation from that rebel army, or from any of the men controlling it, in relation to any peace compromise, has ever come to my knowledge or belief. All charges and insinuations to the contrary are deceptive and groundless. And I promise you that if any such proposition shall hereafter come, it shall not be rejected and kept a secret from you. I freely acknowledge myself the servant of the people, according to the bond of service,—the United States Constitution,—and that, as such, I am responsible to them.

But to be plain. You are dissatisfied with me about the negro. Quite likely there is a difference of opinion between you and myself upon that subject. I certainly wish that all men could be free, while I suppose you do not. Yet I have neither adopted nor proposed any measure which is not consistent with even your views, provided you are for the Union. I suggested compensated emancipation, to which you replied, you wished not to be taxed to buy negroes. But I had not asked you to be taxed to buy negroes, except in such way as to save you from greater taxation to save the Union exclusively by other means.

You dislike the Emancipation Proclamation, and perhaps would have it retracted. You say it is unconstitutional. I think differently. I think the Constitution invests its commander-in-chief with the law of war in time of war. The most that can be said—if so much—is that slaves are property. Is there, has there ever been, any question that, by the law of war, property, both of enemies and friends, may be taken when needed? And is it not needed whenever taking it helps us or hurts the enemy? Armies the world over destroy enemies' property when they cannot use it, and even destroy their own to keep it from the enemy. Civilized belligerents do all in their power to help themselves or hurt the enemy, except a few things regarded as barbarous or cruel. Among the exceptions are the massacre of vanquished foes and non-combatants, male and female.

But the proclamation, as law, either is valid or is not valid. If it is not valid, it needs no retraction. If it is valid, it cannot be retracted any more than the dead can be brought to life. Some of you profess to think its retraction would operate favourably for the Union. Why better after the retraction than before the issue? There was more than a year and a half of trial to suppress the rebellion before the proclamation issued, the last one hundred days of which passed under an explicit notice that it was coming, unless averted by those in revolt returning to their allegiance. The war has certainly progressed as favourably for us since the issue of the proclamation as before. I know, as fully as one can know the opinions of others, that some of the commanders of our armies in the field who have given us our most important successes, believe the emancipation policy and the use of coloured troops constitute the heaviest blow yet dealt to the rebellion, and that at least one of these important successes could not have been achieved when it was but for the aid of black soldiers. Among the commanders holding these views are some who have never had any affinity with what is called Abolitionism or with Republican party politics, but who hold them purely as military opinions. I submit these opinions as being entitled to some weight against the objections often urged, that emancipation and arming the blacks are unwise as military measures, and were not adopted as such in good faith.

You say you will not fight to free negroes. Some of them seem willing to fight for you; but no matter. Fight you, then, exclusively to save the Union. I issued the proclamation on purpose to aid you in saving the Union. Whenever you shall have conquered all resistance to the Union, if I shall urge you to continue fighting, it will be an apt time then for you to declare you will not fight to free negroes.

I thought that in your struggle for the Union, to whatever extent the negroes should cease helping the enemy, to that extent it weakened the enemy in his resistance to you. Do you think differently? I thought that whatever negroes could be got to do as soldiers leaves just so much less for white soldiers to do in saving the Union. Does it appear otherwise to you? But negroes, like other people, act upon motives. Why should they do anything for us, if we will do nothing for them? If they stake their lives for us, they must be prompted by the strongest motive, even the promise of freedom. And the promise being made, must be kept.

The signs look better. The Father of Waters again goes unvexed to the sea. Thanks to the great Northwest for it. Nor yet wholly to them. Three hundred miles up they met New England, Empire, Keystone, and Jersey hewing their way right and left. The sunny South, too, in more colours than one, also lent a hand. On the spot, their part of the history was jotted down in black and white. The job was a great national one, and let none be banned who bore an honourable part in it. And while those who cleared the great river may well be proud, even that is not all. It is hard to say that anything has been more bravely and well done than at Antietam, Murfreesboro, Gettysburg, and on many fields of lesser note. Nor must Uncle Sam's web-feet be forgotten. At all the watery margins they have been present. Not only on the deep sea, the broad bay, and the rapid river, but also up the narrow, muddy bayou, and wherever the ground was a little damp, they have been and made their tracks. Thanks to all,—for the great Republic, for the principle it lives by and keeps alive, for man's vast future,—thanks to all.

Peace does not appear so distant as it did. I hope it will come soon, and come to stay; and so come as to be worth the keeping in all future time. It will then have been proved that among freemen there can be no successful appeal from the ballot to the bullet, and that they who take such appeal are sure to lose their case and pay the cost. And then there will be some black men who can remember that with silent tongue, and clenched teeth, and steady eye, and well-poised bayonet, they have helped mankind on to this great consummation, while I fear there will be some white ones unable to forget that with malignant heart and deceitful speech they strove to hinder it.

Still, let us not be over-sanguine of a speedy, final triumph. Let us be quite sober. Let us diligently apply the means, never doubting that a just God, in His own good time, will give us the rightful result.

His Proclamation for a Day of Thanksgiving. October 3, 1863

The year that is drawing toward its close has been filled with the blessings of fruitful fields and healthful skies. To these bounties, which are so constantly enjoyed that we are prone to forget the source from which they come, others have been added, which are of so extraordinary a nature that they cannot fail to penetrate and soften the heart which is habitually insensible to the ever-watchful providence of Almighty God.

In the midst of a civil war of unequalled magnitude and severity, which has sometimes seemed to foreign States to invite and provoke their aggressions, peace has been preserved with all nations, order has been maintained, the laws have been respected and obeyed, and harmony has prevailed everywhere, except in the theatre of military conflict; while that theatre has been greatly contracted by the advancing armies and navies of the Union.

Needful diversions of wealth and strength from the fields of peaceful industry to the national defence have not arrested the plough, the shuttle, or the ship; the axe has enlarged the borders of our settlements, and the mines, as well of iron and coal as of the precious metals, have yielded even more abundantly than heretofore. Population has steadily increased, notwithstanding the waste that has been made in the camp, the siege, and the battle-field; and the country, rejoicing in the consciousness of augmented strength and vigour, is permitted to expect continuance of years with large increase of freedom.

No human counsel hath devised, nor hath any mortal hand worked out these great things. They are the gracious gifts of the Most High God, who, while dealing with us in anger for our sins, hath nevertheless remembered mercy.

It has seemed to me fit and proper that they should be solemnly, reverently, and gratefully acknowledged as with one heart and one voice by the whole American people. I do, therefore, invite, my fellow-citizens in every part of the United States, and also those who are at sea, and those sojourning in foreign lands, to set apart and observe the last Thursday of November next as a day of thanksgiving and praise to our beneficent Father who dwelleth in the heavens. And I recommend to them that while offering up the ascriptions justly due to Him for such singular deliverances and blessings, they do also, with humble penitence for our national perverseness and disobedience, commend to His tender care all those who have become widows, orphans, mourners, or sufferers in the lamentable civil strife in which we are unavoidably engaged, and fervently implore the interposition of the Almighty Hand to heal the wounds of the nation, and to restore it, as soon as may be consistent with the Divine purposes, to the full enjoyment of peace, harmony, tranquillity, and union.

Address at the Dedication of the National Cemetery at Gettysburg. November 19, 1863

Fourscore and seven years ago our fathers brought forth upon this continent a new nation, conceived in liberty, and dedicated to the proposition that all men are created equal.

Now we are engaged in a great civil war, testing whether that nation, or any nation so conceived and so dedicated, can long endure. We are met on a great battle-field of that war. We have come to dedicate a portion of that field as a final resting-place for those who here gave their lives that that nation might live. It is altogether fitting and proper that we should do this.

But in a larger sense we cannot dedicate, we cannot consecrate, we cannot hallow this ground. The brave men, living and dead, who struggled here, have consecrated it far above our power to add or detract. The world will little note nor long remember what we say here, but it can never forget what they did here. It is for us, the living, rather, to be dedicated here to the unfinished work which they who fought here have thus far so nobly advanced. It is rather for us to be here dedicated to the great task remaining before us; that from these honoured dead we take increased devotion to that cause for which they gave the last full measure of devotion; that we here highly resolve that these dead shall not have died in vain; that this nation, under God, shall have a new birth of freedom; and that government of the people, by the people, and for the people, shall not perish from the earth.

From the Annual Message to Congress. December 8, 1863

... When Congress assembled a year ago, the war had already lasted nearly twenty months, and there had been many conflicts on both land and sea, with varying results. The rebellion had been pressed back into reduced limits; yet the tone of public feeling and opinion at home and abroad was not satisfactory. With other signs, the popular elections then just past indicated uneasiness among ourselves; while, amid much that was cold and menacing, the kindest words coming from Europe were uttered in accents of pity that we were too blind to surrender a hopeless cause. Our commerce was suffering greatly from a few vessels built upon and furnished from foreign shores, and we were threatened with such additions from the same quarter as would sweep our trade from the seas and raise our blockade. We had failed to elicit from European governments anything hopeful upon this subject. The preliminary Emancipation Proclamation, issued in September, was running its assigned period to the beginning of the new year. A month later the final proclamation came, including the announcement that coloured men of suitable condition would be received into the war service. The policy of emancipation and of employing black soldiers gave to the future a new aspect, about which hope and fear and doubt contended in uncertain conflict. According to our political system, as a matter of civil administration, the general government had no lawful power to effect emancipation in any State, and for a long time it had been hoped that the rebellion could be suppressed without resorting to it as a military measure. It was all the while deemed possible that the necessity for it might come and that, if it should, the crisis of the contest would then be presented. It came, and, as was anticipated, was followed by dark and doubtful days. Eleven months having now passed, we are permitted to take another review. The rebel borders are pressed still farther back, and by the complete opening of the Mississippi, the country dominated by the rebellion is divided into distinct parts, with no practical communication between them. Tennessee and Arkansas have been substantially cleared of insurgent control, and influential citizens in each, owners of slaves and advocates of slavery at the beginning of the rebellion, now declare openly for emancipation in their respective States. Of those States not included in the Emancipation Proclamation, Maryland and Missouri, neither of which three years ago would tolerate any restraint upon the extension of slavery into new Territories, only dispute now as to the best mode of removing it within their own limits.

Of those who were slaves at the beginning of the rebellion, full one hundred thousand are now in the United States military service, about one-half of which number actually bear arms in the ranks; thus giving the double advantage of taking so much labour from the insurgent cause and supplying the places which otherwise must be filled with so many white men. So far as tested, it is difficult to say they are not as good soldiers as any. No servile insurrection or tendency to violence or cruelty has marked the measures of emancipation and arming the blacks. These measures have been much discussed in foreign countries, and contemporary with such discussion the tone of public sentiment there is much improved. At home the same measures have been fully discussed, supported, criticized, and denounced, and the annual elections following are highly encouraging to those whose official duty it is to bear the country through this great trial.

Thus we have the new reckoning. The crisis which threatened to divide the friends of the Union is passed.

Letter to Secretary Stanton. Washington. March 1, 1864

My dear Sir, A poor widow, by the name of Baird, has a son in the army, that for some offence has been sentenced to serve a long time without pay, or at most with very little pay. I do not like this punishment of withholding pay—it falls so very hard upon poor families. After he had been serving in this way for several months, at the tearful appeal of the poor mother, I made a direction that he be allowed to enlist for a new term, on the same condition as others. She now comes, and says she cannot get it acted upon. Please do it.

Letter to Governor Michael Hahn. Washington. March 13, 1864

My dear Sir, I congratulate you on having fixed your name in history as the first free-State governor of Louisiana. Now you are about to have a convention, which, among other things, will probably define the elective franchise. I barely suggest for your private consideration, whether some of the coloured people may not be let in—as, for instance, the very intelligent, and especially those who have fought gallantly in our ranks. They would probably help, in some trying time to come, to keep the jewel of liberty within the family of freedom. But this is only a suggestion, not to the public, but to you alone.

An Address at a Fair for the Sanitary Commission. March 18, 1864

I appear to say but a word. This extraordinary war in which we are engaged falls heavily upon all classes of people, but the most heavily upon the soldier. For it has been said, "all that a man hath will he give for his life;" and while all contribute of their substance, the soldier puts his life at stake, and often yields it up in his country's cause. *The highest merit, then, is due to the soldier.*

In this extraordinary war extraordinary developments have manifested themselves, such as have not been seen in former wars; and amongst these manifestations nothing has been more remarkable than these fairs for the relief of suffering soldiers and their families. And the chief agents in these fairs are the women of America.

I am not accustomed to the language of eulogy. I have never studied the art of paying compliments to women. But I must say, that if all that has been said by orators and poets since the creation of the world in praise of women were applied to the women of America, it would not do them justice for their conduct during this war. I will close by saying, God bless the women of America!

Letter to A.G. Hodges, of Kentucky. April 4, 1864

I am naturally anti-slavery. If slavery is not wrong, nothing is wrong. I cannot remember when I did not so think and feel, and yet I have never understood that the Presidency conferred upon me an unrestricted right to act officially upon this judgment and feeling. It was in the oath that I took, that I would, to the best of my ability, preserve, protect, and defend the Constitution of the United States. I could not take office without taking the oath. Nor was it my view that I might take an oath to get power, and break the oath in using the power. I understood, too, that in ordinary civil administration this oath even forbade me to practically indulge my primary abstract judgment on the moral question of slavery. I had publicly declared this many times and in many ways. And I aver that, to this day, I have done no official act in mere deference to my abstract feeling and judgment on slavery. I did understand, however, that my oath to preserve the Constitution to the best of my ability imposed upon me the duty of preserving, by every indispensable means, that government—that nation—of which that Constitution was the organic law. Was it possible to lose the nation and yet preserve the Constitution? By general law, life and limb must be protected, yet often a limb must be amputated to save a life; but a life is never wisely given to save a limb. I felt that measures, otherwise unconstitutional, might become lawful by becoming indispensable to the preservation of the Constitution through the preservation of the nation. Right or wrong, I assumed this ground; and now avow it. I could not feel that, to the best of my ability, I had even tried to preserve the Constitution, if, to save slavery or any minor matter, I should permit the wreck of government, country, and Constitution, all together. When, early in the war, General Fremont attempted military emancipation, I forbade it, because I did not then think it an indispensable necessity. When, a little later, General Cameron, then Secretary of War, suggested the arming of the blacks, I objected, because I did not think it an indispensable necessity. When, still later, General Hunter attempted military emancipation, I again forbade it, because I did not yet think the indispensable necessity had come. When, in March and May and July, 1862, I made earnest and successive appeals to the border States to favour compensated emancipation, I believed the indispensable necessity for military emancipation and arming the blacks would come, unless averted by that measure. They declined the proposition, and I was, in my best judgment, driven to the alternative of either surrendering the Union, and with it the Constitution, or laying strong hand upon the coloured element. I chose the latter. In choosing it, I hoped for greater gain than loss; but of this I was not entirely confident. More than a year of trial now shows no loss by it in our foreign relations, none in our home popular sentiment, none in our white military force,—no loss by it anyhow or anywhere. On the contrary, it shows a gain of quite one hundred and thirty thousand soldiers, seamen, and labourers. These are palpable facts, about which, as facts, there can be no cavilling. We have the men, and we could not have had them without the measure.

And now let any Union man who complains of the measure, test himself by writing down in one line that he is for subduing the rebellion by force of arms; and in the next, that he is for taking these hundred and thirty thousand men from the Union side, and placing them where they would be but for the measure he condemns. If he cannot face his case so stated, it is only because he cannot face the truth.

I add a word which was not in the verbal conversation. In telling this tale, I attempt no compliment to my own sagacity. I claim not to have controlled events, but confess plainly that events have controlled me. Now, at the end of three years' struggle, the nation's condition is not what either party, or any man, devised or expected. God alone can claim it. Whither it is tending seems plain. If God now wills the removal of a great wrong, and wills also that we of the North, as well as you of the South, shall pay fairly for our complicity in that wrong, impartial history will find therein new cause to attest and revere the justice and goodness of God.

From an Address at a Sanitary Fair in Baltimore. April 18, 1864

... The world has never had a good definition of the word "liberty," and the American people, just now, are much in want of one. We all declare for liberty; but in using the same word, we do not all mean the same thing. With some, the word "liberty" may mean for each man to do as he pleases with himself and the product of his labour; while with others, the same word may mean for some men to do as they please with other men and the product of other men's labour. Here are two, not only different, but incompatible things, called by the same name,—liberty. And it follows that each of the things is, by the respective parties, called by two different and incompatible names,—liberty and tyranny.

The shepherd drives the wolf from the sheep's throat, for which the sheep thanks the shepherd as his liberator, while the wolf denounces him for the same act as the destroyer of liberty, especially as the sheep was a black one. Plainly, the sheep and the wolf are not agreed upon a definition of the word "liberty;" and precisely the same difference prevails to-day, among us human creatures, even in the North, and all professing to love liberty. Hence we behold the process by which thousands are daily passing from under the yoke of bondage hailed by some as the advance of liberty, and bewailed by others as the destruction of all liberty. Recently, as it seems, the people of Maryland have been doing something to define liberty, and thanks to them that, in what they have done, the wolf's dictionary has been repudiated.

Letter to General Grant. April 30, 1864

Not expecting to see you again before the spring campaign opens, I wish to express in this way my entire satisfaction with what you have done up to this time, so far as I understand it. The particulars of your plans I neither know nor seek to know. You are vigilant and self-reliant; and, pleased with this, I wish not to obtrude any constraints nor restraints upon you. While I am very anxious that any great disaster or capture of our men in great numbers shall be avoided, I know these points are less likely to escape your attention than they would be mine. If there is anything wanting which is within my power to give, do not fail to let me know it. And now, with a brave army and a just cause, may God sustain you.

From an Address to the 166th Ohio Regiment. August 22, 1864

I almost always feel inclined, when I happen to say anything to soldiers, to impress upon them, in a few brief remarks, the importance of success in this contest. It is not merely for to-day, but for all time to come, that we should perpetuate for our children's children that great and free government which we have enjoyed all our lives. I beg you to remember this, not merely for my sake, but for yours. I happen, temporarily, to occupy this White House. I am a living witness that any one of your children may look to come here as my father's child has. It is in order that each one of you may have, through this free government which we have enjoyed, an open field and a fair chance for your industry, enterprise, and intelligence; that you may all have equal privileges in the race of life, with all its desirable human aspirations. It is for this the struggle should be maintained, that we may not lose our birthright—not only for one, but for two or three years. The nation is worth fighting for, to secure such an inestimable jewel.

Reply to a Serenade. November 10, 1864

It has long been a grave question whether any government not too strong for the liberties of its people, can be strong enough to maintain its existence in great emergencies. On this point the present rebellion brought our Republic to a severe test; and a presidential election, occurring in regular course during the rebellion, added not a little to the strain.

If the loyal people united were put to the utmost of their strength by the rebellion, must they not fail when divided and partially paralyzed by a political war among themselves? But the election was a necessity. We cannot have free government without elections; and if the rebellion could force us to forego or postpone a national election, it might fairly claim to have already conquered and ruined us. The strife of the election is but human nature practically applied to the facts of the case. What has occurred in this case must ever occur in similar cases. Human nature will not change. In any future great national trial, compared with the men of this, we shall have as weak and as strong, as silly and as wise, as bad and as good. Let us, therefore, study the incidents of this as philosophy to learn wisdom from, and none of them as wrongs to be revenged. But the election, along with its incidental and undesirable strife, has done good too. It has demonstrated that a people's government can sustain a national election in the midst of a great civil war. Gold is good in its place, but living, brave, patriotic men are better than gold.

But the rebellion continues; and now that the election is over, may not all having a common interest reunite in a common effort to save our common country? For my own part, I have striven and shall strive to avoid placing any obstacle in the way. So long as I have been here, I have not willingly planted a thorn in any man's bosom. While I am deeply sensible to the high compliment of a re-election, and duly grateful as I trust to Almighty God for having directed my countrymen to a right conclusion, as I think, for their own good, it adds nothing to my satisfaction that any other man may be disappointed or pained by the result.

May I ask those who have not differed with me, to join with me in this same spirit towards those who have? And now let me close by asking three hearty cheers for our brave soldiers and seamen, and their gallant and skilful commanders.

A Letter to Mrs. Bixley, of Boston. November 21, 1864

Dear Madam, I have been shown in the files of the War Department a statement of the Adjutant-General of Massachusetts that you are the mother of five sons who have died gloriously on the field of battle. I feel how weak and fruitless must be any words of mine which should attempt to beguile you from the grief of a loss so overwhelming. But I cannot refrain from tendering to you the consolation that may be found in the thanks of the Republic they died to save. I pray that our heavenly Father may assuage the anguish of your bereavement, and leave you only the cherished memory of the loved and lost, and the solemn pride that must be yours to have laid so costly a sacrifice upon the altar of freedom.

Yours very sincerely and respectfully,
ABRAHAM LINCOLN.

Letter to General Grant. Washington. January 19, 1865

Please read and answer this letter as though I was not President, but only a friend. My son, now in his twenty-second year, having graduated at Harvard, wishes to see something of the war before it ends. I do not wish to put him in the ranks, nor yet to give him a commission, to which those who have already served long are better entitled, and better qualified to hold. Could he, without embarrassment to you or detriment to the service, go into your military family with some nominal rank, I, and not the public, furnishing his necessary means? If no, say so without the least hesitation, because I am as anxious and as deeply interested that you shall not be encumbered as you can be yourself.

The Second Inaugural Address. March 4, 1865

Fellow-countrymen, At this second appearance to take the oath of the Presidential office, there is less occasion for an extended address than there was at the first. Then a statement, somewhat in detail, of a course to be pursued, seemed fitting and proper. Now, at the expiration of four years, during which public declarations have been constantly called forth on every point and phase of the great contest which still absorbs the attention and engrosses the energies of the nation, little that is new could be presented. The progress of our arms, upon which all else chiefly depends, is as well known to the public as to myself; and it is, I trust, reasonably satisfactory and encouraging to all. With high hope for the future, no prediction in regard to it is ventured.

On the occasion corresponding to this four years ago, all thoughts were anxiously directed to an impending civil war. All dreaded it,—all sought to avert it. While the inaugural address was being delivered from this place, devoted altogether to saving the Union without war, insurgent agents were in the city seeking to destroy it without war,—seeking to dissolve the Union, and divide effects, by negotiation. Both parties deprecated war; but one of them would make war rather than let the nation survive, and the other would accept war rather than let it perish. And the war came.

One-eighth of the whole population were coloured slaves, not distributed generally over the Union, but localized in the southern part of it. These slaves constituted a peculiar and powerful interest. All knew that this interest was, somehow, the cause of the war. To strengthen, perpetuate, and extend this interest was the object for which the insurgents would rend the Union, even by war; while the government claimed no right to do more than to restrict the territorial enlargement of it....

With malice toward none; with charity for all; with firmness in the right, as God gives us to see the right,—let us strive on to finish the work we are in: to bind up the nation's wounds; to care for him who shall have borne the battle, and for his widow and his orphan; to do all which may achieve and cherish a just and lasting peace among ourselves, and with all nations.

A Letter to Thurlow Weed. Executive Mansion, Washington. March 15, 1865

Dear Mr. Weed, Every one likes a compliment. Thank you for yours on my little notification speech and on the recent inaugural address. I expect the latter to wear as well as—perhaps better than—anything I have produced; but I believe it is not immediately popular. Men are not flattered by being shown that there has been a difference of purpose between the Almighty and them. To deny it, however, in this case, is to deny that there is a God governing the world. It is a truth which I thought needed to be told, and, as whatever of humiliation there is in it falls most directly on myself, I thought others might afford for me to tell it.

Truly yours,
A. LINCOLN.

From an Address to an Indiana Regiment. March 17, 1865

There are but few aspects of this great war on which I have not already expressed my views by speaking or writing. There is one—the recent effort of "Our erring brethren," sometimes so called, to employ the slaves in their armies. The great question with them has been, "Will the negro fight for them?" They ought to know better than we, and doubtless do know better than we. I may incidentally remark, that having in my life heard many arguments—or strings of words meant to pass for arguments—intended to show that the negro ought to be a slave,—if he shall now really fight to keep himself a slave, it will be a far better argument why he should remain a slave than I have ever before heard. He, perhaps, ought to be a slave if he desires it ardently enough to fight for it. Or, if one out of four will, for his own freedom fight to keep the other three in slavery, he ought to be a slave for his selfish meanness. I have always thought that all men should be free; but if any should be slaves, it should be first those who desire it for themselves, and secondly those who desire it for others. Whenever I hear any one arguing for slavery, I feel a strong impulse to see it tried on him personally.

From his Reply to a Serenade. Lincoln's Last Public Address. April 11, 1865

Fellow-citizens, We meet this evening, not in sorrow but in gladness of heart. The evacuation of Richmond and Petersburg, and the surrender of the principal insurgent army, give the hope of a just and speedy peace, the joyous expression of which cannot be restrained. In all this joy, however, He from whom all blessings flow must not be forgotten. A call for a national thanksgiving is in the course of preparation, and will be duly promulgated. Nor must those whose harder part give us the cause for rejoicing be overlooked. Their honours must not be parcelled out with others. I, myself, was near the front, and had the high pleasure of transmitting much of the good news to you; but no part of the honour for plan or execution is mine. To General Grant, his skilful officers and brave men, all belongs. The gallant navy stood ready, but was not in reach to take an active part.

By these recent successes the reinauguration of the national authority,—reconstruction,—which has had a large share of thought from the first, is pressed much more closely upon our attention. It is fraught with great difficulty. Unlike a case of war between independent nations, there is no organized organ for us to treat with,—no one man has authority to give up the rebellion for any other man. We simply must begin with and mould from disorganized and discordant elements. Nor is it a small additional embarrassment that we, the loyal people, differ among ourselves as to the mode, manner, and measure of reconstruction. As a general rule I abstain from reading the reports of attacks upon myself, wishing not to be provoked by that to which I cannot properly offer an answer. In spite of this precaution, however, it comes to my knowledge that I am much censured for some supposed agency in setting up and seeking to sustain the new State government of Louisiana.

In this I have done just so much as, and no more than, the public knows. In the annual message of December 1863, and in the accompanying proclamation, I presented a plan of reconstruction, as the phrase goes, which I promised, if adopted by any State, should be acceptable to and sustained by the executive government of the nation. I distinctly stated that this was not the only plan which might possibly be acceptable, and I also distinctly protested that the executive claimed no right to say when or whether members should be admitted to seats in Congress from such States. This plan was in advance submitted to the then Cabinet, and approved by every member of it....

When the message of 1863, with the plan before mentioned, reached New Orleans, General Banks wrote me that he was confident that the people, with his military co-operation, would reconstruct substantially on that plan. I wrote him and some of them to try it. They tried it, and the result is known. Such has been my only agency in getting up the Louisiana government. As to sustaining it, my promise is out, as before stated. But as bad promises are better broken than kept, I shall treat this as a bad promise and break it, whenever I shall be convinced that keeping it is adverse to the public interest; but I have not yet been so convinced. I have been shown a letter on this subject, supposed to be an able one, in which the writer expresses regret that my mind has not seemed to be definitely fixed upon the question whether the seceded States, so called, are in the Union or out of it. It would perhaps add astonishment to his regret were he to learn that since I have found professed Union men endeavouring to answer that question, I have purposely forborne any public expression upon it....

We all agree that the seceded States, so called, are out of their proper practical relation with the Union, and that the sole object of the government, civil and military, in regard to those States, is to again get them into that proper practical relation. I believe that it is not only possible, but in fact easier, to do this without deciding or even considering whether these States have ever been out of the Union, than with it. Finding themselves safely at home, it would be utterly immaterial whether they had ever been abroad. Let us all join in doing the acts necessary to restoring the proper practical relations between these States and the Union, and each for ever after innocently indulge his own opinion whether in doing the acts he brought the States from without into the Union, or only gave them proper assistance, they never having been out of it. The amount of constituency, so to speak, on which the new Louisiana government rests, would be more satisfactory to all if it contained forty thousand, or thirty thousand, or even twenty thousand, instead of only about twelve thousand as it does. It is also unsatisfactory to some that the elective franchise is not given to the coloured man. I would myself prefer that it were now conferred on the very intelligent, and on those who serve our cause as soldiers.

Still, the question is not whether the Louisiana government, as it stands, is quite all that is desirable. The question is, will it be wiser to take it as it is and help to improve it, or to reject and disperse it? Can Louisiana be brought into proper practical relation with the Union sooner by sustaining or by discarding her new State government? Some twelve thousand voters in the heretofore slave State of Louisiana have sworn allegiance to the Union, assumed to be the rightful political power of the State, held elections, organized a State government, adopted a free-State constitution, giving the benefit of public schools equally to black and white, and empowering the legislature to confer the elective franchise upon the coloured man. Their legislature has already voted to ratify the constitutional amendment recently passed by Congress, abolishing slavery throughout the nation. These twelve thousand persons are thus fully committed to the Union and to perpetual freedom in the State,—committed to the very things, and nearly all the things, the nation wants,—and they ask the nation's recognition and its assistance to make good their committal.

If we reject and spurn them, we do our utmost to disorganize and disperse them. We, in effect, say to the white man: You are worthless or worse; we will neither help you, nor be helped by you. To the blacks, we say: This cup of liberty, which these, your old masters, hold to your lips, we will dash from you, and leave you to the chances of gathering the spilled and scattered contents in some vague and undefined when, where, and how. If this course, discouraging and paralyzing both white and black, has any tendency to bring Louisiana into proper, practical relations with the Union, I have so far been unable to perceive it. If, on the contrary, we recognize and sustain the new government of Louisiana, the converse of all this is made true. We encourage the hearts and nerve the arms of twelve thousand to adhere to their work, and argue for it, and proselyte for it, and fight for it, and feed it, and grow it, and ripen it to a complete success. The coloured man, too, in seeing all united for him, is inspired with vigilance, and energy, and daring to the same end. Grant that he desires the elective franchise, will he not attain it sooner by saving the already advanced steps towards it, than by running backward over them?

... I repeat the question, Can Louisiana be brought into proper practical relation with the Union sooner by sustaining or by discarding her new State government?

... What has been said of Louisiana will apply generally to other States. And yet so great peculiarities pertain to each State, and such important and sudden changes occur in the same State, and withal so new and unprecedented is the whole case, that no exclusive and inflexible plan can safely be prescribed as to details and collaterals. Such exclusive and inflexible plan would surely become a new entanglement. Important principles may and must be inflexible. In the present situation, as the phrase goes, it may be my duty to make some new announcement to the people of the South. I am considering, and shall not fail to act when satisfied that action will be proper.

Appendix

ANECDOTES

LINCOLN'S ENTRY INTO RICHMOND THE DAY AFTER IT WAS TAKEN

As Described at that time by a Writer in the "Atlantic Monthly"

They gathered around the President, ran ahead, hovered about the flanks of the little company, and hung like a dark cloud upon the rear. Men, women and children joined the constantly-increasing throng. They came from all the by-streets, running in breathless haste, shouting and hallooing, and dancing with delight. The men threw up their hats, the women waved their bonnets and handkerchiefs, clapped their hands, and sang, "Glory to God! glory, glory!" rendering all the praise to God, who had heard their wailings in the past, their moanings for wives, husbands, children, and friends sold out of their sight; had given them freedom, and after long years of waiting had permitted them thus unexpectedly to behold the face of their great benefactor.

"I thank you, dear Jesus, that I behold President Linkum!" was the exclamation of a woman who stood upon the threshold of her humble home, and with streaming eyes and clasped hands gave thanks aloud to the Saviour of men.

Another, more demonstrative in her joy, was jumping and striking her hands with all her might, crying, "Bless de Lord! Bless de Lord! Bless de Lord!" as if there could be no end to her thanksgiving.

The air rang with a tumultuous chorus of voices. The street became almost impassable on account of the increasing multitude, till soldiers were summoned to clear the way....

The walk was long, and the President halted a moment to rest. "May de good Lord bless you, President Linkum!" said an old negro, removing his hat and bowing, with tears of joy rolling down his cheeks. The President removed his own hat, and bowed in silence; but it was a bow which upset the forms, laws, customs, and ceremonies of centuries. It was a death-shock to chivalry and a mortal wound to caste. "Recognize a nigger! Fough!" A woman in an adjoining house beheld it, and turned from the scene in unspeakable disgust.

(The following nine anecdotes were related by Frank B. Carpenter, the painter, who, while executing his picture of the first reading in cabinet council of the Emancipation Proclamation, had the freedom of Mr. Lincoln's private office and saw much of the President while he posed, and whose relations with him became of an intimate character.)

"YOU DON'T WEAR HOOPS—AND I WILL ... PARDON YOUR BROTHER"

A distinguished citizen of Ohio had an appointment with the President one evening at six o'clock. As he entered the vestibule of the White House, his attention was attracted by a poorly-clad young woman who was violently sobbing. He asked her the cause of her distress. She said she had been ordered away by the servants after vainly waiting many hours to see the President about her only brother, who had been condemned to death. Her story was this:—She and her brother were foreigners, and orphans. They had been in this country several years. Her brother enlisted in the army, but, through bad influences, was induced to desert. He was captured, tried and sentenced to be shot—the old story. The poor girl had obtained the signatures of some persons who had formerly known him, to a petition for a pardon, and alone had come to Washington to lay the case before the President. Thronged as the waiting-rooms always were, she had passed the long hours of two days trying in vain to get an audience, and had at length been ordered away.

The gentleman's feelings were touched. He said to her that he had come to see the President, but did not know as *he* should succeed. He told her, however, to follow him upstairs, and he would see what could be done for her. Just before reaching the door, Mr. Lincoln came out, and meeting his friend said good-humouredly, "Are you not ahead of time?" The gentleman showed him his watch, with the hand upon the hour of six. "Well," returned Mr. Lincoln, "I have been so busy to-day that I have not had time to get a lunch. Go in, and sit down; I will be back directly."

The gentleman made the young woman accompany him into the office, and, when they were seated, said to her, "Now, my good girl, I want you to muster all the courage you have in the world. When the President comes back, he will sit down in that arm-chair. I shall get up to speak to him, and as I do so you must force yourself between us, and insist upon the examination of your papers, telling him it is a case of life and death, and admits of no delay." These instructions were carried out to the letter. Mr. Lincoln was at first somewhat surprised at the apparent forwardness of the young woman, but observing her distressed appearance, he ceased conversation with his friend, and commenced an examination of the document she had placed in his hands. Glancing from it to the face of the petitioner, whose tears had broken forth afresh, he studied its expression for a moment, and then his eye fell upon her scanty but neat dress. Instantly his face lighted up. "My poor girl," said he, "you have come here with no governor, or senator, or member of Congress, to plead your cause. You seem honest and truthful; *and you don't wear hoops*—and I will be whipped but I will pardon your brother."

HIS JOY IN GIVING A PARDON

One night Schuyler Colfax left all other business to ask him to respite the son of a constituent, who was sentenced to be shot, at Davenport, for desertion. He heard the story with his usual patience, though he was wearied out with incessant calls, and anxious for rest, and then replied:—"Some of our generals complain that I impair discipline and subordination in the army by my pardons and respites, but it makes me rested, after a hard day's work, if I can find some good excuse for saving a man's life, and I go to bed happy as I think how joyous the signing of my name will make him and his family and his friends." And with a happy smile beaming over that care-furrowed face, he signed that name that saved that life.

HIS SIMPLICITY AND UNOSTENTATIOUSNESS

The simplicity and absence of all ostentation on the part of Mr. Lincoln, is well illustrated by an incident which occurred on the occasion of a visit he made to Commodore Porter, at Fortress Monroe. Noticing that the banks of the river were dotted with flowers, he said: "Commodore, Tad (the pet name for his youngest son, who had accompanied him on the excursion) is very fond of flowers; won't you let a couple of men take a boat and go with him for an hour or two, along the banks of the river, and gather the flowers?" Look at this picture, and then endeavour to imagine the head of a European nation making a similar request, in this humble way, of one of his subordinates!

A PENITENT MAN CAN BE PARDONED

One day I took a couple of friends from New York upstairs, who wished to be introduced to the President. It was after the hour for business calls, and we found him alone, and, for *once*, at leisure. Soon after the introduction, one of my friends took occasion to indorse, very decidedly, the President's Amnesty Proclamation, which had been severely censured by many friends of the Administration. Mr. S——'s approval touched Mr. Lincoln. He said, with a great deal of emphasis, and with an expression of countenance I shall never forget: "When a man is sincerely *penitent* for his misdeeds, and gives satisfactory evidence of the same, he can safely be pardoned, and there is no exception to the rule!"

"KEEP SILENCE, AND WE'LL GET YOU SAFE ACROSS"

At the White House one day some gentlemen were present from the West, excited and troubled about the commissions and omissions of the Administration. The President heard them patiently, and then replied: "Gentlemen, suppose all the property you were worth was in gold, and you had put it in the hands of Blondin to carry across the Niagara River on a rope, would you shake the cable, or keep shouting out to him, 'Blondin, stand up a little straighter—Blondin, stoop a little more—go a little faster—lean a little more to the north—lean a little more to the south?' No, you would hold your breath as well as your tongue, and keep your hands off until he was safe over. The Government are carrying an immense weight. Untold treasures are in their hands. They are doing the very best they can. Don't badger them. Keep silence, and we'll get you safe across."

REBUFF TO A MAN WITH A SMALL CLAIM

During a public "reception," a farmer, from one of the border counties of Virginia, told the President that the Union soldiers, in passing his farm, had helped themselves not only to hay, but his horse, and he hoped the President would urge the proper officer to consider his claim immediately.

Mr. Lincoln said that this reminded him of an old acquaintance of his, "Jack Chase," who used to be a lumberman on the Illinois, a steady, sober man, and the best raftsman on the river. It was quite a trick, twenty-five years ago, to take the logs over the rapids; but he was skilful with a raft, and always kept her straight in the channel. Finally a steamer was put on, and Jack was made captain of her. He always used to take the wheel going through the rapids. One day when the boat was plunging and wallowing along the boiling current, and Jack's utmost vigilance was being exercised to keep her in the narrow channel, a boy pulled his coat-tail, and hailed him with: "Say, Mister Captain! I wish you would just stop your boat a minute—I've lost my apple overboard!"

THE PRESIDENT'S SILENCE OVER CRITICISMS

The President was once speaking about an attack made on him by the Committee on the Conduct of the War for a certain alleged blunder, or something worse, in the Southwest—the matter involved being one which had fallen directly under the observation of the officer to whom he was talking, who possessed official evidence completely upsetting all the conclusions of the Committee.

"Might it not be well for me," queried the officer, "to set this matter right in a letter to some paper, stating the facts as they actually transpired?"

"Oh, no," replied the President, "at least, not now. If I were to try to read, much less answer, all the attacks made on me, this shop might as well be closed for any other business. I do the very best I know how—the very best I can; and I mean to keep doing so until the end. If the end brings me out all right, what is said against me won't amount to anything. If the end brings me out wrong, ten angels swearing I was right would make no difference."

"GLAD OF IT"

On the occasion when the telegram from Cumberland Gap reached Mr. Lincoln that "firing was heard in the direction of Knoxville," he remarked that he was "glad of it." Some person present, who had the perils of Burnside's position uppermost in his mind, could, not see *why* Mr. Lincoln should be *glad* of it, and so expressed himself. "Why, you see," responded the President, "it reminds me of Mistress Sallie Ward, a neighbour of mine, who had a very large family. Occasionally one of her numerous progeny would be heard crying in some out-of-the-way place, upon which Mrs. Ward would exclaim, 'There's one of my children that isn't dead yet!'"

HIS DEMOCRATIC BEARING

The evening before I left Washington an incident occurred, illustrating very perfectly the character of the man. For two days my large painting had been on exhibition, upon its completion, in the East Room, which had been thronged with visitors. Late in the afternoon of the second day, the "black-horse cavalry" escort drew up as usual in front of the portico, preparatory to the President's leaving for the "Soldiers' Home," where he spent the midsummer nights. While the carriage was waiting, I looked around for him, wishing to say a farewell word, knowing that I should have no other opportunity. Presently I saw him standing halfway between the portico and the gateway leading to the War Department, leaning against the iron fence—one arm thrown over the railing, and one foot on the stone coping which supports it, evidently having been intercepted, on his way in from the War Department, by a plain-looking man, who was giving him, very diffidently, an account of a difficulty which he had been unable to have rectified. While waiting, I walked out leisurely to the President's side. He said very little to the man, but was intently studying the expression of his face while he was narrating his trouble. When he had finished, Mr. Lincoln said to him, "Have you a blank card?" The man searched his pockets, but finding none, a gentleman standing near, who had overheard the question, came forward, and said, "Here is one, Mr. President." Several persons had, in the meantime, gathered around. Taking the card and a pencil, Mr. Lincoln sat down upon the stone coping, which is not more than five or six inches above the pavement, presenting almost the appearance of sitting upon the pavement itself, and wrote an order upon the card to the proper official to "examine this man's case." While writing this, I observed several persons passing down the promenade, smiling at each other, at what I presume they thought the undignified appearance of the Head of the Nation, who, however, seemed utterly unconscious, either of any impropriety in the action, or of attracting any attention. To me it was not only a touching picture of the native goodness of the man, but of innate nobility of character, exemplified not so much by a disregard of conventionalities, as in unconsciousness that there *could* be any breach of etiquette, or dignity, in the manner of an honest attempt to serve, or secure justice to a citizen of the Republic, however humble he may be.

Made in the USA
Middletown, DE
10 November 2016